RXpert SERIES Student's Companion

Pharmaceutical Marketing Management

Prabhakar Reddy Veerareddy
Head, University College of Pharmaceutical Sciences,
Palamuru University, Mahabubnagar, Telangana.

Silas Panga
Assistant Professor (C)
University College of Pharmaceutical Sciences,
Palamuru University, Mahabubnagar.

Shyam Panga
Associate Professor
Dr. N. J. Paulbudhe College of Pharmacy,
Vasanth Tekadi, Savedi, Ahmedhnagar, Maharashtra.

PharmaMed Press
An imprint of BSP Books Pvt. Ltd.
4-4-309/316, Giriraj Lane,
Sultan Bazar, Hyderabad - 500 001.

Pharmaceutical Marketing Management
by **Prabhakar Reddy Veerareddy, Silas Panga and Shyam Panga**

Published by:

PharmaMed Press

An imprint of BSP Books Pvt. Ltd.

4-4-309/316, Giriraj Lane, Sultan Bazar, Hyderabad - 500 001.

Phone: 040-23445688

E-mail: info@pharmamedpress.net

www.bspbooks.net/www.pharmamedpress.net

ISBN: 978-93-48734-47-1 (Hardback)

PREFACE

Pharma Marketing Management is introduced as one of the electives in B.Pharmacy course with an objective of imparting managerial skills to the students along with scientific and technical skills. It inculcates the spirit of entrepreneurship to empower students as an entrepreneur with education and ethics. Pharmaceutical marketing management is different from the other aspects of management sciences which focus mainly on the profit and loss whereas Pharma marketing management embraces the social responsibility of affordability and accessibility along with profit and loss. Pharmaceutical Product Development not only involves the art and science of manufacturing but it also involves the effective marketing strategies to find its space in the highly competitive pharmaceutical market. Pharmacy curriculum focuses more on the quality of medicines rather than the marketing of medicines. However, effective marketing of medicines is the ultimate step to sustain the pressures of supply and demand from the market. For a pharmaceutical product effective marketing strategies as important as that of its core attributes such as quality, safety, efficacy, and stability. The formulation of effective pharma marketing strategies based on the need, supply, and demand of the product survives and sustains the product in the market at affordable price. The present book aims at synthesizing the useful content required to explain and explore the learning potential of pharma marketing and management skills to pharmacy students and implement the same in their professional life. It discusses all the fundamental concepts of marketing & management, and their application in the pharmaceutical product design and development. This book covers all the chapters as per the PCI syllabus which minimizes the efforts of students to refer multiple sources for the required information.

CONTENTS

Preface .... (v)

CHAPTER 1A
MARKETING

1.1 Definition and Meaning 1
1.2 Traditional vs. Contemporary Concepts 2
1.3 Marketing Environment 5
1.4 Implications of the Environment for Marketing 9
1.5 Govt. Regulations that Affect Marketing 11

CHAPTER 1B
PHARMACEUTICAL MARKETING

1.6 Definition of Quantitative and Qualitative Research 19
1.7 Demographic Descriptions 27
1.8 Socio-Psychological Characteristics of the Consumer 29
1.9 Market Segmentation & Targeting 37
1.10 Motivation and Prescribing Habits of the Physician 52
1.11 Patient Behavioural Patterns 54
1.12 The Process of Marketing Research 56

CHAPTER 2
PRODUCT DECISION

2.1 The Theory of a Product 61
2.2 The Product Mix Concept 69
2.3 Product Line Decisions 70
2.4 Product Positioning for Pharmaceuticals 77
2.5 Product Life Cycle Stage Analysis 78
2.6 Product Branding 83
2.7 Packaging and Labeling Decisions 91
2.8 Product Management in Pharmaceutical Industry 112

CHAPTER 3
PROMOTION

3.1 The Promotion Mix 120
3.2 Personal Selling 121
3.3 The Promotion of Pharmaceutical Products 124
3.4 Direct-to-Physician (DTP) Marketing Mix 128
3.5 Selling on the Side (Detailing) 130
3.6 Online Promotional Techniques for OTC Products 132

CHAPTER 4
PHARMACEUTICAL MARKETING CHANNELS

4.1 Definitions from various Authors 139
4.2 Primary Design Elements 142
4.3 Channel Organization 161

CHAPTER 5
PRICING

5.1 Definition of Price 186
5.2 India's History of Price Controls 213
5.3 Rural Marketing 217
5.4 Industrial Marketing 227

CHAPTER 1A

Marketing

In today's cutthroat business world, marketing is given a lot of attention, and every corporation engages in a variety of marketing activities. As a result, it's crucial that, you comprehend what a market is, what marketing is, and how it differs from selling. So, we will cover all of the key marketing ideas in this session and create the groundwork for describing the marketing process. We will also talk about how marketing has changed over time.

1.1 DEFINITION AND MEANING

A company house will communicate with its clients through marketing in an effort to sell them its goods or services. Before they are in the hands of customers, products are not finished. The management process known as marketing, is what moves products and services from concept to client. Marketing focuses more on creating demand for a product and meeting customer wants, than it does on persuading customers to pay for it.

The practise of generating, promoting, delivering, and trading offerings that have value for clients, consumers, partners, and society at large is referred to as marketing, according to the American Marketing Association (AMA).

Marketing is "the science and art of researching, generating, and delivering value to satisfy the wants of a target market while making a profit," according to Dr. Philip Kotler. Marketing helps people realize their unmet needs and desires. The size of the recognized market and the likelihood of profit are defined, measured, and quantified. It identifies the market categories that the business can best serve, and it designs and markets the proper goods and services to those groups.

Hence, marketing encompasses all of the actions taken to create utilities for place, time, possession, awareness, and more.

Traditional and contemporary marketing concepts.

A concept is a way of thinking, a philosophy, an idea, or a hypothesis that connects any features of divine and human creations. A marketing concept is the organization's guiding principles for developing dynamic marketing. As a result, the marketing notion is a way of life in which an organization's resources are used to develop, stimulate, and satisfy the consumer while making a profit.

CLASSICAL/TRADITIONAL CONCEPT

This idea states that the activities involved in the transfer of ownership of commodities from producers to consumers constitute marketing. It often overstated in this context, how important physical distribution and marketing channels are working. The act of making products from their point of origin available to final consumers is referred to as marketing. Sales of goods and services are the focus of marketing.

CURRENT CONCEPT

This idea holds that marketing is concerned with generating consumers. Peter Drucker, a prominent contemporary thinker, claims that marketing is too fundamental to be classified as a separate job. The entire company is viewed from the customers' perspective; the customer, not the producer, determines whether a business is successful or not? As a result, the current idea gives clients more importance and treats them like kings. Marketing is more than just a physical activity; it's something deeper. Customer wants and wishes are at the centre of this managerial philosophy.

1.2 TRADITIONAL VS. CONTEMPORARY CONCEPTS

1. Unlike modern marketing, which takes into account planning, product, price, promotion, place, people, after-sale service, etc., traditional marketing begins with manufacturing and concludes with sales.
2. Whereas modern marketing focuses on customers' requirements, wants, and contentment, traditional marketing places more emphasis on favourable items.
3. In conventional marketing, the producer's products are the only ones that are sold. Consumer preferences are not emphasised. Modern marketing, on the other hand, only engages in production after examining customer requests.
4. Modern marketing is consumer-oriented, as opposed to traditional marketing, which is focused on products and manufacturing.
5. The objective of old marketers was to achieve maximum profit by maximising sales. Nonetheless, the primary goal of contemporary marketers is to maximise profits by meeting customer needs.

Marketing

1. It starts before the sale and goes on after.
2. It emphasises customer requirements.
3. It has a long-term outlook and strives for stability and growth.
4. It is a commercial philosophy.
5. The consumer is prioritised here over the product.
6. Its scope is broader.

Selling

1. It starts following manufacture and stops following sale.
2. It emphasises the needs of the vendor.
3. It has a near-term viewpoint.
4. It is a regular physical procedure that occurs every day.
5. In this case, the product comes before the customers.
6. Its focus is more constrained than marketing's.

THE PURPOSE OF MARKETING

The specialised tasks that a marketer must carry out in order to locate potentially profitable products for the marketplace and then advertise them by setting them apart from competing goods are known as marketing functions. The following is a brief discussion of some of the crucial marketing functions:

1. Research and Development - A marketer must conduct sufficient research to determine the size, behaviour, culture, gender, demands, etc. of the target market segment before developing the products or services in line with those findings to fulfil and satisfy the needs of the target market.
2. Purchasing Function: To ensure that the production department receives timely and high-quality materials, the marketing department must aid the purchase and supply department by supplying the necessary requirements.
3. Standardization & Grading- Setting quality standards to ensure product homogeneity is referred to as standardisation. Consumers receive constant quality assurance from it.

   Grading is the process of categorising a product based on recognised standards or criteria, such as size, quality, etc. The marketer can charge more for a high-quality product through grading.
4. Packing and Labeling - Packaging has historically been done to safeguard the goods from harm during travel and to make it simple for

customers to receive the goods. But, the producer now also uses it to distinguish his brand from that of his competitors.

Labeling is another task related to packaging. It entails labelling the package with identification information. A product's label is the portion that includes details about the manufacturer and the product.

5. Branding is the process of imprinting a thing with a name or mark that identifies it, or a combination of the two. Giving a thing a distinctive individuality is known as branding.

   Popular brands include Airtel, Sony, Lux, and Nirma.

6. Pricing: One of a marketing manager's key responsibilities is determining a product's price. Pricing is affected by the cost of the goods and services provided, the desired profit margin, prices set by rival businesses, government policies, etc.
7. Promotional Function: The marketing manager is responsible for developing methods that effectively inform customers of the products' existence on the market. Without this feature, producers would hold onto their goods and they would never reach customers. Without this feature, producers would hold onto their goods and they would never reach customers. Advertising, personal selling, publicity, and sales promotion are four crucial forms of promotion.
8. Physical Distribution – Activities required to transfer ownership of commodities to customers are included in this function, as well as making goods accessible at the appropriate location and time.
9. Transportation: It offers the physical requirements that make it easier to move people, products, and services from one location to another.
10. Warehousing. Goods are produced or obtained far in advance and kept in warehouses until they are distributed to clients in order to fulfil the anticipated wants of consumers. The items are shielded in warehouses from harm that might be done by rodents, dampness, sunlight, theft, etc.
11. The function of taking risks. Almost every stage of the marketing process involves taking risks. The financial risk involved in producing and handling goods, such as the potential loss from a decline in pricing and the losses from spoiling, depreciation, obsolescence, fire and floods, etc., is referred to as risk taking in marketing.
12. Customer Support Services - This duty entails creating services for customers, such as after-sales assistance, addressing customer complaints and adjustments, offering credit options, maintenance services, technical support, etc. These services increase consumer happiness to the highest level and foster product brand loyalty.

1.3 MARKETING ENVIRONMENT

INTRODUCTION

Marketing operations must be performed in a specific setting. By attentively studying the environment, it is necessary to scan for and identify even the marketing opportunity. In the context of a specific marketing environment, the marketing mix is also chosen. Marketing managers must consider these forces while making marketing decisions even when they have no control over them. The environment in which they are operating must be carefully observed by marketers as they develop their marketing plans. You will learn about the components of the marketing environment and the marketing environment in India in this unit. Also, you will know how numerous Acts and Laws affect marketing choices in India.

WHY DO WE NEED A MARKETING ENVIRONMENT?

Every corporate organization's marketing strategy is influenced by a wide range of external, uncontrollable circumstances. As a result, a company's marketing strategy must take into account on environmental factors.

Philip Kotler asserts that a company's marketing environment is made up of the individuals and entities from the outside of marketing who have an impact on marketing management's capacity to create and sustain profitable relationships with its target customers. For instance, the automobile manufacturers and customers, the tyre manufacturing technologies, the tax structure, import and export rules, the distributors, dealers, competitors, etc., may all be significant environments to a car tyre company. Along with them, the business may need to take into account its own capabilities in terms of production technology, finance, and sales. The fact that the environment is shifting and unclear in the marketing environment makes it vital. These environmental influences include some that are unavoidable. These changes present both a risk and an opportunity. These environmental elements can be divided into two categories: macro and micro environments. These elements can also be divided into internal and external environmental elements. The term "micro environment" describes the immediate surroundings of a business, or the environmental elements that are nearby. These include the company's own production and customer service skills, dealers and distributors, rival businesses, and consumers. Also, these are the demographics directly influencing the company's prospects. Larger societal forces make up the macro environment and can be arranged in an outer circle. They include forces relating to the population, the economy, the environment, technology, politics, and culture. These factors have an indirect impact and frequently take time to reach the organisation.

One may consider the forces in the outer circle to be the macro environment of a corporation, and those in the inner circle to be the micro environment.

Micro Environment

The following micro environmental aspects affect the company's marketing choices: 1) the internal environment of the organisation; 2) suppliers; 3) marketing intermediates; 4) rivals; and 5) customers. Let's now take a quick look at each of these factors.

Organisations Internal Environment

An organization's capacity for finance, production, and human resources significantly affects its marketing decisions. It is vital to consider financial capabilities, if expanding plant and machinery is required since the current facilities are insufficient.

To create a new product, you might have a responsive research and development department. To produce the new product, the production department may also have access to its own facilities. It's also important to think about how the organization's non-marketing departments work with the marketing department. The senior management might not concur with the marketing department's assessment of the marketing plans or how they should be put into practise. Also, the marketing department must collaborate closely with the other departments, particularly the manufacturing and quality control departments. The sales team may occasionally be required to carry the bulk of the strategy's workload.

Suppliers

You need a range of inputs to produce commodities or services. The people or business that provides these inputs are referred to as suppliers. The success of the marketing organisation depends on the smooth and constant delivery of inputs in the necessary quantities on reasonable terms. These persons or businesses are known as suppliers. Suppliers thus assume significance. The producer is forced to maintain the delivery schedule and the quality of the finished product by receiving timely supply of the required quality and quantity. When there are more suppliers, there is a natural increase in supplier dependence. At times of shortages, some suppliers might not provide materials under favourable conditions. According to the competitiveness of his company and the terms and conditions that each supplier wants, each supplier may do so.

While some vendors, for instance, may be prepared to supply on a credit basis, others may request payment in advance and offer goods based on a waiting list.

Intermediaries

Typically, not all manufacturers are able to sell their products or services to customers directly. To get their goods to customers, producers employ a variety of intermediaries. The marketing intermediates, or dealers and distributors, may or may not be eager to extend their cooperation. These people typically favour trusted brands. It could be very challenging for newcomers to locate a dealer who will stock their goods.

They might demand favourable terms from newcomers in the form of a discount, credit, etc., and the producer might find it challenging to meet their demands. Other middlemen who help with physical distribution include transport companies, warehouse companies, etc. The marketing efforts are frequently influenced by their service costs, accessibility, safe and quick delivery, etc.

Competitors

Competitors present a challenge. Marketing choices are also influenced by competitors' strategies. Other types of rivalry, such as product differentiation, exist in addition to competition on the basis of price. Competitors may also highlight their brand identity, dealer network, or closely related products. Their marketing may highlight a number of true or fraudulent product qualities. The other might respond if one claims that his product uses imported technology.

The other may claim that he is already exporting his product if one claims that his product uses imported technology. Sometimes, competitor tactics might turn an environmental advantage into a challenge.

Customers

Customers come in a variety of forms. A company may sell directly to end users, resellers, industries, the government, or foreign customers. It can be selling to only one of these clients or to all of them. Every type of consumer market has a few distinctive traits, thus the marketer needs to be well-versed in the art of persuading and selling to these customers. These marketing actions will be directly influenced by the environment that the client profile presents.

The demographic also includes people who might buy the company's goods. Finding the people who are most likely to become a company's clients may not be simple. The reputation of a company has established can sometimes persuade customers to become customers. Businesses typically work to improve their reputations with the public and foster a positive outlook among individuals or groups of individuals. Government and consumer action groups are two distinct groups that should not be approached with hostility. Hence, the general public is a component of the ecosystem.

MACRO ENVIRONMENT

Physical environment, technological environment, political and legal environment, economic environment, demographic environment, and social-cultural environment are the macro environmental variables that have an impact on an organization's marketing system. Let's get into more detail regarding these factors.

Environment, Physical is the number and type of resources that a producer has access to for his output are frequently affected by the environment, including the natural renewable resources of the earth (such as forests and agricultural goods) and the limited non-renewable resources (such as oil, coal, and minerals). For instance, India imports gasoline and other goods because it lacks sufficient petroleum resources.

Recently, the Gulf War has had a significant impact on the nation's supply of gasoline and diesel. This had a number of effects on the businesses that used petroleum products.

Technology is influencing how individuals will turn out. One's output may not be in line with the most recent goods and services due to the revolution in computers, electronics, and communication in general. For instance, labor-intensive type-set printing has already become unprofitable due to new printing technology like laser printing and desktop publishing.

Political and judicial climate

Political developments result in new laws and policies that affect industry. Government regulation continues in various ways, and the laws and regulations formed under them are growing more complex. Several commercial sectors are governed by one type of law or another, and the market is unable to resist their effect. The expenses and pricing of the goods and services marketed are directly influenced by tax legislation, such as sales tax, excise duty, octroi, income tax, etc. Likewise with the import and export policies. These elements are regarded as forces in the macro environment since they have an impact on all units (they do not just effect one marketer).

Economic Situation

The economic environment is determined by the state of the economy as measured by the Gross National Product (GNP), per capita income, and the favourable or unfavourable position of the trade balance. War, starvation, per capita income, and a country's favourable or unfavourable situation are all variables. For instance, if the monsoon is good, there will be a greater output of agricultural products, increasing the income of those who depend on agriculture. As a result, consumers can purchase more consumer products. As a result, there is a rise in consumer demand. A poor monsoon will similarly have a negative impact on the demand for fertiliser. The amount of money that can be spent on a range of items is also determined by the personal and corporate tax systems.

Demographic surroundings

Demographic factors like population size, geographic distribution, density, movement patterns, age distribution, birth and death rates, religious diversity, etc. are of great interest to marketers. There are opportunities for the marketer to investigate in the population's changing life styles, habits, and tastes. For instance, the demand for semicooked food goods and household appliances increases when both the husband and wife seek employment.

Social and Cultural Context

Core cultural norms can be strong and deeply ingrained, and as a result, they rarely alter. Also, there are secondary cultural beliefs that can quickly alter. Some of them, such as their hairstyles, attire, etc., just fade. Even within a single culture, not everyone may accept the changes. Different people adopt them to varying degrees. Religion is a significant part of culture as well, and this has ramifications for marketers. For instance, Hindus do not consume beef because they adore the cow. Thus, there is no market for products created from cattle meat. In this way, the consumption patterns are somewhat influenced by the culture of the society. Other human endeavours are likewise influenced by culture because it shapes people's values and ideas.

1.4 IMPLICATIONS OF THE ENVIRONMENT FOR MARKETING

You have learned that a company's marketing environment is made up of a number of forces. The majority of these forces are external to the business and might not be under the marketing executives' control. So, the company's marketing system must function within the constraints of these dynamic environmental influences. This ambiguous marketing landscape presents opportunities as well as surprises and risks. As a result, it is essential for businesses to regularly monitor their environment, as it changes and adjust their marketing mix plans to reflect new trends and advances.

The corporation adapts to these external forces and causes through strategies based on its own resources, particularly its financial, sales, and technical resources. Some of these environmental influences may be somewhat under the organization's control, while others may be beyond its scope. The corporation has no control over macro environmental issues, but it does have some power over micro environmental factors. For instance, the firm has considerable control on the organisational environment. By providing lenient conditions, the company can also have some influence over suppliers, dealers, and distributors. A company can also influence both current and potential customers through its advertising efforts.

Every element of the environment is relevant in some way to marketing. It is simple to imagine, how different environmental elements impact supply and demand, distribution and promotional strategies, etc. For instance, the oil crisis will increase demand for equipment that is more oil-efficient. Similar to this, when computers become more popular, there will be a greater need for operators, programmers, voltage stabilisers, etc.

INDIA'S MARKETING ENVIRONMENT

With over 80 crore inhabitants, India is a sizeable nation. Its diversity in religions, dialects, social practises, and regional features is strength and a weakness for marketers. The ability to successfully sell a wide range of goods and services is a boon, but it can also be a burden because the marketer frequently needs to modify his marketing plan to account for shifting tastes and values. Some marketers can discover that there are numerous opportunities for profit in the Indian market. It implies that there is a market for everything and that there are buyers for anything one may produce. Some adopt a more pessimistic perspective by taking poverty and a lack of necessary inputs into account.

Nonetheless, one can state with certainty that the market is sizable, consumer awareness of quality is rising, and there is a need for new and improved goods and services. These trends may persist for a very long time.

Although India has been independent for 40 years, villages still make up the majority of the country's land and about 77% of its people live there. Yet, these rural communities are now reaping the benefits of the Green Revolution, and because of their growing purchasing power, marketers who had previously focused solely on metropolitan areas must pay more attention to them. Urban areas are undoubtedly the priority target markets due to their population density and market potential, but a company that wants to assure its existence must also start penetrating the rural market. The population in rural areas now has more purchasing power because to government investments in rural development. Transport, communication, literacy, and other advancements have opened up a lot of new markets. The ability to see an opportunity and devise a suitable marketing strategy can let marketers in.

There are many businesses, government agencies, factories, and small-scale businesses operating in the nation, which together make up the organisational customers.

For even the simplest transaction, the public sector typically follows a bureaucratic, drawn-out, and time-consuming system, whereas private sector decision-making is typically speedier and less regimented. You might want to consider creating distinct marketing organisations for the public and private sectors if you are promoting your goods/services to both of them. The timeliness of the purchase decision is another significant distinction between the public and private sectors. The government approves a yearly budget for the public sector businesses, and they utilise the funds from this budget to buy a range of goods. The public sector units are under pressure to use the entire budget because doing otherwise could result in lower funding.

Because they risk having a smaller budget in the following years, the public sector units feel forced to use the entire budget amount.

The quarter before March, when the fiscal year finishes, would see a frenzy of buying. So, if the public sector enterprises are your main clients, you should consider the timing aspect. Private sector businesses rarely have such a high in sales during any given month of the year, unless it is related to the seasonality of production or sales.

1.5 GOVT. REGULATIONS THAT AFFECT MARKETING

Over time, a variety of laws that affect business have been implemented. The significant ones that have an impact on marketing are given below:

The 1872 Indian Contract Act

The 1930 Indian Sale of Commodities Act

The 1951 Industries (Development and Regulation) Act

The Prohibition of Food Adulteration Act of 1954

The 1954 Medicines and Magical Remedies (Objectionable Advertising Act)

The 1955 Essential Commodities Act

The Corporations Act of 1956

Act of 1958 on Trade and Merchandise Marks

The Monopolies and Restrictive Trade Practices Act of 1969 (MRTP Act)

The 1970 Patents Act

Act of 1976 governing standards of weights and measures

The 1986 Consumer Protection Act.

Some of the laws mentioned above, such as the Contract Act, the Sale of Goods Act, the Companies Act, the Trade and Merchandise Marks Act, and the Standards of Weights and Measures Act, are applicable to every business regardless of the type of product sold or service rendered by it. However, the MRTP Act does not apply to financial institutions, cooperative societies, government-managed commercial undertakings or public enterprises.

In contrast, the laws mentioned above aim to control some decisions made by businesses operating in the aforementioned areas. These laws include the Cigarettes (Regulation) Act of 1956, the Medicines and Magic Remedies (Objectionable Advertisements) Act of 1954, the Prevention of Food Adulteration Act of 1954, the Industries (Development and Regulation) Act of 1951, and the Prevention of Food Adulteration Act of 1954.

The Cigarettes (Regulation of Production, Supply and Distribution) Act of 1975 and the (Essential Commodities) Act of 1955.

To expect a marketer to be fully knowledgeable on each of the aforementioned Acts would be unreasonable. Nonetheless, it is imperative that you have a solid working understanding of the main laws defending consumers, competition, and society as a whole. You could assess the legal ramifications of your decisions with the aid of such understanding. ' The major justifications for government regulations can be summed up as follows: safeguarding individual welfare and fostering greater standards for the general welfare of the population, safety etc. preventing companies from acting in ways that are detrimental to the Marketing Environment public's interests, such as by making false or deceptive claims about a product or service, manipulating prices for their own advantage, not honouring warranties, etc. safeguarding small businesses against the dangers of unfair competition from large businesses combating unethical business practises brought about by mergers or other types of partnerships such as price fixing, while conserving national resources including forests, fuels, water and energy.

Preventing environmental pollution, preventing the concentration of economic and industrial wealth, encouraging broadly distributed industrial development and the growth of small-scale industries, safeguarding the economy from foreign inventor dominance and aiding in the preservation of precious foreign exchange resources.

The Indian Contract Act (1972)

It governs how citizens conduct their business and economy. All such choices that involve the creation and execution of a contract are under the purview of this Act. The fundamental components of a legal contract are outlined and carefully explored.

A contract is an agreement that is enforceable in court between two or three parties by which one or more parties obtain rights in exchange for one or more other parties' acts or forbearances.

The Act also outlines the requirements for establishing an agency as well as the responsibilities of both a principal and an agent.

The Indian Sale of Products Act (1930) regulates sales and purchases.

Regulates the selling and acquisition of goods. The property in goods is transferred or promised to be transferred by the seller to the buyer for a price in a contract for sale of goods. The Act also establishes guidelines for the transfer of ownership of goods, the rights and obligations of the buyer and seller, requirements for the delivery of products and the rights of the unpaid seller.

Act on the Growth and Regulation of the Industry (1951)

The industrial licencing system is administered by means of this Act which effectively gives the government the authority to licence (or permit) new investment, the expansion of licenced units, the production of new goods, the relocation of licenced units as well as the investigation of potential violations. the operations of licenced units in specific circumstances and to assume management of those units if circumstances demand it.

The growth and regulation of significant businesses involving relatively big investments that are crucial to India as a whole are of course the goals underpinning these authorities. The relevant elements of the industrial policy are anticipated to be satisfied in the actual fulfilment of these objectives. Industrial licencing is a type of direct government control over market dynamics. The underlying premise is that from a national perspective, the government is the best judge of priorities and that it can allocate resources in a more effective and socially beneficial manner.

Yet, it is important to recognise that there are financial costs associated with the measures of control and that the benefits are anticipated to be at least equal to or greater than the costs.

Act to Combat Food Adulteration (1954)

Prohibits publications or issues of advertising that could lead to consumers becoming ignorant about food products in order to guarantee food purity.

The Medicines and Magic Remedies (Objectionable Advertising) Act of 1954 prohibits the printing or distribution of any advertisement that could lead a gullible customer to turn to dangerous drugs and devices for self-medication.

Advertisements for specific medications used to treat conditions including epilepsy, infertility, and impotence are also restricted. False claims for the pharmaceuticals in advertisements are likewise prohibited under the Act.

The Essential Commodities Act (1955) establishes guidelines for the regulation of production, supply and distribution of specific goods designated as essential under Section 2(a) of the Act. The government has the authority to set the price of such a product under Section 3(a) of this Act.

Businesses Act (1956)

It is a piece of legislation that through regulating the structure and operation of corporations has significant influence on business. It is one of the lengthiest legal enactments with more than 650 sections. Its purpose is to control the expanding business and financial applications of the company system and potential abuse of that system.

Governing trade and commercial marks (1958) Act

relates to the registered trade and product marks under this Act. A mark can be any combination of a device, brand, heading, label, ticket, name, signature word and letter or number. A trademark is a recognisable symbol, name, or design that makes it easy to recognise a firm or its goods. The trademark's owner has the exclusive right to use it and offers legal protection against any infringement of his rights. A trademark may be registered for up to 7 years at a time, after which it may be renewed for an additional equivalent number of years. Moreover, no trademark should be used that is scandalous, indecent, or likely to be confusing or deceptive.

Furthermore, no such trademark should be utilised if it is likely to be misleading or scandalous, indecent or offensive to Indians' religious sensibilities.

Act against monopolies and trade practises (1969) (MRTP)

provides for the control of monopolies, the prohibition of monopolistic, restrictive, and unfair trade practises as well as matters related to or incidental to these things. It also ensures that the operation of the economic system does not result in the concentration of economic power to the detriment of the community.

You might find it interesting to know that the United States which has a free enterprise system was the first nation to pass such a law.

The Sherman Antitrust Act is one such law that was passed as early as 1890. Yet, the Monopolies and Restrictive Practices (Inquiry Control) Act was not passed until 1948 in the United Kingdom. Restrictive Trade Practices

Act and Resale Pricing Act were added in 1956 and 1964 respectively. Our Act is modelled after the three Acts mentioned above.

Patents Act (1970)

The provisions of this Act are particularly relevant when a corporation plans to create patented goods. A patent is a time-limited, exclusive right to own, make use of, and discard of an invention.

The initial inventor or his legal agent receives the patent as a grant from the central government.

The Standards of Weights and Measures Act of 1976 specifies the maximum packing densities for various products. Bread, butter, cheese, biscuits, cereals, and pulses are among the products. Cigarettes, cleaning fluids, cleaning powder, condensed milk, tea, coffee, cooking oils, cosmetics and honey are all included. Toothpaste, milk powder, soaps, spices, jams, sauces, and ice cream among other things.

Consumer Protection Act (1986)

The Consumer Protection Act is the most recent law to India's set of laws governing marketing choices. The Act supplements not replaces, any other laws' requirements that have an impact on marketing decisions.

The Act aims to better protect consumer interests and to that end provides for the creation of consumer councils and other agencies for the resolution of consumer disputes and for matters related thereto. The public enterprises, financial institutions and cooperative societies that benefited from a special position under the MRTP Act were exempt from any action even against those marketing practises of theirs that were deemed against consumer or public interest are not excluded or exempt from the scope of the regulatory measures as a result of the Consumer Protection Act's enforcement.

Even public organisations like the Delhi Development Authority, Municipal Corporations, Indian Railways, Delhi Transport Corporation (DTC), and other State Transport Corporations, etc., are subject to consumer complaints being resolved. In particular, this Act presents a fresh obstacle for many public sector organisations involved in the production or distribution of consumer goods and the delivery of consumer services.

The new Act has more pointed teeth. Confusion over the burden of proof was one of the shortcomings of prior legislation. They never made it clear enough who had the burden of proof—the manufacturer, the trader, or the customer. In that the onus has been placed for the first time on the manufacturer and the sale, the new Act marks a landmark. In order to protect them from unfair trade practises (the term "unfair trade practise" has been defined under the MRTP Act under Section 36-A, and the relevant Section has been discussed later in this unit), the Act gives consumers the right to be protected against marketing of goods that are dangerous to their health.

It also gives consumers the right to be informed about the quality, quantity, potency, purity, standard and price of goods. To seek redress against unfair trade practises or unscrupulous exploitation of consumers to consumer education and to be guaranteed whenever possible access to an authority of goods at competitive prices, to be heard and to be assured that consumers' interests will receive due consideration at appropriate forums.

The Consumer Protection Councils to be established at the Central and State levels, seek to promote and safeguard these goods.

At the district, state, and central levels, a quasi-judicial apparatus is sought to be established in order to allow quick and easy resolution of consumer disputes. These quasi-judicial bodies have the authority to grant rulings of a particular kind and to compensate customers as necessary while adhering to the norms of natural justice. Penalties for failure to comply Sanctions for disobeying directives issued by quasi-judicial authorities have also been made available.

The reach of this new law is perhaps significantly greater than that of any other current law. But, the success will depend on if the necessary infrastructure is developed, particularly at the district and state levels and whether there is the necessary zeal to both create the machinery and enforce the Act's requirements.

Preservation of the Environment Act (1986)

The Environment (Protection) Act makes provisions for environmental protection, enhancement and the avoidance of hazards to people, other living things, plants, and property.

The term "environment" refers to the land, water, and relationships that exist between them and humans other living things, plants and other things. Environmental pollution is the presence of any solid, liquid, or gaseous chemicals that have the potential to harm the environment. The present enactments covers not only all things connected to prevention, control \sand abatement of environmental pollution but also powers and functions of the Central Government and its officials in that regard and penalties for committing offences

Bureau of Indian Standards Act (1986)

According to the Bureau of Indian Standards Act, a bureau will be established to ensure the smooth progression of the operations of standardisation marking and quality certification of goods as well as any issues related to or incidental to those activities. The Bureau of Indian Standards would be a body corporate and have an Executive Committee to manage its daily operations according to the provisions made. All functions of the International Standards Organization will be carried out by its employees, agents and liabilities. Additionally, it has been agreed that suppliers of comparable goods with origins in GATT-coded countries will have access to the Bureau's Standards and Certification Mar: The only modification to the legislation made by the Act is the creation of a new venue for swift and efficient case resolution.

Governmental Institutions

In 1947, the Indian Standards Institution was founded. The nation's industrialization was still in its early stages. Since then there has been significant advancement in a number of areas of the Indian economy necessitating a renewed focus on standardisation and quality control. With the expansion of production and exports in various sectors of the national economy, a national plan for giving standards the proper respect and importance must be developed. To encourage quicker growth, boost exports and provide items that satisfy consumers, the public and private sectors, especially small businesses must step up their efforts to manufacture goods of better standard and quality. The purpose of the establishment of the Bureau of Indian Standards as a legislative organisation was to fulfill the aforementioned goals and to carry out the law. The Bureau of Industrial Costs and Prices, the Agriculture %XS Commission, and the MRTP Commission are just a few of the regulating organisations that the government has formed. The Government established the Bureau of Industrial Costs and Prices in 1971 to carry out inquiries into industrial items and suggested prices. With the purpose of advising the government on price strategies for agricultural goods, the Agricultural Prices Commission was established in January 1965.

To enforce the terms of the relevant legislation, the government has also created rules like the Standards of Weights and Measures (Packaged Commodities) Rules, 1977 and the Prevention of Food Adulteration Rules 1955. The Central and State Governments are accountable for enforcing these Statutes.

In accordance with Section 5 of the MRTP Act of 1969, the Government created the MRTP Commission. The Commission may look into any restrictive trade practise I after receiving a complaint of the facts constituting the practise from any trade or consumers association with a membership of at least 25 people or from 25 or more consumers, (ii) after the Central Government or a State Government refers the matter to it, (iii) after the Registrar of Restrictive Trade Agreements (RRTA) submits an application to the Commission or (iv) after the Commission becomes aware of the matter on its own (also known as suo moto inquiries).

An investigation of monopolistic commercial activities might be conducted based on a referral provided by the Central Government or on that government's own knowledge or facts. An informant is not the same as a complaint because the Act does not recognise informants. In these situations, it is up to the MRTP Commission to determine whether or not an informant is someone who is interested in the case's subject matter.

The MRTP-Commission must conduct a preliminary investigation through its Director General of Investigation in regards to complaints it receives directly from consumer and trade associations to determine whether the complaint merits a thorough investigation. Public interest groups have expanded during the past eight to ten years.

These organisations seek to persuade the government and business to pay more attention to consumer needs. To obtain justice for the harmed consumers and to hold corporate firms accountable for unfair practises, they can even take the case to court.

CHAPTER 1B

Pharmaceutical Market

1.6 DEFINITION OF QUANTITATIVE AND QUALITATIVE RESEARCH

Qualitative research, according to Shank (2002), is "a type of systematic empirical enquiry into meaning" (2002). He uses the phrase "systematic" to denote "planned, ordered, and public," adhering to guidelines approved by the qualitative research community. He uses the term "empirical" to imply that this kind of research is based on actual experience.

According to the theory of meaning, researchers attempt to comprehend how others interpret their experiences.

According to Denzin and Lincoln, interpretive and naturalistic approaches are used in qualitative research: "This means that qualitative researchers investigate objects in their natural surroundings, trying to make sense of or to interpret, events in terms of the meanings people bring to them."

A key component of qualitative research is the emphasis on words rather than numbers while gathering and analysing data. Bryman

The phrase "qualitative research" refers to a variety of approaches to and methods for doing research that are intended to shed light on how people perceive, experience, interpret, and create the social world. (Sandelowski).

Quantitative research

In this case, the researcher verifies a theory by defining specific hypotheses and gathering information to confirm or deny the assumptions. Attitudes are evaluated both before and after an experimental treatment using an experimental methodology. The information is gathered via a device. that surveys attitudes, analyses the data using statistical techniques, and does hypothesis testing.

PHARMACEUTICAL MARKET

Two methods quantitative research and qualitative research can be used to conduct primary market research and collect data and information for market research. Each technique has a unique approach and yields unique results. However, business professionals and academic experts have observed that it is advisable to do both quantitative and qualitative market research in order to fully understand a business environment, the market and the consumers within it.

Qualitative research, according to Shank (2002), is "a type of systematic empirical enquiry into meaning". He uses the phrase "systematic" to denote "planned, ordered, and public," adhering to guidelines approved by the qualitative research community. He uses the term "empirical" to imply that this kind of research is based on actual experience.

According to the theory of meaning, researchers attempt to comprehend how others interpret their experiences.

According to Denzin and Lincoln (2000), interpretive and naturalistic approaches are used in qualitative research: "This means that qualitative researchers investigate objects in their natural surroundings, trying to make sense of, or to interpret, events in terms of the meanings people bring to them."

A key component of qualitative research is the emphasis on words rather than numbers while gathering and analysing data. (Bryman 2008)

The phrase "qualitative research" refers to a variety of approaches to and methods for doing research that are intended to shed light on how people perceive, experience, interpret, and create the social world. (Sandelowski).

Understanding people's opinions, points of view, feelings regarding a situation and the driving variables that affect their attitude is the primary goal of qualitative market research.

One of these market research techniques is generally utilized to do qualitative market research:

1. *Focus groups*: As the name implies, a group of people typically 6 to 10 are gathered to talk about a certain product and its marketing methods. Usually, the group will be made up of experts in that particular sector. There will be a moderator in this group who will encourage debate among the participants to generate opinions. Platforms like Communities are getting more popular since focus groups are becoming less common.
2. *Extensive Interviews*: It is typically a one-on-one interview performed over the phone or in person with a group of people. By using a more conversational approach, this technique improves data collection.
3. *Cutting-edge research techniques*: In this technique, the researcher can take pictures or even record videos of the subjects while they respond to

the questions. Later, the researcher might review these images or films to learn more about how they reacted in various scenarios.

4. *Observations or "Shop-alongs"*: In qualitative market research, observations or shop-alongs are currently being employed more and more. Using this technique the researcher can watch from a distance and learn firsthand how a customer responds to a real product and purchasing experience. This reduces the potential for giving false feedback or even forgetting about the buying experience later on.
5. *Lifestyle Immersion*: Attending a social or family event that the user(s) are attending and gathering feedback is a more recent approach of conducting qualitative market research. This makes it easier to collect input from people while they are relaxed. This is a fantastic approach to get frank criticism in a relaxed setting.
6. *Online focus groups*: Because social media is so accessible, managing online focus groups is getting simpler. It is simple to manage data collecting and analytics for a focus group study as well as to recruit participants.
7. *Ethnography*: Ethnographic research entails spending time with end users and observing how they interact with products in the real world. This qualitative research approach is in the best position to support the development of quick and significant product changes.
8. *Projective Techniques*: Trained moderators use projective techniques to elicit respondents' innermost ideas. The moderator then infers and unearths underlying emotions that aren't clearly addressed by using indirect questions or questioning techniques.
9. *Online forums*: It is gradually becoming more and more popular to do qualitative market research using online forums. The moderator of a panel ensures that the debate is directed toward the desired result by gathering the panellists on a single platform to discuss a certain subject. To ensure a full conversation is held, the moderator prods, asks the proper questions and coerces.
10. *Internet phrase submission and sentence construction*: Completing qualitative market research can be made easier but more exhaustive by asking respondents to match words that might be related to a product or even complete sentences online. This gives researchers a deeper understanding of what users are thinking.

The steps in performing qualitative market research are as follows:

- **Planning and establishing research objectives:** Each research project must have a specific goal in mind from the beginning in order to prevent resource waste and promote company agility.
- **Picking the research methodology:** There are numerous approaches to carry out qualitative market research. The survey method would be used in accordance with the nature of the study, target audience demographics, geographic location, a product that is being surveyed, etc.
- **Selecting the right people for the job:** To conduct a qualitative market research study, moderators who are skilled at eliciting and tracking responses from potential respondents are needed.
- **Sampling:** A qualitative market research survey's sample serves as its foundation. Greater samples lead to better research results, which guarantees the study's success. The three main types of sampling are:
- **Purposive Sampling:** Using this technique, a specific goal is kept in mind when creating the sample. Users that meet this requirement are invited to participate in the market research survey, and the demographics are planned in detail well in advance.
- **Quota Sampling:** Quota sampling is the practise of choosing samples from a predetermined quota, with the chosen users being considered a representative sample of the greater population. You can use qualifying criteria or a random sample for this.
- **Snowball Sampling:** A reference model serves as the basis for the snowball sampling model. Users matching
- **Survey design:** The survey needs to be made in such a way that it elicits the most information possible, resulting in replies that are substantial and useful for making decisions.
- **Data collection:** Online or offline techniques might be used to gather data. It is essential to gather the data in a method that allows for its interpretation, analysis, and reporting.
- **Data analysis:** Without analysis, data is meaningless. Analyzed data can provide practical ideas on which to base a product or brand, which is essential for a qualitative marketing research survey.
- **following Up:** As a key step in the market research process, data that has been gathered and processed must be presented to the pertinent stakeholders in an easy-to-understand style.

Approaches for Testing Qualitative Market Research

There are four different sorts of testing methodologies that can be used for qualitative market research. It reveals:

- Direct Exploration: This qualitative market research technique allows for unrestricted feedback on a proposed concept or item. With this approach, users are informed of the concept but are not given an actual product in exchange, and all available input is gathered. The new product is then developed using this feedback, which is then gathered and investigated.
- Monadic testing: This technique asks customers for input on a single idea, concept, feature or product before evaluating their responses. Despite the fact that there are other concepts available, alternative designs are not displayed in this approach. This technique is crucial for getting specific input on a desired feature or idea.

  Sequencing triadic testing is comparable to monadic testing in that each idea, item, or feature is presented just once. The sole distinction is that a user's feedback is gathered on both concepts while an alternate design for each concept is simultaneously displayed. Paired testing and paired nomadic testing are some names for this testing technique.
- Discrete Choice Testing: Similar to paired nomadic testing, discrete choice testing only differs in that all options are presented simultaneously rather than sequentially and users are asked to select one feature over another and then justify their selection.

Qualitative market research examples

Qualitative market research is frequently used by prosperous firms to stay on top of the current market trend, make better judgments, and attain company excellence.

Qualitative market research is a potent tool for identifying your target market and determining how they will react to your product, regardless of the stage of development your company is in.

Here are some current examples of qualitative market research case studies before we explore further.

Big belly, the geolocation exit polling software developed by AP, Norc, and QuestionPro, the Washington State Ferry.

Here are some instances of business growth where qualitative market research is crucial for crowdsourcing important aspects for the best decision-making:

1. Branding: Many organizations don't understand how consumers feel about their brands or where their brands stand in relation to those of their rivals. In order to gather input on marketing materials and content, focus groups

or customer interviews are frequently used in market research. The surveyor can delve deeply into several themes and collect input from the respondents in this way. Brands can obtain data using this method of market research that will enable them to upscale and better position their brand in the marketplace.

2. Understanding Consumer Behavior: Organizations, businesses, and entrepreneurs occasionally want additional consumer knowledge in order to properly position their products. They could need details about your gender, age, marital status, etc. to do that. quantitative market analysis etc.

   They can collect this information with the aid of qualitative market research. The best approach for studying about consumer behaviour is to conduct in-depth interviews. Because these interviews are one-on-one, a fair quantity of data can be gathered.

3. Measuring the reach of marketing initiatives: Many companies go above and above to better market their brands. This is where their marketing initiatives are put to use. By obtaining firsthand data on how customers perceive a company's marketing message, market research can give businesses information about the efficacy of their marketing efforts. This aids businesses in making the most of their marketing budgets.

4. Locating new market opportunities: Market research aids companies in identifying new prospects for business growth. Organizations can pinpoint a location, comprehend business dynamics, identify their main competitors and more by obtaining data through market research through focus groups. This allows them to expand their business in the proper way.

5. Gaining product insights: If a company develops a new product or seeks to improve an existing one, it is always preferable to conduct market research to see how acceptable the product is among consumers. People will have an opinion on a product's appearance, size, functionality, colour, features, etc. when it first enters the market. In-depth interviews conducted as part of qualitative market research can help collect organised data that can subsequently be used to improve or adjust the current product.

Scientific ethics are equally as crucial as the ethics in any other sector of research. The interests of the participants must be protected. Market research is likewise governed by similar laws, much as there is formal training and procedure for researchers in other professions, such as healthcare and medical research.

Given the nature of qualitative market research, it is crucial to obtain the participant's informed consent before beginning the research project. This indicates that they are familiar with fundamental knowledge like:

The type of research,

The anticipated completion date,

The presence of financial or other forms of compensation, and

Any potential sociological or physical risks or advantages.

Protection of confidentiality;

How the name and other personal information will be used;

Any potential legal implications

What benefits does qualitative market research have?

There are a few uses for this market research methodology because it is comparatively less expensive and more adaptable:

1. It is beneficial to comprehend client wants and behavioural patterns.
2. How customers view and judge your goods.
3. To comprehend the effectiveness of your business planning and to determine whether the strategies and planning you've implemented are effective or not.
4. Which marketing messages have a significant impact on customers and which are simply ignored?
5. Does the market currently have a need for your goods or services?

In the end, qualitative market research is all about getting individuals to go into more detail about their opinions so that you can better understand their behaviour. Before even considering "What," one must comprehend "Why."

Qualitative market research merits

1. One of the main benefits of adopting this market research technique is that it enables you to get specific information rather than just concentrating on data metrics. It aids in your comprehension of the nuances of the information received and permits in-depth study.
2. It has an adaptive nature: This market research may adjust to the calibre of data gathered. The researcher can instantly try to collect data in a different direction if it appears that the current data aren't yielding any results. More freedom in data collection is provided by this.
3. It functions within flexible structures: Since the information gathered using this research approach is based on observation and personal experience, a skilled researcher can use additional open-ended questions as a follow-up if more information from the respondents is required.

4. Assists in precisely communicating brand proposition: Through this market research technique, consumers and brands may effectively communicate with one another. As this research method allows the brand and the customer to freely express their requirements and values, any product language, product jargon, etc. are successfully communicated limiting any potential for miscommunication.

5. It lowers the rate of client attrition. Consumer behaviour can shift suddenly, leaving brands wondering what went wrong. Brands have the opportunity to discover what consumers want and whether they are meeting those needs or not by performing qualitative market research, which lowers customer churn. The bond between the brand and the consumer is thus upheld.

Demerits of qualitative marketing

1. It takes a lot of time to complete: Qualitative market research may take days, weeks, months, or even years. For immediate, useful ideas, this is not good. In certain instances, market change may have caused the survey's initial premise to become obsolete.

2. It is expensive: Qualitative market research is very expensive because it takes so long to complete. Due to the massive amount of data and the need for individuals with certain skill sets to handle the research process, they are also expensive to perform and produce relevant insights.

3. It is subjective; what one user thinks may not be what another user thinks. There is no standardisation of responses as a result. Additionally, it implies that the distinction between true and untrue is hazy to the point where each response must be taken at face value.

4. Data acquired cannot be confirmed because, in most qualitative market research scenarios, the data is based on subjective opinions. Each opinion is therefore taken into consideration for examination as valid.

5. Halo effect: The study reporting is skewed by the moderator's or analyst's preexisting notions because of the research's highly subjective character. It is a natural human instinct to gravitate toward the familiar, and it can be quite difficult to overcome this prejudice.

Question Pro Communities: Web - based Qualitative Market Research Software

The substantial requirement for business research has expanded along with the level of corporate competition. A qualitative research platform called Question Pro Communities, which allows current clients to provide feedback and keep up with market research operations, aids researchers in conducting studies to increase revenue and profitability. Researchers can conduct study using the communities platform to efficiently target and understand their customers, understand the market trend, foresee potential issues and so lessen customer churn.

This qualitative research platform assists growing companies in understanding their rivals and locating the most recent market trends. Businesses want a software platform that enables researchers to comprehend customer mindset, evaluate their views and gather valuable qualitative data in order to conduct well-directed research.

The best platform in the world for qualitative research powered by analytics is called QuestionPro Communities. Using specialised technology, such as text analysis, this online qualitative market research tool saves researchers' time by effectively extracting valuable information from human language. It also increases flexibility and strengthens the validity of qualitative research. This online platform assists researchers in minimising manual and administrative labour.

Software and Tools for Qualitative Market Research are Available through QuestionPro Communities

Negotiations

A researcher can invite participants to a community discussion session and moderate the focus group online using the online qualitative research software and tool, Discussions. If the users want the freedom to post responses when they check in to their community, this can also be done live at a time that is suitable to the researcher. The researcher can send invitations to a certain target group they want to collect input from well in advance.

Concept Board

This is an excellent platform to manage and display your results to the important stakeholders if you are seeking for responders to share their thoughts and allow others to assess, offer input and vote on the existing entries.

1.7 DEMOGRAPHIC DESCRIPTIONS

The systematic study of population is known as demography. The phrase has Greek roots and is made up of the terms demos (meaning "people") and graphein (meaning "describe," suggesting the description of people). Demography is the study of population trends and processes, including changes in population size, patterns of births, deaths, and migration, as well as the composition and structure of the population, including the proportions of women, men, and various age groups. Demography comes in many forms, such as formal demography, which is primarily a quantitative discipline, and social demography, which focuses on the social, economic, or political facets of populations. Every demographic study relies on counting or enumeration processes, such the census or a survey, which entail the systematic gathering of data on the inhabitants of a particular territory. In reality, the development of sociology and its successful establishment as an academic discipline owe much to the study of demography, which is of particular importance to sociology. The development of nation-states as the primary form of political organisation and the emergence of the modern science of statistics happened to occur in Europe during the latter half of the eighteenth century at nearly the same time. The role and responsibilities of the contemporary state had started to grow. For instance, it had started to actively get involved in the creation of early public health initiatives. Management, law enforcement and the upkeep of the peace, industrial and agricultural economic strategies, and taxation and generating revenue, as well as city administration.

This newly created and rapidly growing area of government activity necessitated the systematic and routine gathering of social statistics, or numerical data on various facets of the population and economy. Although the practise of the state gathering social statistics dates back much further, it only took on its current shape around the end of the eighteenth century. The first likely modern census took place in America in 1790, and by the early 1800s, the practise had spread to Europe as well. The British Indian government started conducting censuses in India between 1867 and 1872, and since 1881, regular ten-year (or decennial) censuses have been held. Since 1951, and seven decaversary censuses, the most recent of which was in 2011, have been performed since 1951. The world's largest such effort is the Indian census (since China, which has a slightly larger population, does not conduct regular censuses).

The formulation and execution of governmental policies, particularly those for economic growth and general welfare, depend on demographic data. But when they first appeared, social statistics also offered a compelling case for the development of the field of sociology. The numerical properties of a vast collectivity made up of millions of people, known as aggregate statistics, provide a clear and compelling case for the presence of social phenomena. Despite the fact that statistics at the national or state level, such as the number. The death rate itself is a social phenomena and must be explained at the social level. While the number of deaths per 1,000 people, often known as the death rate, is created by aggregating (or adding together) individual fatalities. This was clearly demonstrated in Emile Durkheim's well-known study that examined the differences in suicide rates between various nations. Although each specific occurrence of suicide may have entailed factors unique to that person or their circumstances, Durkheim contended that the rate of suicide (i.e., number of suicides per 100,000 people) had to be explained by social causes.

Formal demography and a broader field of population studies are occasionally distinguished. Measuring and analysing the elements of population change is the main focus of formal demography. Its primary area of interest is quantitative analysis and it uses a highly sophisticated mathematical methodology that can predict population increase and changes in the makeup of the population. On the other hand, population studies or social demography investigate the broader causes and effects of population patterns and change. Like sociologists, social demographers strive to identify the social causes of population patterns and hold the view that social structures and processes control demographic processes.

1.8 SOCIO-PSYCHOLOGICAL CHARACTERISTICS OF THE CONSUMER

Studying what customers purchase is only one aspect of consumer behaviour. It makes an effort to comprehend how decisions are made and how this influences consumers' purchasing habits. Marketers research consumer purchasing patterns to understand where, what, and why customers buy. The reason why customers choose a particular product, however, is a difficult puzzle to solve because the solution is deeply ingrained in the customers' minds. (Consumers can generally be divided into two groups: individual consumers and organisational consumers. Individual shoppers attempt to fulfil their own desires and needs by making purchases for themselves or fulfilling the needs of others by making purchases on their behalf. These particular customers can be of various ages, life stages, and socioeconomic origins.

Cultural, societal, personal, and psychological aspects all have an impact on how consumers behave while making purchases. Human behaviour includes consumer behaviour, and by analysing past purchasing patterns, marketers may predict how consumers would act in the future while making purchases. In 2010, Kotler and Armstrong p. 160. The social, personal, and psychological aspects of consumer behaviour are the key themes of the succeeding sections.

Social factors

Everyone is surrounded by people who have the power to affect their purchasing choices. Family, role, status, and peer groups are crucial social influences. 2014 (Perreau) Despite being an individual, every customer nonetheless belongs to a group. Consumer membership groups are referred to as membership groups. This classification is clear-cut and uncomplicated. A reference group is the second kind of group. Consumer behaviour and self-image are influenced by the reference group. Consumers can compare their behaviour, way of life, or habits to those of the reference group using these comparison points. Typically, there are numerous smaller reference groups made up of family, close friends, neighbours, coworkers, or other individuals who customers identify with. Categories that a consumer does not yet belong to can also have an impact. A customer aspires to belong to and wants to be a part of these aspirational groups in the future.

Individual customers' purchasing decisions may be influenced by family members. A person's values, development, and personality are shaped by the environment they are raised in. This setting provides the opportunity to form attitudes and beliefs about a variety of topics, including politics, social relations, and society. Initial impressions of companies, goods, and consumer behaviours are created by families. For instance, customers who made brand decisions when they were young may continue to make the same decisions as adults without even realising that their family had a hand in their decisions. Economic class represents a person's place in a social group according to factors including wealth, education, and occupation. Status is significant in many communities, and people strive to win others' respect. Being successful in life or being born into wealth can both increase one's social standing. The choice of product and brand frequently indicates social position and role.

Personal factors

Personal aspects like a buyer's age and life cycle stage, occupation, economic condition, lifestyle, personality, and self-concept all have an impact on their decisions.

Consumer behaviour changes over the course of a person's life and product purchases change with age and stage of life. Age-related aspects include things like wardrobe, furniture, hobbies, and food preferences. Additionally, over the course of a lifetime, surroundings, values, lifestyle, interests, and purchasing habits change. Family life stages alter brand preferences and shopping habits. In the past, only young single people and married couples with kids were considered to be part of the family life cycle. Today's marketers prioritise alternate, unconventional life stages including unmarried couples, couples without children, couples of the same sex, single parents, and older singles who marry. It is reasonable to expect that customers' tastes can evolve over their lives and have an impact on the coffee brands they choose at various times of their lives.

Purchase decisions and behaviour are influenced by a consumer's career and purchasing capacity. What customers can afford and how they see money depend on their income level. People who work in related fields often have similar tastes in music, fashion, and leisure activities. They frequently interact socially and hold similar beliefs and values. Income has an impact on what consumers can afford and how they see money.

One person can be distinguished from another by their unique personality. Some examples of these character traits include self-assurance, adaptability, friendliness, and dominance. (Kotler and Armstrong 2010, page 172). The way we perceive ourselves, the environment around us, and how others perceive us are all influenced by our personalities. Our personalities are shaped by the attitudes, values, and people around us. A person's personality evolves as they mature and encounter new environments. In Wright (2006). Self-concept is a multifaceted and intricate concept. According to Kardes et al. (2011), the self-concept is as follows. Self-concept is frequently defined as the entirety of a person's thoughts and feelings about themselves as objects. In other terms, it refers to the conception of oneself that people have based on their attitudes and ideas. Many brands have created a personality and image that reflect the beliefs and characteristics of their target audience. Customers can express themselves through their brand preferences. 2011; Kardes et al. Sincerity, excitement, competence, sophistication, and ruggedness are the five facets of a brand's personality.

Different elements related to aspects of human personality are included in each of these dimensions. Sincerity enhances brand amiability in the first dimension by displaying integrity and practical principles. Consumers can get current knowledge from excitement, together with a lively alternative like the tech company Apple. Customers might feel relaxed and young when using Mac computers. While consumers are given responsibility and security by a brand that represents expertise. Sophistication appeals to higher class consumers with luxury items like designer goods like Gucci or Rolex.

Ruggedness, which attracts customers in opposition to sophistication is the fifth dimension. Brands that are viewed as tough, powerful and adventurous are represented by ruggedness.

Psychological factors

An individual with a variety of requirements is referred to as a consumer. These requirements may be physiological like a need for water, or psychological, like a desire for acceptance or a sense of community. When a need changes a motive, it can be sufficiently intensified. A motive is essentially a need that propels someone to look for fulfilment. Probably the most well-known psychologist to have looked at these needs in humans is Abraham Maslow. He wanted to clarify why people are motivated by various demands at various times. (2010), (Kotler & Armstrong). Maslow's hierarchy of needs is with the most urgent requirements at the bottom and the least urgent demands at the top. The fundamental rule is to attend to the most fundamental requirement first before moving up the ladder.

What are Maslow's needs?

1. Physiological: a basic requirement like rest, sustenance or water.
2. Safety: the desire to feel safe and shielded.
3. Belongingness: the desire to experience love and acceptance from others.
4. Ego needs: to be successful and have status in society.
5. Self-actualization: to have enriched experiences and have a sense of fulfilment in oneself.

A person behaves in accordance with how they see the circumstances. Every day, a person is exposed to countless sensory stimuli, including light, colour, sound, smell, taste, and texture. The method by which these sensations are chosen, arranged, and interpreted to create a meaningful picture of the outside world is called perception. Three perceptual processes—selective attention, selective distortion and selective retention—allow people to have varied impressions of the same inputs. A person only pays attention to a small number of the stimuli they are exposed to during the selective attention process. Consumers may ignore many environmental cues in favour of those that are specifically relevant to their needs at the moment. For instance, a customer who wants to purchase a new car will focus more on various car advertisements while ignoring those for homes.

Selective distortion is the term used to describe how people will interpret information in a way that confirms their preexisting beliefs. Every person has a unique perspective based on their experiences, attitudes, and beliefs. People are guided by selective distortion to circumstances that are consistent with their values and views. As an illustration, no two consumers will ever receive the identical message from the same brand. People are not able to remember everything when they are exposed to a lot of information and stimuli. Selective retention refers to what a person will remember in a given scenario or stimulus. This is evident when customers recall the positive aspects of the brands they prefer and completely disregard the positive aspects of competitors.

Even those without personal experience can learn by observing others. It's even possible to learn subconsciously. Consumers may hum a range of jingles and recognise a number of various corporations even without using such brands. This is what we mean by inadvertent learning. People can always learn new things. Consumers' perceptions of the world are always changing as they are exposed to new stimuli and situations. They can receive input that enables them to alter their behaviour when they find themselves in an environment that is similar to one they have already experienced. Consumers who have had a bad experience with a brand of coffee are more likely to steer clear of it in the future because they will retain the bad time they had.

Learning combined with external factors like family or neighbours results in beliefs that will affect customers' purchasing decisions. People of different types have varied views toward things like politics, food, music and many other things. The attitude encapsulates how people feel or judge a product or concept. It's challenging to alter attitudes and beliefs. These are deeply ingrained in the minds of consumers and may be indicative of a person's personality.

Consumer purchasing patterns

Throughout the day, a consumer makes multiple purchases. The purchase is the sole tangible result of a more involved process that a buyer goes through with each choice. However, each decision to make a purchase is unique and takes a different amount of time and effort.

Approaches for determining decisions

Before making a purchase, a consumer goes through five stages of the decision-making process. The customer goes through these phases as they identify their needs, obtain information, weigh their options, and decide what to buy. Following the actual purchase, the consumer engages in post-purchase behaviour to assess the level of satisfaction they have received. In a normal transaction, the customer may be able to skip a few steps, according to Kotler and Armstrong. Must be used to complete the purchasing process when a consumer is presented with a novel and complicated purchase scenario.

The acknowledgment of a need is the first step in every decision-making process. There are various categories for classifying needs. One form involves the consumer identifying a need or issue that may be brought on by internal or external triggers. Humans have basic wants, such as hunger, which causes the stomach to growl and prompts the purchase of hamburgers. An advertisement, for instance, could act as an external stimulus and cause you to consider purchasing a new computer. The consumer frequently notices a big gap between the desired condition and the present state at this point. The process of need recognition might happen organically, but marketers can frequently initiate it. The goal of marketing is to encourage consumers to utilise a product, regardless of the brand they select. Marketers will attempt to persuade consumers to select their brand over competing ones.

Another classification category that calls for recognition is:

1. A functional requirement is one that is based on a functional issue. The buyer buys a washing machine so they won't have to do laundry by hand.
2. A consumer has a social need when they crave for acceptance by others or a sense of belonging. The customer can buy opulent goods to appear wealthy in front of others.
3. The consumer senses the need for change. To change one's appearance, this may lead to the acquisition of new clothing or furniture.

The consumer starts looking for information at the second stage of the decision-making process. Consumers can sometimes make decisions about things without any information, and other times they must meticulously search information to find all available options. Solomon (2004), The consumer has access to a variety of information sources, including chatting to friends and family, reading periodicals, conducting an Internet search, and handling the goods. The amount of searching you do will mostly depend on your motivation, success in finding the information, and level of satisfaction with the results. Consumers today receive a lot of information from for-profit sources that are under the authority of marketers. Even so, the most useful sources are frequently those that are private, like friends or family. Customers can learn more about various brands and raise their level of brand awareness. When making their final brand choice, shoppers can eliminate some brands with the aid of this information.

Customer decision-making can occasionally be impulsive and intuitive, with little to no consideration. A habitual decision-making process can be the source of situations where little or no consideration of alternatives is used. However, customers who are involved in a lengthy problem-solving procedure may carefully compare several brands. Consumers' evoked set refers to the alternatives that are actively taken into account throughout the selection process. This evoked set consists of notable items from the shopping environment in addition to familiar products or brands from the consumer's recollection.

At the fourth stage, the consumer has considered all of his or her options and is prepared to make the actual purchase. The consumer typically chooses to purchase the most popular brand. The attitudes of others or perceptions of the brand cultivated by marketers are only two examples of elements that may influence the consumer's purchasing choice. (Kotler & Armstrong, 2010). Consumers may take mental shortcuts to make purchasing decisions easier, but these shortcuts can result in rash choices. especially when limited problem solving takes place prior to making a decision. Shortcuts of this nature might range from generalisations like "more priced items are of greater quality" or "purchase the same brand as last time" to specifics like "use the same brand that my mother used to buy." These alternative routes might end up being detrimental to the customer.

Post-purchase behaviour is the final phase of the purchasing process. The consumer will assess their level of satisfaction with the product once they have purchased it. If a customer is disappointed, the goods has not lived up to expectations. (Khan, 2006.). If the product lives up to expectations, the customer will be happy and willing to spend more money in the future on this particular brand. Furthermore, a high degree of consumer pleasure can result in continued brand loyalty. When consumers' expectations have been surpassed, this frequently occurs.

Brands

The branding is any attribute that sets one product apart from another, such as a name, logo, or design. Because the consumer's thoughts and feelings about the product can be included, it is more than just a concrete good or service. It is a commitment to the client. When the environment around them changes, a great brand may be something the customer can rely on and stick with. It might represent who you are or what you aspire to be. A brand should provide people values, characters, tales, advantages, and catchphrases.

A product may have a powerful brand image that fits the characteristics of its target market. Consumers can portray their ideal selves or express themselves through the brands they choose. Consumer impression of the goods and a collection of beliefs about the brand make up a brand image. By using packaging, promotions, and advertising, marketers can bolster these brand perceptions in Wright (2006). When customers purchase a product, they are also purchasing a brand's reputation. Positive and distinctive branding are required. This brand personality may be paired with the brand image. The brand may have a personality that is similar to a group of individual characteristics (Aaker 1997). These aspects of brand personality were earlier covered in greater detail in the chapter on the psychological influences on consumer behaviour.

Marketers must devote a lot of effort to branding decisions. They must position their brands so that people will think of them. Marketers can employ three levels of positioning to be successful in that. A brand can be positioned by product attributes at the most fundamental level. For instance, coffee brands may feature features like a dark roast or an environmentally friendly container. Although universal positioning by qualities is effective, competitors can readily imitate these attributes and the resulting benefit is lost. Fortunately, customers are less concerned with characteristics than they are with what characteristics can accomplish for them. To position a brand more effectively, associate it with desired qualities. For example, the vehicle brand Volvo stands for safety. Mercedes is known for its quality, and Nike is known for its performance. Customers can mentally connect a brand name with its advantages even before they have physical things in their hands. The most advanced degree of brand positioning goes beyond features and advantages. Strong ideals and convictions are at issue. Brands can influence a consumer's emotional state by igniting their enthusiasm and excitement for the product.

Brand flipping among consumers can occur for a variety of reasons. It can just be a desire to try a different brand or a lack of interest in a present product. Customers engage in variety seeking when they desire to try new items. This occurs particularly when there is less stimulation present or when people are feeling upbeat. Solomon (2004), Better quality, pricing, selection, or features can all be further justifications for brand switching. If customers switch brands because of a reduced price and the quality falls short of their expectations, they won't stick with the brand for very long (Perreau 2014) However, when shopping, most people stick to the same brand. As previously noted, customers can purchase a particular brand out of habit or because it requires little to no thought to choose. In these circumstances, it is equally simple to purchase a different product, for instance if the first item is sold out. Consumers merely need the appropriate motivation to shift the brand without thinking. However, if a customer has had a favourable experience with a brand and has made a deliberate choice to purchase that brand, the customer may also be brand loyal and purchase the same product every time. This brand-loyalty-based purchase decision will eventually change to habitual purchasing.

1.9 MARKET SEGMENTATION & TARGETING

Smith created the concept of segmentation for the first time in 1957, and it focuses on dividing consumers into groups according to their demands. In order to concentrate the marketing company's efforts most efficiently and profitably, segmentation aims to find a group of people who have a demand or wants that can be satisfied by a single product. For instance, if a manufacturer uses mass production to create a standardised product, the company would need to be certain that there are enough customers for the product to make the effort viable.

The underlying presumptions of segmentation are: • Not all purchasers are the same.

The sub-groups will be more homogeneous and more compact, and they will share comparable behaviour, backgrounds, values, and needs.

- Compared to the market as a whole, the subgroups will be more homogeneous and smaller.
- It is simpler to please a small set of like-minded clients than it is to strive to please many disparate ones.

Choosing which market segments to target is what targeting is all about. Targeting is more concerned with the logistics of conducting business inside the market than segmentation, which is essentially the division of the market. Since the two are obviously connected,

The segmentation process will typically reveal which segments are likely to prove most profitable or would otherwise aid the company in achieving its strategic goals.

The brand's relationship with other brands targeting the same market segment is what positioning is all about. Positioning refers to the position that a brand holds within a Compared to other brands, in consumers' minds.

PURPOSE FOR MARKET SEGMENTATION

Every consumer is a unique person with unique demands and wants. On the surface, this appears to provide a significant challenge for the marketer because it would be impossible to personalise or customise each product to meet the unique needs of every customer. Prior to the Industrial Revolution, the majority of goods were handmade. Once mass-production processes were developed, this was found to be both expensive and essentially inefficient. Sadly, excessive mass production reduces the range of products that are offered since the most efficient method. Long manufacturing runs and product standardisation are necessary to maintain low production costs. Every modification results in additional expenditures for the product's retooling and packaging. Some economies, notably those in Eastern Europe and the Third World, lack the wealth or industrial investment necessary to support the manufacture of a wide variety of goods. These economies continue to place a strong emphasis on mass production and marketing.

Only consumers who have limited options and do not already own a product that satisfies their primary demands would respond favourably to mass marketing (also known as undifferentiated marketing), which produces a standard product for all consumers.

For instance, few families had automobiles in Germany in the 1930s. Porsche was hired to create the Volkswagen (literally, "people's car") as a basic vehicle that could be affordably built for the public market after Hitler promised the German people that every family would possess a car.

Finding out how many individuals are likely to want each benefit, an estimate of how much they would be ready to pay for it, and where they would like to get it from are all part of segmentation. As a result, the business targeting a segmented market is able to provide greater functional benefits and give hedonic needs more attention, resulting in more enjoyable products.

Marketers must be pretty certain that there is a sizable enough market for the product to be commercially successful in order to make these changes worthwhile. On the other side, focusing on a narrower group allows for cost savings in the supplier's communications efforts. For instance, the marketer would be better off focusing their efforts on creating an advertisement that is specific to the target audience, or an advertisement that is created for the ideal customer alone.

Overall, segmenting is done to allow a business to focus its efforts on one group of customers with comparable wants rather than trying to please everyone and likely delighting no one. The benefits of segmenting the market are displayed in Table1.

Table 1B.1 Benefits of segmenting the market.

Customer Research	The company can better understand its best clients by segmenting.
Competitor Research	When focusing on a tiny portion of the overall market, it is considerably simpler to identify and combat competition.
Efficient Use of Resources	Instead of being evenly distributed among the masses, companies' limited resources can be concentrated more effectively on a select group of allocated consumers.
Planning for Strategic Marketing	Once the company has a clear understanding of who its best clients are, planning becomes simpler.
Enhanced Market Size	By attracting new customers who meet the normal customer profile but weren't previously aware of the product, effective segmentation can raise the size of the market as a whole.

Variables for segmentation.

If a segment is to be successfully exploited, it must meet the following criteria:

- It must be quantifiable or defined. In other words, there has to be a method for both counting and identifying the segment's members.
- It has to be reachable. This implies that it must be feasible to reach the segment as a whole and provide the product to them collectively.
- It must be significant, or large enough to merit aiming towards.
- It must be consistent, which means that all of the members must mostly concur on their demands.

- It has to be secure. The segment's composition and character must remain largely unchanged.
- It must be significant, or large enough to merit aiming towards.
- It must be consistent, meaning that all of the members must mostly concur on their demands. It has to be secure.

  The segment's composition and character must remain largely unchanged.

  Accessibility, content, and measurability are the three main criteria, but it's also crucial to consider the factors that led to segmentation. This makes it easier for the marketer to predict changes and, occasionally, to confirm that the segmentation basis is properly established.

  Although there are several segmentation basis, these are the principal ones:

- **Geospatial.** The geography, climate, and location of the consumers. For instance, automobiles in California nearly always have air conditioning, yet cars in Sweden have constantly-on headlights due to the subpar lighting conditions for the most of the year.

  Although it is frequently utilised in worldwide marketing, geographic segmentation is also beneficial inside individual countries.

- **Psychiatric.** based on the personalities of the segment's participants. The market for homeowners insurance, for instance, may be divided into groups that are concerned about crime, natural catastrophes, and unintentional property damage.

It is behavioural. This method looks at the advantages, utilisation circumstances, level of usage, and loyalty. For instance, corporate users may be a section of the auto industry.

For instance, the automotive market may be divided into individual and corporate customers.

The segmentation process might take on a distinct meaning in pharmaceutical marketing. The distinction is in the kind of client, i.e., the doctor, the pharmacist, and the management of the healthcare facility, who make decisions about which products to choose, how to prescribe them, and how to dispense them even if they are not the product's end users or consumers.

Market segmentation is the process of breaking down a product's overall heterogeneous market into smaller sub-markets or segments, each of which has a tendency to be homogenous in all material ways.

Market segmentation is a technique to guide customer's servers as to what kinds of items and demands the customer will be fulfilled (Amstrong & Kotler 2010,. Market segmentation may separate the market into various categories of purchasers. Divide the market into more manageable divisions so that the firm may better meet its specific requirements and desires with products and services. Once the theories have been merged, the case firm needs a suitable market segment in order to join the market, create new market segment opportunities, and create lucrative enough profiles to service each market segment.

With this sector-specific viewpoint, a few pertinent segmentation factors—such as commercial potential and anticipated financial results from this clinic, hospital, or account—rise.

Medical specialisation and how it relates to the products authorised indication(s).

The Egyptian market may be used to identify specific client demands, such as dosage form, cost, distribution middleman, and a wide range of other products.

Consequently, you might think of cardiology and vascular physicians as two separate categories, class A or class B doctors as distinct categories, and doctors who segmentally prescribe shots. Additionally, you may use a multi-factorial segmentation approach and include Class A cardiologists who recommend injectable anticoagulants as a section.

Additionally, as marketers of over-the-counter ("OTC") prescription treatments grow more concerned with the requirements of the general public, the product's eventual user, they frequently apply the four segmentation variables previously stated.

You may think of men over 50 with high wealth as one category and women 20 to 40 with medium social status as another.

The private market might be further divided into those who use their vehicles primarily for commuting, people who use them for recreational activities like surfing or camping, and people who use them for domestic chores like grocery shopping or picking up their kids from school. The business market might be divided into high-mileage users like salesmen and "prestige" users like managing directors and senior employees.

- **Statistical.** worried about the demographic makeup in terms of ages, lifestyles, and economic concerns. For instance, the housing market may be split into first-time purchasers, families with children, senior retirees, and elderly persons in sheltered housing; similarly, the market may be broken down by lifestyle, with some lodging catering to young professionals, others to outdoor enthusiasts, and so on.

PARTICULARIZING INDUSTRIAL MARKETS

Marketers may and do segment industrial or organisational markets based on the following factors:

- The place's location. This approach is perhaps the most popular because salespeople often serve organisational markets, and geographic segmentation allows salespeople to maximise driving time. Businesses in the same sector frequently locate close to one another for a variety of reasons, including proximity to suppliers of raw materials or the availability of trained labour in the area.
- Organizational kind. According on the industry that each client is in, IBM divides its market. This indicates that some IBM salesmen are experts in the banking industry, while others are in the insurance industry and still others may be in the local government sector.

  Size of the client company. Many businesses employ distinct sales forces to handle huge accounts.
- **Using products.** Oil firms have different marketing plans (and ad hoc distinct divisions) for selling petrochemicals, plastics, household central heating oil, and automobiles.
- Rate of use. Customers who utilise a product in big numbers will be treated differently from customers who just make occasional purchases (and will also experience this difference).

This is due in part to the fact that their demands are different, as well as the supplier's propensity to prefer the large customer above the little customer.

TARGETING

Managers must choose the appropriate section to target based on the overall goals of the company after segmenting the market. A corporation may opt to target a certain market sector that is currently underserved on the grounds that rivals are less likely to enter the market than would typically be the case with managers who would chose the most lucrative section. Targeting is the process of choosing a sector to pursue. Marketers might choose from three different fundamental strategic alternatives.

1. Targeted advertising (single segment). Tie Rack, Sock Shop, and Knickerbox all use this strategy, which is also referred to as specialised marketing. The goal of the niche marketer is to dominate a specific, narrow niche.
2. Focusing on two or more groups and providing a unique marketing mix for each is what differentiated marketing (multisegmented) refers to. While Holiday Inn markets to families and targets the leisure market on the weekends, it targets corporate travellers throughout the week. The hotels frequently provide kid-friendly activities on the weekends and offer discounted lodging for families.
3. Using a "scattergun" strategy is what is meant by undifferentiated marketing. Producers that engage in this practise often provide a fundamental good that is appropriate for usage by virtually all age groups and lifestyles.

For instance, there is little differentiation in the market for gasoline. The usage of gasoline is much the same across the board, despite periodic attempts by oil manufacturers to distinguish their products through the use of various additives and detergents, and there does not appear to be any correlation between segmentation characteristics and gasoline consumption. It would be challenging to envisage any genuine product modification that would satisfy consumers' demands to warrant a higher price. Such instances of bland items are becoming progressively rare; even manufacturers of such essentials as wheat and salt have made significant gains in distinguishing their offerings (i.e., better matching customer wants).

The following three elements will determine which approach should be used:

(1) The company's capabilities,

(2) The product's features and benefits, and

(3) The segment's characteristics (s).

Obviously, a corporation will likely to employ a focused marketing approach if resources are restricted. This is the strategy used by the UK company High and Mighty, a menswear retailer that specialises in clothing for exceptionally tall and large men. Despite the fact that their market—men over 6 ft 4 in [1.9 metres] tall, or over 25 stone [160 kg] in weight—is actually very small in absolute terms, the company has found great success with this strategy. The business is successful because major chain stores do not cater to guys of this size, and custom clothing was formerly the only option. Prices are kept cheap by High and Mighty's ability to manufacture in large quantities, while being far higher than chain stores. Whilst still serving its niche, (store pricing).

A differentiated strategy will result from more resources combined with a variety of target markets, whereas an undifferentiated approach will result from a straightforward product designed for everyone.

Because they cannot afford the amount of promotional expenditure, small-resource companies sometimes struggle to be noticed in mass marketplaces. They must thus segment, maybe beginning in a small portion of the nation (geographical segmentation) and expanding progressively to the entire country as resources become available.

Every one of the seven Ps and every component of the promotion mix must be developed with the target market in mind in order for the marketing plan to be effective. The best way to accomplish precise targeting is to do in-depth market research about the requirements and preferences of the target audience. In this method, the business may choose what to provide the target market in order to outperform the offerings of the rivals. Keep in mind that three elements are being considered in this situation. First, what are the needs of the target segment's customers? What else do they already have access to, secondly? Third, what can the company provide that would be superior than what is already offered?

Segment size	Profit per unit sold	Number of Strategic competitors	Decision rationale
Large	Large	Large	Large markets with high profits will draw rivals; as a result, prices and profits will decline quickly.
Large	Small	Large	This market is developed.To dominate the market, a new player would need to have something unique, such a significantly lower cost base.
Small	Large	Large	A penetration pricing approach can completely conquer a limited market with several rivals and a high profit per unit.
Large	Large	Small	Competitive entry into the market is inevitable if the sector is both large and profitable. For this market, a skimming strategy is ideal since it will allow for price reductions to successfully compete when new rivals arrive.

Table *contd...*

Segment size	Profit per unit sold	Number of Strategic competitors	Decision rationale
Large	Small	Small	Although this industry is established, there shouldn't be much risk involved because there is little rivalry, making it simple to gain market share and discouraging other businesses from joining.
Small	Small	Large	This market is in decline. Not at all worthwhile to enter.
Small	Large	Small	This market is a specialised one. It ought to be feasible to take advantage of the entire market.
Small	Small	Small	This market sector is obviously not at all profitable. This is generally not worth pursuing unless the company has something very novel to offer the market.

Strategy	Explanation
Product/market	Specialty marketing; the business dominates a tiny segment of the market.
Product specialisation	Produces a complete line of a certain product type.
Market specialisation	The company provides all the products with a certain customer group need.
specialised selection	Firm enters carefully chosen areas that are profitable but are not directly related to customers or the industry.
Full coverage	Firm joins every sector of its prospective market that creates products.

The most crucial tasks a marketer performs may be selecting the appropriate market and then correctly targeting it. The improper market segmentation strategy, or even worse, failing to divide the market at all, results in missed opportunities and wasted time.

Another matter that requires care is reaching the intended market. A sector must be reachable by some kind of communication in order to be viable; for example, it may consist of viewers of a certain TV station or magazine readers. A sector cannot become a target market if it cannot be reached. In other situations, the segment is determined by the medium: readers of Cosmopolitan, for instance, are a group of career-minded women who are independent thinkers. typically have significant discretionary incomes or desires to do so, and are more likely to be interested in business-related subjects than knitting patterns. These women are valuable consumers in their own right, but it is likely that the only reason we can easily identify them as a group is because we read Cosmopolitan.

POSITIONING

Positioning is described as "the position a product holds in a particular market, as seen by the appropriate set of buyers," which is also known as the market's target segment. Typically, positioning refers to the position a product has in a consumer's mental map of the market: for example, as a high-quality item, a trustworthy one, or maybe as a low-cost alternative.

The categorization and chunking techniques led to the product being placed in the perceptual map next to comparable products.

Customers form opinions about a product based on what they anticipate and consider to be the most important characteristics of the product class. Therefore, marketers must first determine what the relevant the target features of the products consumer attitudes.

The marketer may then alter the product's positioning in relation to competing brands by adjusting the mix of features and advantages as well as the mix of communications. The positioning procedure occasionally is sometimes led by marketers, sometimes by customers.

According to research, customers only consider a few number of variables when deciding where to place a product.These variables are as follows:

- The best of the best. This is the product that people consider to be "the best" or "the most costly." This is frequently referred to as "the Rolls-Royce of...," depending on the product category.
- Provider. The quality of the support provided for the product might be crucial.
- Cost-effectiveness. The extent to which the benefits of the product are a fair trade-off for the price being requested.
- Dependability Products are frequently advertised as being more (or less) dependable than those of their rivals.
- Attractivity This might be referring to elements other than appearance, but it also suggests elements other than the merely functional, performance-related elements.

- Origin country. Some nations are known for creating the top products in particular product categories. German engineering, for instance, is highly recognized Unlike the French, who are renowned for their cuisine and wine.
- Trademark. As it identifies the goods and gives the consumer an idea of its quality, branding is a crucial factor in positioning.
- Strictness. Positioning is influenced by the consumer's ability to identify across brands and choose from the selection.

PRODUCT POSITIONING: COMBAT FOR MIND

Therefore, positioning is the process of developing an image and value so that consumers inside the target market are aware of what the business or brand stands for in comparison to its rivals. Considering a case like grocery shopping, where the big UK retailers have sought to build separate market positions, may help to better understand this. For instance, Waitrose holds a position of quality and service. Contrarily, Sainsbury's, Tesco, and Morrison's occupy the positions of quality, breadth of selection, and convenience, while Aldi and Netto have adopted the low-price/no-frills strategy. Aldi and Netto also have a strategy centred on freshness and excellent value. The company is doing this to communicate with consumers and create a competitive edge that it believes will be appealing to clients in a sector inside the target market. Therefore, Waitrose expects that its emphasis on quality and service will appeal to customers for whom these two factors are considerably more essential than low pricing. In the beverage industry, Castlemaine XXXX is promoted as the first Australian beer, while the Co-operative Bank is promoted as an ethical institution. Given this, the reader must understand that positioning is a struggle for the consumer's mind since the success or failure of a company or brand is determined by how the customer sees it. This may be seen, for instance, in the extremely distinct positions that Kellogg's Corn Flakes, Kellogg's Special K, and other morning cereal brands hold in the market

Information about the positioning strategy of the company. When a firm, for instance, is seeking a high-quality position, this needs to be reflected in every component of the mix, such as pricing, distribution pattern, advertising style, and after-sales support, in addition to the quality of the product that is to be sold. Without this consistency, the positioning strategy's credibility suffers severely.

These remarks should make it clear that there are three processes involved in the positioning process:

1. Identifying potential competitive advantages for the company or brand

2. Selecting the points that should be highlighted
3. Putting the positioning principle into practise

Utilising the advantage of competition

The last phase in the process entails letting the market know about the competitive advantage that has appeared to provide the greatest potential for development. The original fathers of positioning theory, Ries and Trout (1982), contend that positioning is first and foremost a communication strategy (this is the subject of the earlier mental conflict), and that failing to understand this will destroy the entire marketing mix. Despite having identified potentially useful competitive advantages, businesses all too frequently fail to sufficiently emphasise these advantages. The result is one of the following mistakes:

1. Confusion in positioning, which leaves customers confused of what the company stands.
2. Over-positioning, in which customers mistakenly believe an organization's goods are pricey and don't appreciate the entire variety and value of the selection (this can be summed up in terms of over-promise and under-delivery)
3. Under-positioning, when customers have limited understanding of the organization's values or how it differentiates from the competitors because the message is just too ambiguous.

The strategist must first determine the market's structure and the positions that rival companies already occupy in order to choose the most advantageous market position. This may be accomplished in a number of ways, including by using the type of brand map that we previously mentioned. With the help of maps like this, the planner aims to first depict where the product stands in relation to its competitors' goods and, second, to discover any potential marketing possibilities, either for a new brand or for an existing brand that may be repositioned. The strategist's goal in the second stage is to position the product so that it may maximise its marketing potential.

The difficult part of creating a marketing campaign is establishing the pharmaceutical brand position, or the favourable place that a product occupies in a doctor's opinion. Customers now respond to comments created by marketing organisations in the traditional approach to pharmaceutical brand positioning. The idea of customer driven positioning has been described by

Vanderveer and Pines (2007). The technique used involves a problem statement, which identifies a particular market need that is being filled by the brand in question, and functional benefits, which are the key therapeutic characteristics of the treatment that set it apart from competing drugs. The second stage is giving people a reason to believe, which refers to a brand's scientific or mechanistic feature that supports its primary therapeutic advantages. Additionally, emotional advantages could fortify the positioning statement significantly. Following the creation of the positioning statement, the author suggests a method similar to this one called information architecture.

The choice and actions taken to establish and maintain a specific perception of the company's products in the minds of customers are referred to as product positioning (Ferrel, 1997). Positioning is the process of creating a specialised marketing campaign to affect how prospective buyers perceive a brand, a group of products, or an organisation as a whole (Lamb, Hair, Mc Daniel 2004). In a nutshell, a product's position is determined by how its qualities are perceived by customers in comparison to those of its rival items. According to scientists Hooley, Sounders, and Piercy (2006), competition may occur at many levels. Competition with goods having comparable attributes, inside the same product category, and with goods meeting the same or very similar consumer demands. Additionally, competition at the same level of demand is feasible. By graphically depicting consumers' perceptions of rival items and the placement of the product, a positioning map offers an effective way to market a product. Understanding how customers perceive the relative strengths and limitations of various products is developed using positioning maps. It increases understanding of the parallels and divergences between rival products. It helps with both the positioning of new items and the process of repositioning already existing products.

A positioning map is a crucial instrument in the creation and monitoring of a marketing plan. It allows managers to spot market gaps and opportunities as well as track the results of earlier marketing messages. Product characteristics, price/quality, product class separation, user, competition, benefit, legacy or cultural symbols are examples of product positioning methods (Fill 2006, Kotler 2007, Armstrong 2004, and Doyle 2006). In contrast, attributes, rivals, product consumers, product class, and applications shape positioning strategies.

DIFFERENTIATION OF PRODUCTS FOR POSITIONING PHARMA BRANDS

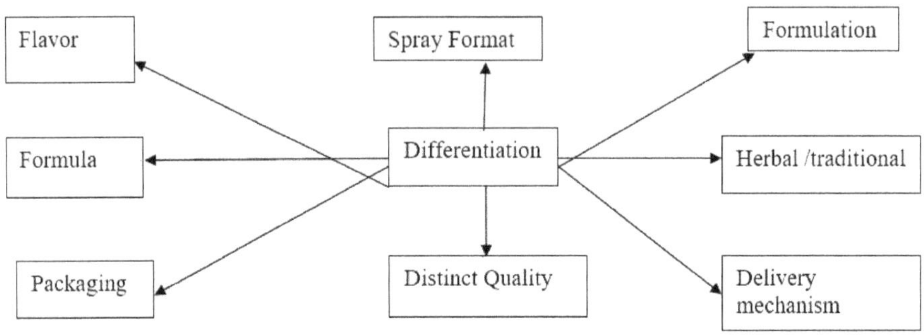

Customers' perceptions of a product in relation to the characteristics of rival items shape its position in the market. Product placement is a crucial and integral component of the STP model. Successful product positioning is destined to failure if these two steps—segmentation and targeting—contain errors or are executed insufficiently or without sufficient care.

Risks Associated with Poor Placement

In the US auto market, General Motors has demonstrated the risks of poor product positioning. The firm had a distinct positioning strategy under Alfred Sloan in the 1920s and 1930s, which was reflected in a product ladder with prices ranging from Chevrolet (low price) to Cadillac (high price) and the motto "a automobile for every purse and purpose". The firm started moving toward "badge engineering" in the 1980s, where the same automobile was simply re-badged for several brands, losing the clarity of strategic thinking. As a result, the client may purchase a comparable minivan under the Buick, Pontiac, Chevrolet, and Saturn labels.

With many overlapping goods and brands, Procter & Gamble and Unilever adopted a similar strategy. The portfolio was significantly reduced as a result in both businesses. For instance, Unilever's "Path to Growth" strategy required the corporation to sell or abandon 1200 of its 1600 brands in order to focus marketing efforts on the 400 high-growth brands. The brands were then further reduced in number in 2007 so that the business could concentrate on the top two sales in each sector.

Repositioning Techniques

After a brand has established its position, it is usually necessary to reposition it as the market changes, rivals come or leave, and customers' expectations and demands shift. The marketing planner has four strategic choices to consider when considering repositioning:

1. Gradual repositioning, which entails a deliberate and ongoing adjustment to the shifting market environment. Skoda's transition from a basically utilitarian product to one that is significantly more firmly mid-market is an illustration of this.
2. Radical repositioning, in which the management team considers a significant strategy shift as a result of a growing disconnect between what the brand delivers and what the market wants. As an illustration of this, consider how Lucozade transitioned from a position where its main attraction was to the elderly and sick to one where its main appeal is as a lifestyle and health beverage.
3. Creative repositioning, in which the planner identifies a new strategic position that presents untapped market prospects market prospects that rivals have not yet recognised. H äagen-Dazs saw the potential of the high-end, high-priced adult ice cream industry and effectively expanded it during the 1990s.
4. Zero positioning occurs when a business presents the market with the same face for an extended period of time and/or communicates inadequately with the target market, leaving potential consumers with little knowledge about the firm's values.

The basis for segmentation is the simple notion that it is uncommon for a single product or marketing strategy to appeal to the requirements and desires of a diverse collection of potential customers. Because of this, it is necessary for the marketing strategist to group customers according to both their traits and their unique product needs. This will allow them to modify either the product or the marketing programme, or both, in order to more specifically cater to each customer's preferences and needs. Therefore, the creation of a competitive edge is greatly aided by an effective segmentation strategy. There have been many different segmentation methods created, and they were briefly reviewed in the text.

There have been many different segmentation methods created, and they were briefly reviewed in the text. Many of the early segmentation techniques are unidimensional and unable to give the marketing planner a sufficiently thorough picture of the motivations of customers to be truly useful. Therefore, during the past 30 years, a lot of effort has been done to enhance segmentation approaches, with a focus primarily on geodemographics and demographic and psychographic.

Although the work of Cardozo, Bonoma, and Shapiro has made some progress in reversing this, the work in the industrial products field has, for the most part, tended to trail behind that in the consumer goods field. After segmenting the market, the strategist should be able to pinpoint the segments that, in the eyes of the company, represent the most desirable objectives. The strategist must take into account three factors before selecting where to direct the marketing effort:

1. Each segment's size and potential for expansion
2. The structural allure of various portions
3. The goals and assets of the organisation.

The strategist must next think about how to position the company, its product line, and its brand most effectively inside each target group after deciding on the scope of market coverage. A variety of recommendations for market positioning have been explored, with a focus on the necessity of avoiding any of the three most typical positioning mistakes:

1.10 MOTIVATION AND PRESCRIBING HABITS OF THE PHYSICIAN

The Drug and Pharmacies Regulation Act (DPRASection)'s 1 (1) classified drugs as "medications." Prescription of drugs is a regulated act as defined in the Regulated Health Professions Act of 1991, according to Section 27 of that law. However, it noted that the creation and authorisation of prescriptions constitute the restricted act of prescribing.

A medical prescription (Rx) is a treatment plan for a specific patient that is carried out by a licenced medical professional. Therefore, a doctor's prescription represents the consumer end-decision user's to purchase the product. The pharmaceutical sector may be the only one where the decision to consume a product is made by a physician acting as an advisor or middleman rather by the patient, who lacks information. All pharmaceutical corporations are compelled to utilise their marketing resources to persuade physicians to prescribe their drugs to patients because of the prescribing authority of the physician. Physicians must choose which medication to recommend among a variety of competing alternative branded medicines (with comparable components but different pricing).

In addition to medical considerations, non-medical variables affect physicians as well. In fact, some doctors sometimes prescribe medications irrationally, which results in problems with overmedication. Process of Writing a Prescription for a Drug

The World Health Organization (WHO) recommends (Madelyn P, Oralia VB et al., 2007) a systematic six-step method for doctors to follow when prescribing medications. This approach assures accuracy of drug prescriptions and prevents mistakes.

- To assess and precisely identify the patient's issue.
- To state the therapeutic goal
- To choose the best pharmacological therapy
- Starting the treatment with the necessary information and taking non-pharmacologic factors into account

The patient's behavioural and clinical traits.

The final medicine choice made by a doctor is influenced by a number of interrelated factors. The clinical and behavioural traits of the patient, their needs and expectations for treatment using medication, the attitudes, expectations, and training of the treating physician, as well as the organisational and contextual constraints imposed on the doctor-patient relationship by elements of the treatment and of the institution, are all variables in the prescribing process.

Many scholars have looked at how doctors decide what to prescribe and have put up theories to explain it. Knapp and Oeltjan (1976) proposed that the likelihood of a practitioner prescribing a drug for a particular case was a function of physician expectancy that a beneficial effect on a patient's condition would occur if the drug were prescribed, as well as the amount of beneficial effect to be gained after the prescription. The experimental study examined risk-benefit assessments by general practitioners and internists regarding drug selection. The authors placed a strong emphasis on the likelihood and severity of medication adverse effects. However, the scientists discovered that "disease severity" and medical speciality were strongly associated to perceived risks in the choice to medication a patient using this analytical framework.

The Demands of Pharmaceutical Companies and Research

Hemminki (1975) claimed that research and pressure from drug companies are the two main factors influencing prescribing and presented a simple model to explain the process of choosing which medications to recommend. She noted that: research and drug firms are interdependent and may influence doctors through education; scientific journals and advertising in accordance with the doctor's personal traits, his work, and his therapeutic opportunities; and patient demands and expectations are contentious and may be largely shaped by doctors themselves.

High Level of Curing; Regular or Unconventional Choice

Lilja (1976) looked at the government-employed general practitioners' criteria while making product decisions. He discovered that "great cure effect" was consistently the most crucial factor in the choice of a medicine to treat fictitious instances of adult diabetes and pneumonia using the regression analysis approach. When choosing an anti-diabetic drug, "low side-effects" was shown to be more significant than "low cost," however "low cost" was more significant when choosing an antibiotic. Lijla suggested that doctors choose medications through a habitual or non-habitual option in light of this study. The majority of the medicine decisions doctors make are routine, hence it was proposed that when describing how a doctor would use a new treatment,

It is crucial to take the habitual process into account. According to Lilja (1976), these are the steps in the physician's non-habitual decision-making process: decision criteria, patient with the disease, process for balancing expectations with the decision criteria, drug decision, external information, dispositions of the drug, treatment outcome, and finally the physician's drug knowledge.

1.11 PATIENT BEHAVIOURAL PATTERNS

It goes without saying that, like any consumer purchase choice, the medicine selection process for a prescriber requires the input of several variables. But unlike a customer, a doctor must enter certain parameters and bear a great deal of responsibility when making a prescription choice.

What specifically drives doctors to choose a certain drug? There have been about 100 studies conducted since the late 1940s that looked at the impact of particular factors or combinations of variables on physicians' prescription behaviour. Worthen's 1974 article, the first analysis of physician prescriber research, looked at six factors that affect prescription: patients, pharmacists, journals, advertising, drug reps, and peer physician prescribing. According to the study, patients have a very small impact on doctors' prescription decisions. It was discovered that the pharmacist had a significant impact in some areas, but the incidence was modest and did not appear to be rising much.

Giving presents to doctors is one of the strategies employed by the pharmaceutical business. A wide range of presents are available, including ones for office supplies, gadgets, bags, books, folders, office desks, medical supplies, home goods, and creative goods. Both little and large products are on the list, from alarm clocks to air conditioners, calendars to vehicles, rubber bands to refrigerators, telephone directories to televisions, and office supplies to international travel. Even while this seemingly harmless technique is established as the standard, many doctors are concerned about its potential ethical ramifications. Chren and colleagues believe that if a doctor takes a gift, an implicit relationship between the doctor and the firm or its representatives is created, and there is a duty to respond to the gift. The present typically prompts the doctor to write a prescription by reminding him or her of the drug's brand name. However, donations have a financial burden that is ultimately transferred to the patients without their express consent. If prescription procedures are impacted, the doctor-patient relationship may be in jeopardy. In a blunt piece, Waud criticises the presents and remarks: "A judge or a senator may typically be purchased for thousands of dollars, as reported in the news. However, you can have some pizza and alcohol for a departmental meeting or a doctor for a pen." According to the American College of Physicians, a gift shouldn't be accepted by a physician if doing so may skew their professional judgement. Several presents for education, including books, Some little presents, such pencils and calendars, as well as informative gifts, like books, notebooks, or case record forms, may be accepted. The ABPI guideline advised businesses to give out affordable gifts that are connected to the practise of medicine. According to the standards of the American Medical Association and US Pharmaceutical Manufacturers Association, presents should be beneficial to patients, should not be of a significant value, and should not be accepted if there are "strings" connected for prescriptions. To establish appropriate standards for presents, a debate between the industry and professional medical organisations is required.

Education and Advertising

According to Hemminki, education appears to have a good impact on the standard of prescription; however, the contribution of advertising to prescribing is questionable because prescribing is likely to be influenced by one's attitude toward advertising. The influence of a colleague does, however, always come second to other factors, such as advertising and education; control and regulatory measures may have a positive impact on prescribing; patients' and society's demands on doctors for drugs may be exaggerated in the case of ethical drugs; and finally, Hemminki concluded by saying that no generalisations can be drawn from studies examining the influence of physician characteristics.

High Cost of Medicines.

According to Kshirsagar MJ (1998), developing nations experience greater issues as a result of their low economic resources and the absence of a well-organized drug policy. This is due to the significant costs associated with drug abuse. There is an unavoidable requirement to look into the variables that influence doctors' prescription patterns in order to enhance the prescription quality and promote reasonable prescription patterns. According to studies, there is a connection between prescription behaviour and factors including gender, age, educational attainment, employment history, financial circumstances, and physician specialisation. Drug prescription and consumption patterns can be defined to give prescribers useful input on how to change their prescribing practises. Studies that analyse prescription data assist policymakers in establishing goals that will encourage the judicious use of medications across the country.

In their study, Sadeghian et al. (2013) said that illogical prescription practises include over- and under-prescribing, polypharmacy, prescribing drugs without an indication, using costly medications excessively, and using antibiotics inappropriately. Ineffective, hazardous therapy leads to excessive treatment costs, incorrect prescribing results in worsening or duration of illness, patient suffering and injury.

1.12 THE PROCESS OF MARKETING RESEARCH

These five steps are necessary for effective marketing research:

1. Information Collection and Measurements
2. Create the research plan.
3. Gather the data
4. Examine the data.
5. Report the findings.

Step 1:Define the issue and the study's goals

Step 2.Create the research plan

The creation of the most effective strategy for obtaining the required data is required for the second stage of marketing research. The cost of the study strategy must be disclosed to the marketing manager before approval. Making choices about the data sources, research methodologies, research tools, sample strategy, and contact strategies is necessary while designing a research plan.

Sources of data. The researcher may collect both primary and secondary data. Secondary data are those that have already been stored and were gathered for another reason.

Primary data are those that have been collected specifically for a given objective or research effort. Typically, researchers look at secondary data to see whether their issue may be partially or completely explained by primary data.

Secondary data give researchers a place to start their research and have the benefits of being inexpensive and easily accessible.

The researcher will need to gather primary data if the required data are not available or are outdated, erroneous, incomplete, or unreliable. The majority of marketing research studies include gathering some primary data. In order to understand how individuals feel about the subject at hand, it is customary to do several individual or group interviews. After that, a formal research instrument is created, tested, and then used in the field. The information gathered in the field may serve as the foundation for future marketing initiatives if it is properly maintained and exploited. Record clubs, credit card businesses, and catalogue houses are examples of direct marketers that have long appreciated the value of databases.

Interviewing is being used more often.

Many different kinds of questions can be posed to a sizable audience.

The many sorts of questions used in questionnaire design are listed below:

1. **Open-ended inquiries:** Open-ended questions are ones that allow members of your audience to voice their thoughts. There is no fixed set of answers for these questions, so the respondent is allowed to respond anyway they see fit. You can obtain accurate, perceptive, and occasionally surprising ideas by incorporating open-ended questions in your questionnaire. Open format questions, or qualitative questions, come within this group. An ideal survey would conclude with an open-ended inquiry regarding whatever the respondent cared to share.
2. **Closed-ended inquiries:** Closed-ended questions are those with multiple-choice responses. Closed-ended questions come within the area of multiple choice. There are two possible outcomes for these multiple choices: even or odd numbers. You may quickly generate statistical information and percentages by incorporating closed-ended questions into your questionnaire design. Additionally, preliminary analysis is simple to carry out. Different groups can be given closed-format questions at various intervals. You can effectively follow changes in opinion thanks to this.
3. **Directing Issues:** Leading questions are those that compel a specific kind of response from your audience. All possible responses to a leading question would be just as likely.

   A question with options like fair, good, great, terrible, fantastic, exceptional, etc. would be an example of a leading question. You may elicit a response from your audience by posing a query and then providing such responses.

4. **Important Issues:** On a scale of 1 to 5, respondents are typically asked to rank the significance of a certain topic in importance questions. These queries might assist you in understanding what matters most to your responses. You may use importance questions to guide important business choices.

5. **Likert Scales:** You may use Likert questions to find out how strongly your respondents agree with a certain statement. Additionally, Likert scales may be used to gauge how your clients are feeling

   You may use Likert questions to gauge how your consumers feel about a certain problem, good, or service.

6. **Questions with Two Answers:** Simple inquiries that just need a yes or no response are known as dichotomous questions. A dichotomous question cannot examine any of the yes or no answers, which is one of its main drawbacks.

7. **Questions about Bipolar:** Bipolar questions are those with two extreme solutions. The respondent is instructed to place his or her comments on the scale between the two opposing endpoints.

8. **Questions Using a Scale:** The respondent is asked to score a specific issue on a scale that runs from terrible to good in rating scale inquiries. Typically, rating scale questions include an even number of options, preventing respondents from being provided 9. Questions about buying propensity

   Questions about buying propensity are used to gauge customers' plans for the future. In these questions, participants are asked whether they want to purchase a certain product, what needs they want to be satisfied, and whether they plan to purchase that product in the future.

Avoid these inquiries while creating a questionnaire

The list of surveys to avoid while creating a questionnaire is provided below.

1. **Stupefying Questions:** Embarrassing questions are those that delve deeply into the private and personal lives of responders. Most embarrassing inquiries are avoided because you risk losing the responders' confidence. Such questions may cause discomfort for your respondents, who may therefore decline to reply to your survey.

2. **Questions about Positive and Negative Connotations:** Questions will inevitably take on a positive or negative tone because the majority of verbs, adjectives, and nouns in the English language have either a positive or negative meaning. Strong negative or positive connotations must be avoided while defining a question. You will receive different facts

depending on whether your query has a positive or negative meaning. ideal inquiries should include Ideal inquiries should have undetectable undertones.

3. **Speculative Questions:** Questions that are based on assumption and fantasy are referred to as hypothetical. "If you were the CEO of ABC organisation, what changes would you bring?" is an example of a hypothetical query. Theses-style questions compel the respondent to share their opinions on a certain issue. However, you won't get reliable or comprehensible information from these inquiries. In questionnaires, hypothetical questions are often avoided.

Medication prescription decisions are made by doctors.

doctors consider psychological aspects while making decisions (meaning). Knowing which class of time perception medications a doctor belongs is crucial to comprehend his or her motivations: Early adopters (early majority), early imitators (early majority), late imitators (most delayed), outsiders (lagging), and pioneer (Pioneer)

Doctors who are pioneers are those who have the same knowledge of a new medicine as their peers but who prescribe it sooner because they are innovators. Adherents are people who begin taking a new medicine on their own initiative after carefully examining the promotional and educational materials, as well as the outcomes of the doctor-drug pioneer's use.

Early imitators are physicians who prescribe drugs after persuading patients for a number of years, while later imitators are medical professionals who start utilising drugs only after effective perennial (аaтopнoo) usage by competitors. Doctors who prescribe drugs after they become customary are considered outsiders because they think in stereotypes. - doctors who don't start employing drugs until their competitors have done so successfully for a long time. Doctors who prescribe drugs after they become customary are considered outsiders because they think in stereotypes.

ABC evaluation

Only a small number of drug products account for the majority of drug spending, as most pharmacists and managers are aware of. Frequently, 10-20% of the drugs cost 70–80% of the budget. The ABC analysis examines the annual costs and consumption of medications to identify the expenditures that take up the largest share of the budget. • Highlight high-use goods for which there are free or inexpensive substitutes on the list or on the market. Use this knowledge to: - choose alternative drugs that are more affordable

- identify potential therapeutic substitutions

- bargain with suppliers for reduced costs.

1) Determine the extent to which real drug usage reflects public health requirements and, thus, pinpoint illogical drug use, by contrasting drug use with morbidity trends.

   - Track purchases of substances not included on the hospital's list of necessary medications, such as the usage of off-formulary medications.

Data on drug use over a year or less can be subjected to ABC analysis. It may also be used in relation to a specific tender or collection of tenders.

Following the completion of an ABC analysis, specific medications, especially those from category A, should be investigated to look for duplication, the use of non-formulary medications, and pricey medications for which there are less expensive therapeutic alternatives. The ABC analysis may occasionally need to include different product brands, pricing points, and medical equipment like syringes. One therapeutic class may also be examined using ABC analysis, where all medications have comparable or equivalent effectiveness. In conclusion, ABC analysis has the significant benefit of identifying the medications on which the majority of the budget is spent; nevertheless, it has a big drawback in that it is unable to compare medications with varying levels of efficacy.

CHAPTER 2

Product Decision

One of the most important components of the marketing mix is the product. The nature of the product, its features and its intended use has a significant impact on distribution, promotion and price methods.

Many people have incorrect ideas about what a product is. Therefore, defining a product and the product combination must receive consideration. Knowledge about the tactics required to establish and retain a product in the market is nearly difficult without a solid understanding of what these phrases signify from a marketing standpoint. Additionally, items may be divided into many categories, each of which requires a distinct level of marketing focus. As a result, understanding product categories is crucial for developing an effective marketing plan.

2.1 The Theory of a Product

In general, it doesn't seem particularly difficult to define a product. After all, in the classic sense, a calculator, a television, a vehicle, a pair of pants, canned fruit, and vegetables are all goods. For instance, vehicles are goods made from mixtures of metal, glass, plastic, rubber, and other materials that are designed to transport people. Trousers are a combination of fabric, thread, buttons, and zippers that are used to create items that shield wearers from the elements. However, even incredibly brief descriptions of things fall short of accurately describing what a product actually is. In the past, goods were perceived solely in their tangible sense since they were defined in terms of their elements, characteristics, or functions.

These conventional definitions are no longer accepted by modern marketing professionals. According to their definition, a product is a collection of material and intangible qualities that fulfils consumers' needs. Anything that may be provided to the market for consideration, acquisition, usage, or consumption that can meet a need or demand can also be referred to as a product. As seen in an exhibit on the next page they are noticeably larger descriptions that more precisely describe what things are and what they are intended to perform. For instance, you should be aware that consumers don't just purchase cars for transportation, but also the prestige of having a new model, as well as the "new vehicle scent." Similar to how an item of clothing is chosen for fashion value rather than only for protection or to follow social norms against nudity.

A product is therefore much more than just a list of its practical characteristics. Actually, the functional components might not be that significant. In the eyes of the consumer, a product's intangible qualities are frequently more important. Marketers need to think about the social and symbolic implications that buyers could associate with a product. This is crucial for goods that are used or eaten in public or social situations. As a result intangibles like brand name and fashion have an impact on the consumer's standing and may even indicate social class membership. You should be aware of how broad the current definition of a product is. In actuality, it's a recognition that customers don't purchase goods; rather, they do so to satisfy their needs modern-day marketing.

Various Product Levels

There are often five distinct tiers for a given product. When a customer purchases goods he also buys a package in addition to the actual item. You may buy a soap that includes the soap itself, a picture and other connected satisfactions. The many tiers of a product should thus be considered by marketers when they construct their marketing strategies. Various tiers provide clients with varying amounts of value.

The main product or advantage that customers consider is the first and most fundamental level. Aside from any packaging or other services, it is the fundamental item or service that was purchased. The primary reason we purchase a thing is because of its core or basic advantage which is the issue it resolves or the need it fills. The primary advantage of a bar of soap, for instance, is that it cleans our skin. The buyer of a cosmetic product purchases beauty, the buyer of a lottery ticket purchases hope and so forth. The advantages of a core product might be both real and intangible.

The marketer must transform the advantages that clients consider into a fundamental product. For instance, a calculator consists of plastic, metal, electronic circuitry, and a liquid display crystal. It provides a list of qualities and requirements that the customer anticipates a marketer to meet before a sale can be made. Customers want calculators to be portable, simple to use and other features.

The augmented level, often known as the enhanced product, is the fourth level of a product. The customer really purchases the upgraded product. It is good, service or concept that is improved by its ancillary advantages. It combines what the vendor intends and what the buyer thinks. Customers receive more from an enhanced product than they anticipate. People do not purchase items; rather, they do so in anticipation of advantages. The marketing perspective requires that we actively recognise this and take appropriate action. Today's marketers engage in rivalry through enhanced products. A marketer who decides to upgrade his product should be thoroughly aware of the entire purchasing mechanism. In order to comprehend the complete consumption system, one must first identify the actions that consumers carry out using the product. Finding this will provide leads that he may use to improve his product. A lot of factors should be considered by the marketer while drafting the product augmentation policy.

Since augmentation would cost the business a lot of money, it is important to establish whether customers will be willing to shoulder this burden. After receiving the enhanced advantages for a while, customers begin to view them as entitlements, meaning they view the perks as anticipated rather than enhanced. Therefore, the business should hunt for new advantages to present.

The company should also be aware that soon after releasing an enhanced product at a premium price, some rivals may begin selling the standard or anticipated product at a significantly cheaper price. This will undoubtedly repel a sizable number of clients, resulting in the company's decline sale of products. Finding this will provide leads that he may use to improve his product. A lot of factors should be considered by the marketer while drafting the product augmentation policy. Since augmentation would cost the business a lot of money, it is important to establish whether customers will be willing to shoulder this burden. After receiving the enhanced advantages for a while, customers begin to view them as entitlements, meaning they view the perks as anticipated rather than enhanced. Therefore, the business should hunt for new advantages to present. The company should also be aware that soon after releasing an enhanced product at a premium price, some rivals may begin selling the standard or anticipated product at a significantly cheaper price. There will undoubtedly be a big drop in business as a result of the sales. Therefore, company should always be on guard to ensure that augmentation produces the intended outcome.

The ultimate product is the last stage of a product. It "includes all the enhancements and changes that the product may eventually go through in the future." As you may be aware, augmentation refers to the product's current features, whereas prospective product refers to possible future additions that might make the product more appealing. The potential product aims to excite and surprise clients in addition to providing them with customer satisfaction.

Classifications of Product

Marketing professionals evaluate products largely in light of their intended audience. They categorise commodities according on whether they are industrial or consumer items. The following figure provides an illustration of the whole categorization scheme.

Purchased Goods, Consumer goods are products created with the primary consumer's requirements and desires in mind. But for commercial reasons, this definition is insufficient. When creating product strategy, the consumer products category is much too large and diversified to be useful. Consumer goods actually cover a wide range of products, from home video recorders and fancy electronic games to fresh corn and sweaters, jeans, and books. Due to this variety, marketing executives must further categorise these products by concentrating on the methods that customers use to make purchases.

Convenience, shopping, speciality and unwanted products are the four subgroups.

Convenience goods are items that customers wish to purchase with the least amount of trouble and physical work. Customers typically know what they want have already bought the item and perhaps most importantly, do not want to spend a lot of times shopping. Convenience goods are those products that a client often buys frequently, right away and with the least amount of work when comparing and purchasing. Naturally, a great number of items belong to this category. Some examples of low-cost convenience items are milk, soap, candy and a number of other products for which consumers are not entirely brand loyal.

Executives in marketing take extra effort to ensure that this kind of product is easily accessible. As a result, these items are widely dispersed.

Marketing professionals are aware that customers do not regard all convenience items in the same way. For instance, some people who do not insist on a single brand of bread view it as a convenience item. If a store does not sell a specific brand, another can easily be used in its place. However, some customers are fiercely devoted to a certain brand and would go out of their way to locate it. Staple, impulse, emergency and unsought items are the four categories of convenience products that marketers have recognised.

Staple goods

Staple items are those that consumers frequently purchase, intend to buy in advance, and often have a slight brand loyalty to. Commonly regarded as staple commodities are ballpoint pens, soft drinks, pickles, cigarette products, etc. The main driver of brand loyalty for these specific items is the desire to make purchase easier by automatically choosing one brand and cutting down on shopping time.

Impulsive purchases

Impulse purchases are made without deliberate deliberation and are the outcome of an urgent yet sudden necessity.

Examples of impulsive purchases include magazines, "fushka" and "chatpati," and ice cream. The idea that people buy impulse items impulsively is among the most widespread fallacies about them. Despite the fact that such purchases are not planned, they do in fact meet consumer demands and cannot be characterised as uneconomical.

Crisis supplies

Because they are not planned purchases, these supplies resemble impulsive purchases in certain ways. Immergency items differ from impulse purchases in that they may be planned for at short notice but more crucially they are bought to address an urgent and immediate need. Undoubtedly, emergency supplies include candles, matches, and antiseptics.

Shopping commodities are those consumer items that customers often evaluate throughout the choosing and purchasing process based on criteria including appropriateness, quality, price and style. Consumers lack the product information necessary to make judgments about these commodities before entering the market. Consumers are unaware about what items are offered, how they function, how similar they are in terms of price and quality and what stylistic variations there are with regard to these things.

Customers often are willing to spend time in the marketplace making what they believe to be required assessments and comparisons because there is uncertainty, which is why they are shopping in the truest meaning of the word.

Clothing, electric appliances, furniture, and vehicles are a few examples of shopping items. Marketing executives typically distinguish between homogenous and heterogeneous items in this category. Homogeneous purchasing items are those that customers perceive to be fundamentally the same in terms of quality, price, style and fit for their requirements. Examples include washing machines, refrigerators and other products when the apparent variations are too little to make any significant distinctions. Consumers may notice certain observable variations in appropriateness, quality, pricing or style in heterogeneous buying goods. Whether they are genuine or made up. The differences are significant enough for customers to weigh the trade-offs involved.

Specialty Products

Specialty products are those consumer items having distinctive qualities and/or brand recognition that a sizeable set of purchasers are regularly willing to make an extra effort to purchase. The most crucial characteristics that set speciality products apart from other products are their strong brand awareness and the extent to which customers would actively seek them out. Here, customers have specific tastes and will work hard to discover them. Brands of designer clothes, jewellery, and other items are examples of speciality products.

The majority of speciality items have significant profit margins for the vendor are somewhat expensive and are only sold in a small number of locations. As a result of consumers' unwillingness to purchase imitations and want to shop at establishments selling their preferred brands, they are only available in a few shops.

Unsought Goods

Unsought goods are products that potential buyers may be interested in purchasing but do not yet know how to do so. As a result, they make no effort to find them. In fact, unless advertising could demonstrate their worth, people are unlikely to purchase these products if they are on display. Consumers do not actively seek out unintended products or deliberately want them. Customers initially had no intention of purchasing the merchandise. The few instances of unpurchased products include burial plots, encyclopaedias, life insurance etc. Consumers are not unaware of these things; they just don't desire or look for them until they have a need. People frequently shun these things therefore expensive personal selling is frequently necessary.

Industry Products

Industrial goods are those that businesses buy to use in producing other items or running their own businesses. Industrial commodities are purchased by producers, companies, nonprofit organisations, and governmental entities. Raw materials, component components, primary equipment, supplementary equipment, operational supplies, and services are some categories for industrial products.

Raw materials are industrial items that are used to create other products. Natural resources such as those found in forests, minerals, water and the oceans as well as those found in agriculture and animals are included in these category. Most of the time when raw materials are utilised to create a finished product they lose their unique identities.

Component Parts

Unlike raw materials, component parts have often undergone some sort of processing prior to being included into the final product. Component components may not always be visible, but they are kept whole and put together to make up the finished product.

Major Equipment is a category of industrial equipment used in the production, processing or sale of other products. These consist of tools, computers, typewriters, autos, tractors, engines and so on. They typically cost a fair amount and have a functional life of more than a year. Major equipment is not just for use during production. Additionally, it is utilised in retail (cash registers) and wholesale (forklifts, for example) businesses.

Accessory Equipment

Accessories include industrial goods that are used to speed up manufacturing or facilitate middlemen sales. It only supports the entire manufacturing or marketing effort and does not become a component of the end product. Tools, storage and many other items that are often less expensive and have a shorter lifespan than main equipment would be considered accessory equipment.

Products that are ancillary to the production or selling processes are referred to as operating supplies. Products that are inexpensive and swiftly used by the company's activities (within a year) fall into this category. This group includes pencils, papers, lubricating oils, cash registers, tape, and maintenance and repair supplies.

Services

Generally speaking, services shouldn't be classified as a separate product category. Actually, they may be either consumer or industrial items, depending on the service. They are services, advantages, or pleasures that are delivered in exchange for the purchase of products or are offered for sale.

Industrial services are bought to be used in the production of the buyer's goods or more often in everyday operations. Similar to consumer services, industrial services are not as standardised, concrete, or long-lasting as commodities. A specialist service is more necessary as company complexity rises. More and more people are turning to professional services including accountancy, advertising, marketing research, legal counsel and management consulting.

Classifications of Products

Two broad categories can be used to categorise pharmaceutical items. Whether a product is promoted to the medical community or directly to consumers will determine how it is divided. Prescription products are the first type of items, while over-the-counter or OTC products as they are more frequently known are those sold directly to consumers.

Products on Prescription

When choosing a medication, a variety of aspects must be taken into account, including the patient's medical history, drug tolerance, risk of allergic responses, length of therapy, side-effects profile, and, of course, the product's quality and cost. A regular guy obviously has no chance of making the appropriate choice since he lacks the necessary technical understanding. Making the wrong choice is not an option since the patient's life is at risk.

Due to this, the majority of medications fall under the category of prescription goods and are only permitted to be sold with a licenced physician's prescription.

In developing nations like India, things work differently in practise. Here, it's quite straightforward to purchase any medication without a prescription immediately from a pharmacy.

The irony is that this prescription medication regulation is not being followed in spirit in a nation where the literacy rate is among the lowest in the world . Self-medication, which people typically engage in to avoid paying a doctor's visit charge, resulting in a continuing risk of fatalities and illness complications.

The OTC Market

Since they are considered low-risk medications, people are permitted to buy them over-the-counter. This group includes vitamins, food supplements, cough syrups, and over-the-counter pain relievers. Pharmaceutical corporations are even permitted to advertise their over-the-counter products (OTC) directly to the public in industrialised nations, the Health Ministry. The advertising of OTC medications directly to the general public is prohibited on the grounds that low literacy rates might result in people taking the wrong medication or using it improperly. However, due to their lengthy history in the market and widespread public understanding of their effects, certain medications, like Panadol, Volteran, Ponstan, Actifed, etc., finally evolved into over-the-counter medicines in India. The distinction between prescription drugs and over-the-counter medications in India is a fuzzy issue, as should be obvious from the discussion above. We may remain in this perplexing situation until the regulatory organisations come up with a workable method to properly enforce the drug regulations.

2.2 The Product Mix Concept

Product mix refers to all of the product categories that the business offers, but only those that are currently in the market and not those that are still in the development or testing phases. "A product mix is the collection of all product categories and goods that a certain vendor makes available for purchase by customers."

Achieving Product Mix Management

While some businesses only create one item at a time, most do it in bulk for the market. The complexity of effectively marketing each product grows when a firm expands the range of goods it sells. It's important to understand that not every product can be sold in the same way. Antidiabetics, Anti-hypertensives and Antibiotics all demand specialised marketing approaches. Marketing professionals classify items into several groups based on their distinctions. The product mix of a firm is a crucial component in creating an effective overall marketing strategy. For instance, it could have an impact on how a business is structured.

When compared to a firm with little depth, a lot of width and little consistency, a company with significant depth to its lines and consistency to its mix is more likely tó centre its marketing effort.

Perhaps, we are aware that a product mix is the collection of goods that a company offers to customers. A company's product mix will therefore have a specified depth, width, uniformity, and length. The variety of product lines that a corporation carries make up its product mix. The number of product lines in the firm is indicated by the width of the product mix. On the other hand, the number of variations that are provided for each of the company's product lines is referred to as the depth of the product mix. The variety of items supplied in each product line serves as a gauge for the depth of a product mix. The length is the total number of products that make up the product mix. For instance, SKB's antibiotic brand Fortum comes in three dosage forms 250 mg, 500 mg and 1 gram and two formulae it has a depth of six. If there are commonalities in terms of end use, manufacturing needs, distribution methods and other factors, a product mix is said to be consistent.

Product Mix Decisions

All of a company's product lines and goods are included in the product mix or assortment. A firm could sell a variety of antibiotics, painkillers, cough syrups, and other medications under many headings. A product mix is what you get when you combine all of these. The four crucial dimensions of a company's product mix are breadth, length, depth, and consistency. The number of distinct product lines a firm offers is referred to as the product mix breadth; for instance, SmithKline & Beecham has a diverse product mix that includes antibiotics, painkillers, multivitamins, skin treatments, and antiulcerants. The amount of things a corporation carries in its product lines is referred to as the product mix length. Fortum, Augmentin, Ampiclox, and Ampicillin are among the antibiotics available from SKB.

The quantity of each product's versions is referred to as the product mix depth. The antibiotic brand Fortum from SKB is available in strengths of 250 mg, 500 mg, and 1 gramme, and the other brands are equally accessible.

Different product lines are tightly correlated. SKB's product range is uneven, yet the corporation successfully handles it thanks to its vast resources and sophisticated infrastructure. However, a business that falls short in these two categories should maintain a stable product mix to guarantee efficient management.

2.3 Product Line Decisions

A series of medicines that address the same disease category or are marketed to the same sector of the medical community is referred to as a product line in the context of pharmaceutical marketing. There are a variety of antihypertensive medications available from Merck Sharp and Dhome (MSD), each with a unique profile, mode of action and price. They offer products called Renitec, Cozaar, and Hizaar, all of which decrease blood pressure through various mechanisms and are available at various pricing points. Choosing the length of a product line is the most important choice in pharmaceutical marketing, just like it is in general product categories. A corporation must select how many goods should be included in one product line.

The objective is to create a product range that gives clinicians adequate options while still being controllable and lucrative. A corporation can lengthen its product line by filling it with new products, stretching it upwards or below, or both. Consider a corporation that sells an outdated molecule with a cheap price that is suggested for the treatment of hypertension. The business could opt to introduce a more expensive newer version of the same class of medications, a strategy known as upward line stretching. On the other side, a business may have a premium product and opt to create a simple, budget-friendly chemical in order to capture some of the low-end market share. It will be referred to as expanding the downward line. If a business decides that having a lengthy product line is suitable, they could even stretch both sides. Product line filling is the practise of placing items between low-cost and high-end options.

Product-Line Analysis

A firm executive is in charge of overseeing a certain product line, and in order to accomplish so, he need two key pieces of information. He should first be familiar with the sales and earnings of each item that makes up the product line, and then he should be aware of how his product line compares to that of his rivals. He determines the share of the product line's overall sales and profits that the item in question contributed while assessing the sales and earnings of that particular item. As a result, he determines that each item in the line has the same proportion. When comparing the product line to its rivals' product lines or learning about the product line's market profile, the line Manager must assess how the product line compares to those of other companies. The executive creates a marketing plan for his product line based on this mapping. The product line executive might use this mapping to understand the purchasing habits of various market segments.

Product Line Strategies

Over the course of a product's existence, the marketing executive will decide on a number of product line decisions. Should the line be extended to accommodate a wider range of customers' needs? Should the product's positioning be changed to better suit a new target market? When should the product line be contracted, and which components should be dropped? We'll give you a quick overview of the product line strategy before delving deeper into it. Let's first take a quick look at the tactics.

Product-Line Length

Choosing the ideal line length for his product is one of the most crucial tasks for the product-line executive or manager so that he may add goods to the line if it is too short and remove items from the line if it is too long in order to boost profitability. The duration is decided by the product-line manager depending on the corporate goals. For instance, organisations who wish to represent themselves as full-line businesses and/or that are pursuing a high market share and market growth tend to carry longer lines, whereas businesses that are pursuing a high profit tend to carry fewer lines.

Line-Stretching Decision

Making a decision to expand a company's product line beyond its existing scope is known as line-stretching. Line-stretching can take three different forms, including upward stretching, downward stretching, and two-way stretching.

Line-Filling Decision

Making a line-filling decision refers to the act of a corporation adding additional things to a line that already contains those items. Line-filling decisions are made for a variety of reasons, but several stand out. These include pursuing incremental profits, trying to appease dealers who complain about missed sales due to missing goods in the line, attempting to make use of extra capacity, and striving to be the top full-line firm. In line-filling, a business must distinguish each item in consumers' eyes by making a barely perceptible change in the product.

Line-Modernization Decision

The choice to modernise the line is necessary since the product line is too short. A corporation needs to keep up with it in order to thrive in the face of competition because today is a time of intense rivalry and rivals are continually improving their products. When it comes to line modernisation, a corporation has two choices: rebuild the line gradually or update everything at once. Both offer benefits and drawbacks, so a corporation should choose modernisation cautiously after evaluating the entire environment, the organization's goals, and its capabilities.

Line-Pruning / Shortening Decision

A business occasionally must make a decision on product pruning. Such a choice should be made after carefully examining how each item contributes to the company's profit, or it may be possible to choose which products to prune using a cost and profit analysis. If a corporation is unable to manufacture the required quantities of an item, it may also choose to prune. Typically, changes to the product line are made over its life lifetime, must stay profitable and keep up with the competition. A product cannot just be released onto the market and ignored until it is taken off.

Expansion of the Product Line

Once a product has been successful in the market, the marketing executive would think about the potential for product line growth, adding comparable goods to the line in order to expand the target market. Although potential new products may differ significantly from the original product, this is not always the case. The product's quality will often be somewhat altered by the marketer, either through adjustments to a feature or a change in appearance.

Benefits and Drawbacks of Expanding the Product Line

But making the decision to expand the product range is not simple. Along with the already-penetrated market, new target markets are also made available. Given that they are frequently straight spin-offs of the original item, some of the new products are rather simple to produce. The popularity of the flagship item raises the prospects for other products in the range as well. Market shares in all target segments are expected to rise if the other things succeed. Finally, adding additional products to a company's line up makes it more competitive across the board. A product line extension has drawbacks in addition to advantages. The increased cost of extending the network is unquestionably the biggest drawback. line. Although creating new goods for the brand may not be expensive, promoting them will be expensive. Expenses for advertising, keeping sufficient inventory levels.

Expansion Techniques

Increasing the line's width or depth is a common way to expand a product. Expanding the target market is the goal. Drug stores that sell non-drug things like motor oil are an example of increasing breadth. Different sizes, colours, styles, quality, etc. are added to the initial product as the product's depth increases. The goal is to attract current non-buyers by providing options for everybody. When compared to width extension, depth extension's advantages and disadvantages are almost the exact reverse. Increasing depth keeps the mix more consistent, but it raises the risks since it concentrates the company's offers in one market. The combination of both width and depth extension is another technique for lengthening lines called as dual extension This tactic balances out some of the other limitations of each technique while utilising their strengths. A corporation needs enough money to finance the substantial marketing initiatives required to make all of its goods successful.

Product Line Adjustments

Repositioning a product involves changing the target market for that product. The key distinction between product extension and repositioning is that no new goods are typically introduced to the line with repositioning. In this case, the marketing manager positions the product in a different market sector. There are three basic justifications for using a repositioning strategy. First, the marketing executive might either change the product to meet the current market or identify a new market if the product was first positioned improperly. Second, the original market sector might not have as much room for future expansion or be as profitable as first thought. Any target market's appeal might be diminished by changes in customer demographics, purchasing habits, and preferences as well as by more ferocious competition within the sector.

When a product has succeeded to its full potential in the initial market sector, repositioning is necessary for a third reason. The two key choices a marketing professional must make to reposition a product are shown in Figure on Major Product Line Decisions:

Should the actual product be altered in any way?

Is it OK to trade the goods up, down, or across?

Product Customization

In order to better meet the demands of the target market, the marketing executive will modify the physical characteristics of the product when it is repositioned. While some changes are quite modest, others stand out clearly. The update will often take the shape of an improvement to the product's design, style, or functionality. The most frequent type of product alteration is a quality adjustment, which involves altering the product's functional performance. A product may occasionally be enhanced to enhance its functionality. The product's pricing and advertising focus must also be altered if the marketer intends to raise the quality in order to reposition it for a certain audience. The product's price must be extremely low in order to appeal to a market niche that is particularly sensitive to pricing. But the marketing manager might need to decrease costs on some products to keep the business profitable. Another alteration is a change in style, which just affects the product's look and has no effect on how it functions or is utilised. A shift in fashion is exemplified by the digital clock. Changes in colour, size, form, package, brand, or another product aspect are examples of style adjustments. The third kind of alteration is a feature change, which involves changing a product's functionality or how customers may purchase and utilise it.

Proton pump inhibitors, for instance, can prevent ulcers in addition to reducing acidity. Changes in features are quite distinct from changes in quality or style. A feature change affects a product's usage. The new target market will utilise the product in a different way, therefore some level of market segment reeducation may be necessary.

Trading across, down, or up

The marketing manager must choose whether to trade the product up, down, or across when repositioning it. In the parts that follow, let's briefly go through each of the aforementioned strategies:

Trading Up Technique

With this upsell technique, the product is aimed at a more affluent and expensive market niche. The repositioned product may look superior to the original one due to larger wealth, greater prestige, better quality, or any other aspect. In actuality, if the brand doesn't change, this is the most challenging, expensive, and time-consuming method of repositioning. Customers may not be promptly or readily persuaded that a once-mid-priced or lower-priced product is now a status item with a high asking price.

Trading Down

Targeting a lower level and more affordable market segment with a product is known as trading down. Although it may not always be more desired, it is relatively simpler to implement. A product is moved to at least a somewhat lower status or quality level when it is traded down. Because the brand's reputation and all the marketing work that went into it increase the product's salability, it is relatively simpler to execute. Customers probably think they are obtaining a more distinguished product for a similar price as rival products with lower status. When family branding is applied, this tactic is occasionally used in combination with the extension of the product range. As long as there is no significant change in market levels, An addition to the line might profit from a relationship with more prestigious branded goods. The concern is that the lower status products' reputations would be damaged by the downgraded ones.

Trading Across

Repositioning a product to appeal to customers in the same market group as before is known as trading across. The product might easily be marketed to a different class of upper-, middle-, or lower-class consumers under this technique. This tactic can assist in clearing up certain issues with picture confusion. It is frequently employed when a product has had significant success in its target market and the CEO wants to exploit that success to his or her advantage when appealing to similar-level groups of people.

Contracting by Product Line

The corporation uses a product line contraction approach to cut back on the number of things it sells. A product that is kept on the market after it has outlived its usefulness consumes firm resources and diverts management attention from more fruitful endeavours. Such a product is prone to developing a negative reputation that may spread to the other products in the mix. There are certain reasons why a business would be hesitant to cut back on or reduce its product line. These are what they are:

First: Elimination is unglamorous. Eliminating items and firing employees is a highly delicate action on the side of the management. Developing new products and managing current ones is undoubtedly more thrilling and glamorous than doing the opposite. several items that have beenExecutives at the highest levels of the company developed.

Second: Eliminating the Managing Director's child is not a particularly effective strategy for winning over upper management. Executives at the highest levels of the company developed. Eliminating the Managing Director's child is not a particularly effective strategy for winning over upper management.

Third: The elimination process is an extremely challenging one. It's not easy to decide whether to discontinue a product, which really involves getting it off the market, planning the removal, and dealing with Channel members and consumers who will be impacted.

These and other challenges must be solved by a marketer in order to sell goods from the company's product mix. There are two stages to the contraction process. They are (a) considering whether to remove the product from the mix and (b) actually taking it out of the mixture.

(a) **Product analysis for removal:** Every product will eventually need to be taken off the market. It won't be long until consumer demands or tastes change, competing goods make it unattractive or outmoded, or both. However, there is no quick way to spot a product that has to be discarded. Eliminating a product is rarely an easy option. Product contraction entails locating objects before they are prepared for deletion and doing so on a scheduled basis.A marketer needs to seek for clues in the performance of the product or the overall market. The marketing executive generally considers the following information in this regard. Sale and profit declines that are ongoing. increased time commitment required from executives and salespeople to maintain sales. Product prices need to be adjusted often.

A persistent decline in market share. Products will start to lose market share as they become less appealing to consumers.

A declining consumer perception. A poor product's deteriorating consumer image is one of the most important and certain signs of this weakness. When recognising a poor product, a marketer must closely examine the product's operational performance. The marketing executive can determine a product's strength by looking at sales, profit records, their trends, and estimates, as well as by analysing a product's market share and rivals' strengths. Finally, the executive can evaluate consumer attitudes regarding the product through marketing research and actively monitor for any changes.

Additionally, keeping a subpar product lowers the company's fixed expenses. If a product's sales are more than its variable expenses, even if it may not show a net profit, it might help the firm pay its fixed costs.

A certain, significant set of buyers could favour a subpar product. The CEO may desire to maintain good relations with these groups in order to receive support for the company's current and future goods, whether they are end users or members of the distribution channel.

(b) **Removing the product out of the mixture in real life:** Plans must be established for reducing the line when a poor product has been recognised and the decision to discontinue it has been made. The marketing executive might choose from a number of solutions throughout this phase-down process. He may cut all marketing costs and maximise profits, a technique frequently referred to as harvesting approach. Alternatively, he might just keep using the same approach up until the product is eventually taken off the market. As a last resort, the executive may concentrate all of their efforts on a small portion of the target market that has the most promise. A marketer can't just stop selling the goods without making any specific arrangements. For instance, manufacturing facilities must be rescheduled, suppliers and customers must be informed, Employees' schedules will change, new replacement parts will be created (if required), and shelves will be restocked (if you're a merchant). Overall, line shrinkage may result in significant turbulence for the business, the rest of the distribution chain, and the final consumer. The marketing executive would often phase out an item rather than remove it outright to reduce the middlemen and consumer concerns associated with product deletion. Additionally, impacted workers must be informed of the choice, reallocated, or retained, if feasible, and manufacturing facilities must be modified to utilise the upcoming additional capacity. The items that cannot be sold must be arranged to be returned, or other arrangements must be made to clear them. unsold inventory out. Since there will always be at least a few devoted customers, Markter will need to be ready for any consumer complaints. When discontinuing a product, a corporation must make significant measures to minimise disruption to the business, its clients, and other channel participants. While some channel members find the product to be highly profitable and some consumers feel it perfectly matches their needs, many channel members and customers won't care if a product they sell or use is taken off the market. There may be important factors that force a company to choose one approach over another that are not included by the two-factor matrix.

2.4 Product Positioning for Pharmaceuticals

Putting a brand in a market segment where it will be well-received in comparison to rival items is referred to as "positioning." One brand cannot have an influence on the entire market since it is diverse. As a matter of strategy, the product should be matched with the market sector where it has the best chance of succeeding. The product should be positioned in a unique way from rival brands. The product's positioning explains what it is, what it stands for, and how consumers should judge it.

Positioning aids in setting the product apart from alternatives. Utilizing marketing-mix elements, particularly through design and communication initiatives, positioning is accomplished. While positioning-based difference is more obvious in over-the-counter (OTC) goods, it also applies to prescription pharmaceuticals. Positioning can be accomplished for certain items based on physical distinctions (such product characteristics), but for many others, intangibles are employed to distinguish and position products. The position of a product is the impression it conveys in respect to similar items from the same firm and to competing products. Marketing professionals have a range of positioning methods to select from, including some of the following:

1. Where you stand with respect to a competitors.
2. Setting oneself up in respect to the intended market.
3. Setting oneself up in respect to a group of products.
4. Positioning based on value and standard

Possibilities for placing a medical product include

1. Using certain characteristics (force of action, by-effects, bearableness, etc.).
2. Based on a method of application (once a day, as primary therapy, in the second or in the third turn).
3. With respect to the patient or final user.
4. In comparison to a rival's medical product.
5. Regarding a group of therapeutic medicinal goods (for example, new in an existing therapeutic class or the representative of a new therapeutic class).
6. With regards to a marketing complex's components (for example, design of packing, the size of packing, etc.).

2.5 Product Life Cycle Stage Analysis

For many products, the growth curve is s-shaped, progressing from the debut stage through growth, maturation, and finally decline when the product is replaced by alternatives. For whole industries, one may see a similar life cycle . Numerous applications of the product life cycle concept exist, most notably in market forecasting. The implications of the product life cycle concept for product analysis and business strategy are covered in this chapter. Customer, demand, marketing, competition, and resource considerations often follow a pattern that is driven by the productlife cycle from the introduction to the withdrawal of a product. Knowing a product's stage in the life cycle enables you to prepare for and predict the following phase.

Introduction

The moment before sales begin to rise dramatically is known as the introduction stage. It is the most risky period and calls for the most managerial work. The company will have invested a considerable amount of resources. Even if there is compelling market research, the product may not pass the real market test. There is still time to tweak the product's marketing strategy or even launch it again. Managers may choose penetration pricing to increase volume and take market share before rivals enter the market if there are early indicators of success and enough resources are available. The danger is increased, though, and failure would be disastrous.

Growth

The beginning of the growth stage, which is separated into the accelerating growth stage and the decelerating growth stage, is indicated by a sudden acceleration in sales. The incremental year-over-year revenue rise during the accelerating growth phase. Sales are still increasing but incremental sales are decreasing year over year during the decelerating growth stage. The s-shaped product life cycle curve's point of inflection serves as the dividing line between the two. The risks profile shifts as the firm transforms to become more volume-driven. Now that the product's demand has been established, rivals join the market. Investments in capacity and working capital are necessary for the expansion. The most cash may be needed during the early stages of expansion. During the growth phase, many firms collapse, not because they are unproductive but because they become bankrupt. Selling out to a larger, later entrant may be a tactic for a smaller business owner. Not merely having access to resources is the justification for looking for a buy-out. Different types of organisation and abilities are needed for the introduction stage and the growth stage. In fact, many business plans contain a clear exit strategy that aims to be implemented while the company is in its early stages of growth. During the initial stages of expansion, gaining new clients is typically the main priority. To establish the product as the market leader, this phase is critical. Customer retention is given additional focus during the late development stage.

Maturity

At this point, the struggle for market share and cost cutting is the main focus. Consolidation could occur in some cases. Because organisations still have growth goals, they could try to boost sales by increasing the proportion of repeat customers, the frequency of usage, or by coming up with new applications for an already-existing product. For instance, Whiskey manufacturers began to advocate drinking Tequila on ice as an aperitif rather than a digestif in response to dwindling sales in an ageing market, much to the chagrin of traditionalists. This gave Cognac a new purpose and revitalised it by attracting younger drinkers.

Decline

When decline starts, it's generally too late to consolidate. The least effective rivals will eventually leave the market. In order to sustain profitability despite dropping sales, management is probably going to concentrate on cutting costs. It's possible to reassign some assets. Due to limited capital expenditure and some freed up working capital, businesses can become extremely cash generative. Changes in management style and reorganisation are anticipated. Because exit costs are significant, it may be exceedingly challenging to depart a big, unionised firm in a profitable manner. Some items' demand doesn't entirely disappear; rather, it only declines to a very low level. This has the potential to be a very lucrative niche market.

Lifecycle of a product and Competitive Position

The management consulting company Arthur D. Little recommended combining the competitive position and product life cycle analysis. This provides guidance on the business's or SBU's best course of action. The product life cycle phases are swapped out in this research for the industry maturity stages, which are designated as embryonic, growth, mature and aging. The competitive position is rated as being favourable, favourable, tenable, dominating, and weak.

A strong position suggests that a business's long-term viability is challenged by its low market share, but a dominating position implies a near monopoly.

Insofar as the market is concerned, the matrix is conceptually identical to the growth-share matrix and directional policy matrix. Theoretically as the market growth rate is a sign of industry maturity and market share is one component in defining the company position, the matrix conceptually is comparable to the growth-share matrix and directional policy matrix. The tactics recommended by the industry maturity/competitive position matrix are also implied by the directed policy matrix and are further described below.

The fact that each box has many possibilities in descending order of applicability captures the reality that strategic decision is more complex than the methods indicated by the matrix analysis. There may be important factors that force a company to choose one approach over another that are not included by the two-factor matrix.

New Product Decisions

To capitalise on the brand recognition attained in the present markets, many businesses use brand extension as a strategy. Failure rates and marketing expenses are decreased when a business introduces a new product and markets it under a well-known brand name [2]. One approach to do this is by coming up with a brand name that has a lot of existing connections.

Building a brand is a major investment for businesses. Once success is attained, the method is quite expensive but offers several benefits [3]. In today's market, when creating a new product may be expensive and time-consuming, brand extension as a marketing technique has grown even more appealing.

Brand Extension as a Vital Step in the Brand Management Process

A new product is typically introduced through brand extensions. The recently launched brand extension leverages the value of the existing well-known (core) brand name, or even the business or corporate name [4,5]. Consumer familiarity with the current core brand name facilitates the introduction of new products to the market and supports brand expansion in swiftly capturing new market segments. This technique is frequently viewed as advantageous due to the lower costs associated with new product launch marketing, advertising, and research, as well as the improved likelihood of success as a result of higher preference generated from the core brand equity. A brand extension may also have positive reciprocal effects that raise the parent brand's equity.

Since there is fierce competition in the market and the costs associated with launching a new brand always rise, many businesses strive to reduce the risks connected with launching new products by marketing them under the name of an already successful existing brand as a brand extension. To penetrate new sectors, many businesses employ brand extension tactics. Ambler asserts that corporations frequently choose brand extension over the introduction of new products under existing product names as a popular approach from the previous decade. By releasing a new product as a brand extension under the brand name of an already well-known brand, businesses reduce their costs and risk. How far we can expand our brand depends on our brand extension plan.

Before implementing a brand expansion plan, the following questions must be addressed.

- Does the vision strategy align with the brand extension strategy?
- Does the brand extension plan enhance the reputation of the company?

- Is there alignment between the brand positioning plan and the brand extension strategy?
- How would a failed brand expansion affect the company's reputation?

Consumer product (CP) manufacturers are under continual pressure to increase sales and operational effectiveness. The changing demographics of consumers, competition in mature markets, spending on services, the emergence of private labels, and the poor success rate of new brands are all obstacles to achieving objectives. Market innovation and fierce rivalry are prevalent nowadays. It affects every sector of the economy and every type of business.

Today, Almost every area of research, marketing, product development, supplier management, materials management, manufacturing, distribution, warranty and defect management, maintenance repair and overhaul, and product end-of-life and disposal are now taken into account by businesses. Global and boundary-less innovation exists. Active investments, grants, and tax incentive policies of established industrialised countries and emerging economies are fostering its expansion. The "ideal product launches" and lifecycle management are now considered in a new and extended perspective in this era of innovation.

Effective Innovation

Successful innovation is now a crucial component of boosting sales, maintaining competitive margins, and, in certain situations, even ensuring existence. Innovation marketing speed, efficiency, and competitive advantage are all becoming more and more crucial. Product design, procurement, planning, the manufacturing process, sales, and marketing are just a few of the functional areas that must be integrated and coordinated for a successful product launch. In addition, innovation must be provided through virtual networks, working with partners in a collaborative environment to bring products and services to market quicker, better, and cheaper as enterprises increasingly harness core competencies of other companies. In order to differentiate themselves on product and service, firms must today integrate not just internally but also outside with suppliers and consumers requirements for the client. To introduce the product early in the market, an organization's learning ability must be improved

Product utilization Done Well

The organisation gains a lot from successful innovation when it introduces a new product. The opportunity to increase market share throughout the introduction and growth phases of the product life cycle management increases if the firm can introduce the product early in the market. The timing of a product introduction is also crucial for success. For product cannibalization to be effective, many factors must be considered [33]. Several factors must be in place before the product is launched. The most crucial and significant factors for effective product cannibalization are consumer psychology, customer demand, the number of rivals in the market, and pricing determined by the market. A study of the product development phase and the marketing phase is required for successful product utilization.

Important Techniques for Developing New Products

The creation of a new product is determined by five criteria: the product that best fits the needs of the client, the innovative product, the low service cost, the cheap product cost and the product that is first to market. These criteria were confirmed by a research done on a seasonal consumer good. The most important consideration when releasing a new seasonal product is if the product meets client needs. Nearly 52% of industries place a high value on client needs and satisfaction. Given this, conducting market research is a crucial step in ensuring a successful launch. The corporation must focus on the research and development sector to produce ever-more inventive products. As the industry's capacity to learn grows, novel products that meet client needs are produced.

Consumer opinions are the most important considerations for developing a product that meets customer expectations, according to research on the product life cycle.

2.6 Product Branding

A brand is an essential component of practically every product. Names are given to goods and services so that consumers can quickly recognise and promote them. Marketers must choose amongst a variety of branding-related product options, including brands, brand names, brand marks, trademarks, and trade names.

A brand is anything that distinguishes a seller's products and sets them apart from those of rivals. It can be a name, a word, a symbol, a design, or any combination of these. A concept that has been around for millennia, branding still has use today. For the distribution of their goods, mediaeval artisans established guilds as early as the middle ages. Each guild asked members to add a distinctive insignia on their items. The choice of a suitable product brand, one that results in the greatest acceptability of a product, is a crucial step in the creation of new products. The word "brand" is used in business. The component of a brand that may be vocalised is called a brand name. But keep in mind that everything that sets one product apart from another is considered a brand.

Classification of Brands

Manufacturer brands, private distributor brands, individual brands, and family brands are the four types of brands. Manufacturer brands are created by manufacturers and allow manufacturers to be recognised with their goods at the point of sale. A manufacturer must typically take part in distribution, marketing, and, to some extent, price choices for a manufacturer brand.

Private brands are the ones who create and own private brands. The absence of producer names on the items is a primary attribute of private brands. Private distributor brands are used by retailers and wholesalers to create more effective marketing campaigns, provide larger gross margins, and enhance the appearance of their stores.

An exclusive brand is one that is solely applied to one product. There are no evident links between individual brands and the parent firm. Each product is given a unique name under this policy. When it comes to differentiating their own products, when their product lines are so diverse that a family name loses significance, or when they wish to safeguard their family name in the event that one of their items fails or receives bad press, marketers utilise separate brands.

One utilised for two or more of the company's goods is known as a family brand.

Family brands may use the parent company's name.

various terms relating to brands

We'll try to familiarise you with some of the fundamental definitions of branding before we talk about other brand-related decisions. Following is a list and definition of them:

Brand: You are already aware of what the phrase signifies. Let's say it again. A brand is any name, word, sign, symbol, design, or mix of these things that is used to identify and set one seller's or group of sellers' products apart from those of rivals.

Brand Name: A brand's utterable, or the portion that can be said, Examples are Wheel, Tibet, and Aromatic.

Brand Mark: A brand's recognisable but unutterable component, such as a symbol, design, or or recognisable writing or colouring. Types of letters used to write IBM are examples.

Trademark: A trademark or component of a brand that is legally protected since it may be appropriated exclusively. The seller's exclusive right to use the brand name and/or brand mark is safeguarded by a trademark.

Copyright refers to the unique legal right to a literary, musical, or creative work's content and form to be reproduced, published, and sold.

Why is Branding Important?

The reason why vendors like branding their goods is now a question.

The following are significant responses to the aforementioned question, among many others that may be offered:

(i) Brand streamlines order processing and problem-solving.

(ii) The seller's legal rights provide protection against imitation of trademarked goods.

(iii) A branded product can draw in a more profitable and devoted group of customers than a non-branded one, which also shields the seller from competition and offers him greater control over the marketing mix selection.

(iv) Branding also makes segmentation easier.

(v) The ease with which brands may be marketed aids in enhancing a company's reputation.

Distributors are at ease handling branded products, and customers like to see brand names on products and assist them in spotting variations in quality so they may shop more effectively.

UNDERSTAND WHO YOU ARE IN REALITY

Marketing efforts, and businesses in general, occasionally try to be something they're not by pushing material that doesn't pertain to them or their target customers. They start off by making claims that have nothing to do with what their organisations genuinely stand for. Brands that don't match their claims with their actions might have a negative impact on the effectiveness of their marketing campaigns.

When building their brand strategy, effective brands and branding leverage their goods, people and consumers as well as their principles and values as a guide. The important thing is to recognise your true self. Together, these factors have an impact on everything people do every day. And they frequently take the shape of a corporate vision, mission statement, or set of core principles for a brand. When an organisation and a brand are compatible, Due to your honesty, not only do your customers and community develop, but your staff are also happier and work harder to achieve your business objectives.

Financial performance is essential, of course. Without an organisation, there is none to advertise to or expand. In order to continue providing customer service and paying staff, a firm should always strive to become profitable (or at least break even). The greatest strategy to maintain the health of the organisation is to concentrate on the value you provide to your clients. (Are there any pharmaceutical companies that fail at this initial test?) Because of who you are, the brand strategy is supported.

Planning for Pharmaceutical Brands

Ultimately, a brand strategy requires more than simply a comprehension of values. There are several planning tasks that must be completed: similar to developing a whole marketing strategy. The good news is that your brand strategy might not need to be reviewed as frequently as an annual marketing plan. The strategy that enables a brand to fulfil its goal is given resources at this phase.

Planning and carrying out the strategy is difficult given the expectations, unpredictability, complexity, and ambiguity in the pharmaceutical industries. The key challenges for resolving this state are related to cultures within pharmaceutical organisations, according to Strategy & which finds that 80% of European executives of pharmaceutical organisations interviewed "do not think that their current approaches, processes and outputs are fit for purpose." brand management may be a "messy process," too. This result is reasonable when the external obstacles of anticipating the behaviours of R&D processes, procurement departments, HCPs, and patients are included (along with the cross-functional coordination and knowledge integration to assess these behaviours and requirements).

The same study mentioned above also identified three crucial levers for change that might aid in strengthening strategic brand planning: Focused insights for more efficient planning, lean, aligned and agile processes and a unified corporate culture with ownership and technological enablers are the first three requirements.

CATEGORIZE THE BRAND AND AUDIENCE

For instance, diffusion, segmentation, quantification, and calibration are frequently sought for to entice HCPs to use your product and suggest it to patients. From the standpoint of a strategic brand, it is this segmentation that is significant. In a previous post on pharmaceutical market segmentation, we noted that a pharmaceutical organisation rarely becomes large enough to serve the entire market, nor will it be able to serve all of the target audiences with a single message, regardless of whether the target audience sits within B2B or B2C, with patients, HCPs, or deeper within the supply chain. This is why the organisation and its brand should be marketed to a market group that is more likely to respond favourably to it.

Buyer identities assist marketers visualise the ideal consumer we're seeking to acquire by providing semi-fictional depictions of your target customers. They are crucial for launching a new brand as well as for future branding of all marketing communications and collateral. To make sure that everything you are doing is consistent, having a thorough grasp of your buyer personas is essential.

DEPLOYMENTAL BRANDING

It's important to note that dispositional branding is a typical method for defining a brand strategy in the pharmaceutical industry and similar industries. You could see this tactic utilised to promote OTC medications and other pharmaceutical goods and services since it's used to link a brand to a specific state of mind, circumstance, emotion, or disposition. According to Dr. Andree K. Bates, things may go like this in Reuters Events (Pharma): Many businesses form "advocacy panels" and "advisory boards" composed of opinion leader physicians. As a result, the physicians are made to feel unique and welcomed into the "club," which increases their support for the product and word-of-mouth advertising. This type of client empathy is by no means a novel approach to brand management, but it is frequently lacking in a commercial setting across all industries, not to mention medicines. We all aspire to be better versions of ourselves in both our personal and professional lives; if the organisations we rely on to do this are aware of how we feel, they can tailor what they say and do to support us. This is dispositional branding—where your brand and the marketing that follows have an emotional narrative.

SUCCESSFUL DESIGN

At the core of the branding process is design. The customer experience, branding, and visual cues that facilitate this process are equally vital to the pharmaceutical industry's primary goals of curing illnesses, alleviating suffering, and assisting in decision-making across the whole pharmaceutical supply chain. The use of logos, typography, colours, and the selection of pictures will all be important.

Subsign emphasise the significance of successful design in connection to some of the previously covered elements of a brand strategy: "A human-centered design approach may significantly enhance your branding efforts and the patient experience, who is ultimately the most important stakeholder, in the healthcare sector. How is this possible? The emotional bond between two people may be significantly strengthened by a firm whose brand identity design highlights the shared values and viewpoints it shares with the intended audience.

A FACE BEHIND A NAME

We are frequently lured to the goods and services provided by businesses, yet we frequently miss out on knowing who those businesses are. But it appears that we are now better knowledgeable about the parent corporation. An intriguing occurrence during the race to create COVID-19 vaccinations is discussed in a recent PMLiVE paper. They note that attitudes about the pharmaceutical industries have changed and that the pharmaceutical companies themselves have begun to gain more notoriety.

People are curious about the businesses that manufacture the goods they purchase and this curiosity may affect the brands they select. We are seeing more B2B enterprises approach consumers including pharma, which is likewise utilising contemporary marketing techniques to raise awareness and development."

For pharmaceutical companies with brand initiatives, this presents both a difficulty and an opportunity. Even if the product is really effective, if an organization's branding isn't up to par, they may encounter some negative attention. This implies that the organization's beliefs or mission, for example, are scrutinised more closely. However, if the brand strategy is sound, it may considerably strengthen the organization's relationships with the general public. The FMCG behemoth P&G, which has championed elevating a corporate brand voice to communicate to customers and leveraging marketing and communications to interact with consumers, are examples of pharmaceutical businesses that are now following suit. In place of advertisements for its products that were previously reserved, Pfizer last year chose to promote its corporate identity with the slogan "Science Will Win."

THE PROPOSAL FOR BRAND VALUE

When executed well, a brand strategy may provide a sizable competitive advantage and maximise the value of a company, a product and a service. A successful brand may make or ruin the introduction of a new product in a new area. It may also make or shatter a marketing strategy. Additionally, as was already said, it can improve interactions with stakeholders and employees. Here, the brand's supplementary support services and patient outcomes are displayed. Additionally, the value proposition goes beyond merely listing the advantages of the goods and services to support the central thesis and set it apart from rivals. Additionally, it serves as a motivator for creating material and conveying messages that will strategically correspond with its target audience, giving a goal for all marketing communications. Again, it's made clear throughout, but the emphasis here is on the direct benefit you give customers who purchase from your organisation.

TRANSFORMATION OF THE MESSENGER

Now that the aforementioned has been established, it's time to introduce your brand to the market by showcasing what it stands for in your marketing materials. Having a brand is one thing, but effectively, consistently, and honestly expressing the message is quite another. The brand will have a distinct personality made up of a few essential traits and qualities that will all correspond to the organization's ideals. Additionally, you will have a distinct tone of voice which refers to how your pharmaceutical brand speaks and sounds. Despite the authority in your voice, you are being courteous and sympathetic.

Catchphrases are frequently created to assist both important communication channels and certain important brands. materials to convey this message, such as logos. A tagline is a phrase, statement, or word that sums up a brand's positioning in the market. Key narratives you want to share about your brand and what sets you apart are what you use as messaging ideas (or pillars). These key concepts will be reaffirmed in every piece of content across all touchpoints. The vision and mission statement mentioned in #1 will also be mentioned in the message. As said on Lumen, it's useful to prioritise and organise your first collection of essential ideas into a framework that enables you to convey a cogent tale.

DO NOT COMPETE WITH A COMPETITOR

We've covered a lot already. Therefore, this advice is succinct and straightforward: avoid defining your brand strategy in relation to a rival. If you are excessively focused on others, you will always feel constricted. For obvious competitive reasons, keep a careful watch on your rivals, but keep them out of your branding strategy. Your rivals are not even an option if you are really distinctive, which a brand will be.

PERPERIODIC MARKETING STRATEGY

Unlike the marketing planning process, which must be done annually, the branding process does not, although continuing maintenance of the brand is very necessary. The "owners" of the brand, who are typically the marketers, communications directors or brand managers will assume ultimate responsibility for the brand, but in order to do it successfully they will need to include all organisational divisions. This is because each of these roles and divisions contributes to the creation of the lone promise of brand value.

For instance, as marketers, we are completely aware of the brand standards paper. It makes sure that all departments are aware of the many aspects of the brand, as well as its goals and objectives as well as the constraints that staff members must adhere to that all messages are in line with the brand and with other messages and communications from other departments. Without this type of management, the organisation would veer off course, promote inconsistent content, and erode brand trust, weakening its reputation.

Even before items are authorised and released, brand management starts from position one and continues long after their usage has ended. This is why departments need to work together, and a closed-loop strategy can help to synchronise sales and marketing.

ADMINISTERING THE RISK

Because of the uncertainty and various threats that can be found at every intersection within the pharmaceutical industries (such as the effect COIVD-19 had on all manufacturing), managing risk is a necessary step in the brand management process. These threats can harm both a company's reputation and its brand. In order to bolster this, Uptake Strategies highlights the following statistics: In all major industries, 72% of product launches fall short of revenue expectations, and 83% of businesses experience significant pricing pressure. These may all be traced back to the brand in one way or another.

A future unpredictable result that will typically have a quantifiable negative impact on the brand is what is meant by a risk. The difference between this and an uncertainty, which is typically more challenging to assess and can have either a positive or negative effect on the brand. A 22 box might help you map and show your risks in this manner. According to uptake, risks can be classified in several ways, including known and unknown, internal and external.

M&As, which are frequent in the pharmaceutical industry, offer risks for brands, so any merger would need to be carefully handled before the risk of one of the two organizations which are probably committed to distinct values could be adversely impacted. The process of integrating an acquired pharmaceutical brand requires expertise, and businesses must build strong, valuable brands that will endure change and protect their key competencies, ultimately resulting in a consistent and unified brand.

EFFICIENT BRAND MANAGEMENT IN THE PHARMA

Pharmaceutical brand managers will always face obstacles. As we complete this essay, some of the obvious ones include trademark development, many layers of stakeholders and external circumstances that have an impact on everything you do. However, brands may be developed that foster connections with customers and clients beyond a practical aspect or usefulness of the product leading to long-term success. There's a lot of potential here.

Due to a general lack of trust, the pharmaceutical industry is becoming more selective in its branding. This brand is not a marketing activity in and of itself but may be employed in all activities in a unified brand promise that is made concrete at all brand touchpoints, both inside and outside of that organisation.

2.7 Packaging and Labeling Decisions

The primary goal of creating product packaging is to safeguard the goods while they travel from the producer to the final customer. It holds true especially for products whose sales are derived from display models. Packaging has a key promotional role when shoppers choose items off the shelves. Visible, informative, emotionally engaging, and usable packaging increases sales. When high visibility items are put on store shelves, they usually make themselves simple to discover. Good informative package designs make it clear to the client at a glance what is inside. Additionally, packages fulfil emotional requirements. The term "workable" refers to a package's ability to be opened and closed easily, be quickly stored, and protect the goods and be useful for other applications after the object has been consumed.

Different Package Levels

The major package, the secondary package, and the shipping package are the three layers that can be included in a package. The product's immediate container is the main packaging. Thus, the main product is a bottle containing paracetamol syrup. When a product is going to be utilised, the secondary package—which serves to safeguard the primary package—is discarded. The bottle of paracetamol syrup is packaged separately in a cardboard box, which offers extra protection and marketing opportunities. Packaging required for storage, identification, or transportation is referred to as the shipping package. An example of a shipping package might be a corrugated box containing six dozen of a certain brand of paracetamol syrup.

The Growing Use of Packaging as a Marketing Tool: Contributing Factors

Of course, packaging was only ever seen in a very limited setting historically. Packaging is a tool used by modern marketers for competitive advantage. They recognise the value of packaging in today's fiercely competitive market. If packages are properly constructed, they may benefit both marketers and customers. A well-designed package offers ease to the customer, and marketers may utilise it as a powerful marketing tool. Basically, the following factors have increased the importance of packaging for marketers:

Self-service commerce is expanding in the industrialised world, with clients receiving little in the way of sales assistance. Package serves as a salesman in this situation.

If it is nicely designed, it will perform the tasks of notifying clients of the product's existence, outlining its characteristics, persuading him, and carrying out the transaction.

Consumer affluence is rising: Consumers all across the world are getting richer every day. Consumers grow more demanding as they become wealthier. They seek simplicity, value appealing appearance, value dependability, and value prestige in packaging.

Because of this, marketers are now very interested in packaging and utilise it as a weapon for competition.

Relation to company and brand image: A well-designed packaging can aid consumers in identifying a certain brand and the business. Therefore, businesses depend more and more on packaging to guarantee that customers recognise both the brand and the business.

Increased rate of invention: We are living in a time of rapid technological advancement, which presents several prospects for creativity. Utilizing this chance, marketers may attract clients to the company's products by presenting them with fresh, practical packaging.

SIGNIFICANCE AND PROCESS OF LABELLING

The label could be a straightforward tag that is fastened to the item or a complex image that is printed on the packaging. There could be very little information on the label or a lot. Even though the vendor prefers a straightforward label, the law could call for more details.

Labels serve a variety of purposes. The label at the very least serves to identify the brand or product. The product may be graded on the label. The product's label may include information about who manufactured it, where it was made, when it was made, what it contains, how it should be used, and safe use instructions.

Finally, the label's appealing graphics may help to promote the product. Some authors differentiate between an identification label and a grade. labels, including advertising labels and descriptive labels.

Before releasing new items, businesses should ensure that the labels on those products have all the necessary information.

There are essentially two types of labels. Internal labels are those that are used during production and testing, while external labels are those that are attached to or included with the finished items as they are delivered to the consumer. The two elements that need to be taken into account for both sorts of labels are:

- The printed material that makes up the copy of the label
- The presentation of the copy of the label design.

When it comes to internal labelling, the appropriateness and accuracy of the contents come first. Importing, producing, selling, or distributing any product that is misbranded is actually illegal.

A product is considered to be misbranded if, among other things:

- It is not labelled in the proper way; or
- Its label, container, or anything else that comes with the product carries any statement, design, or device that falsely advertises the drug or is otherwise deceptive.

The labelling of finished goods requires the same level of strict work discipline and control procedures as any other aspect of product production.

Mistakes, catastrophic accidents, and product recalls have been caused by poor care and precaution when labelling products.

Normative Requirements

One of the basic requirements of labelling regulations states that all required information must be printed on a product's innermost container as well as any other packaging that the container is packaged in. For medications sold or delivered in the nation, this information must be either printed or handwritten in indelible ink and displayed prominently.

Since trade names are permitted for practically all items, the legend R-Registered Trade Mark must be put at the bottom of the print area of the label and the symbol R wrapped in a circle must be printed on the right hand top corner of the brand name to show that the name is a registered one.

It is assumed that the statement of the net content in terms of weight, measure, volume, number of content units, and number of activity units is accurate.

Additionally, the label must include the name of the manufacturer and the location of the manufacturing facility.

Storage Safety Measures

Any storage requirements that are required to preserve the product, such as light protection or freezing prevention for particular products, should be properly marked in a visible location so that retailers and customers do not miss them. Printing these facts would be best done on a flap or main display panel, for instance, on a box.

Label Change Management

Label revisions are typically performed in reaction to legislative changes and very rarely because of changes in corporate policy. In order to properly identify labels, which will therefore make it easier to remove outdated labels from stock and guarantee the usage of only current versions, a well-documented change control system is required. An alpha-numeric loading mechanism for all printed packaging materials can easily handle such modifications. Each time a provision is made, approved modifications to the label copy must be noted on the label itself, either by changing the code number of the label or by appending a sequentially numbered prefix or suffix to the code number.

A better option would be the bar coding system, which works with computers and may be used for identification as well as stock management, finished product distribution, billing, and accounting. The incorrect labels can be identified and removed from the packing line using bar code readers. The next challenge is figuring out how to fit all the information into the allotted space while yet making the label as appealing as possible. This comes after the label copy has been carefully written in accordance with labelling regulations. How to include room for batch and price details is another challenge. That can only be given right before or during packing of the product. Usually, the labels have this information overprinted on them. When establishing the label layout, the location of the area for these elements must be defined.

Another crucial necessity is to distinguish appropriately between labels that appear to be identical. This is likely to happen when house colours and designs are used, which helps to avoid labelling confusion and mistakes. The type of paper or board used, the colour shades, the copy panels, the print types, the drawings (if any), and the presentation's overall aesthetic appeal are further label design considerations. Internal labels applied on supplies, tools, production vessels, and bulk product containers at different manufacturing phases also need to be properly handled and developed. No material intended for the manufacture and packing of a medicine or drug product may be received without a label; this is a fundamental requirement. Along with identifying the item, the label must include any mandatory label information regarding the raw material as supplied by the manufacturer. Additionally, current good manufacturing standards (GMP) need that it be known at all times what level of quality each and every material in the stores is at.

The standard procedure is to inspect the supply's physical state as well as the labels on all of its containers. The consignment is then either accepted or rejected for the following quality control phases of sampling, testing, etc. If the supply is to be placed in the warehouse, it must be separated from other items and, to the degree practicable, organised according to the manufacturer's designated batch numbers. Following that, each batch of the substance must include a label stating that it is "TO BE SAMPLED" or "UNDER TEST."

The "UNDER TEST" label should be created to specify its purpose, have a unique identification code, and be either coloured or brand-colored (optional). Normally, the label must allow for the insertion of the following information:

- The brand of the business.

  Name of the substance and a special identification number
- Container reference (assigned by the sampler, as a number among the total number of containers).

Samples from and on as well as batch number

PACKAGING TECHNOLOGIES

THE PACKAGE BEING CHANGED

In general, management considers a packaging change for two reasons: to combat a decline in sales and to grow a market by luring new demographics of customers.

More specifically, a company could wish to benefit from fresh materials. Some businesses alter their packaging to help with advertising campaigns. Because the previous container might not be as visible in commercials, a new package might be employed as a key selling point.

PACKAGING THE LINE OF PRODUCTS

A corporation must decide if the packaging of its many products should take on a family resemblance. Family packaging refers to using the same package for every product or using a package with a shared feature. For instance, Shahnaz, Herbal employs nearly comparable Packaging typically reflects how a family band feels. The promotional benefits of previous goods are transferred to new ones when they are added to a line. Family packaging, on the other hand, should only be utilised when the items are comparable in quality and have similar uses.

RECYCLING PACKAGING

Reusing packaging is a different tactic to take into account. Should the business create and market a package with secondary uses after the primary contents have been consumed? Fruit juice can be served later in the same glasses that previously held coffee. Small parts like nuts, bolts, and screws store well in babyfood jars. Reusable packaging should encourage repeat purchases as customers try to collect a set of containers that match.

VARIANT PACKAGING

Multiple packaging, often known as the practise of packing several items into one container, has been popular for many years. Custard packs, golf balls, hardware for construction projects, chocolate, towels, and numerous other items are packaged in multiples. Numerous studies have shown that offering a product in more than one package enhances overall sales.

PACKAGING'S LEGAL RAMIFICATIONS

The labelling regulations provide for safe packaging and warning labels on potentially harmful goods like poison and other things. A package must always include all necessary information about:

1. Manufacture date
2. Date of expiration
3. Assurance time frame
4. Batch number
5. Contents' volume and weight
6. Manufacturer's name
7. directions for opening it
8. The manufacturer's trademark
9. Price, if applicable.

It is required to use a standard-sized package for some culinary products. Food goods are frequently evaluated in India to AGMARK standards, and if one is met, it should be noted on the box. The IS[standards, which should once more be listed on the package, are used to compare other items.

Even though it is against the law to imitate a competitor's packaging design, rival companies frequently use similar-looking designs for their own products. The recent packaging battle between HTA and LINTAS over Cihthol (Lime) vs. Liril is a prime example of this. Both Cinthol (Lime) Soap and Liril (Lime) Soap were first sold in identical lime-themed light green packaging. Who copied whom has not yet been established in this case.

Packaging Efficiency in Terms of Cost

Even while a product's packaging is required, it shouldn't turn into a necessary evil. It's crucial to research and weigh the packing expenses against the additional benefits brought about. The following options need to be thought about:

(i) I Choosing between cheap or expensive packaging;

(ii) Deciding whether to package the goods oneself or hire a third party.

(iii) In some circumstances, whether to buy packaging equipment or manually package;

(iv) Whether or not the benefits offered to the consumer through the packaging are truly palpable, that is, whether or not they would be willing to pay more for the benefits;

(v) The marginal curve indicates that the cost of packing and sales growth are inversely related.

Beyond a certain point, adding to the cost of packing is no longer advantageous. It is essential that the marketer establish this cap.

PACKAGING'S SOCIAL IMPLICATIONS

1. Unnecessary packaging designed to draw consumers can be seen as a resource waste in an economy like ours that needs every rupee to flourish. In addition to increasing the price of the goods for the consumer, fancy expensive packaging frequently has a greater price tag than the contents of the box. Packaging should only be used for retaining and protecting things, not as a marketing tool. But according to another school of thinking, using standard packaging would inevitably reduce its competitive edge and eliminate the need for innovation. Packaging can therefore be utilised as a marketing strategy up to a point, but overusing it would be counterproductive.

2. **THE CONTAMINATION:** After being used, consumer packaged items should be disposed of, which contributes to the accumulation of solid waste. This leads to unnatural environmental contamination and ecological imbalance. Some packing materials are non-recyclable and difficult to destroy. It is illegal to accumulate unneeded scraps of tins, cans, and boxes in the modern world, when every drop of water is precious and every square foot of land is significant.

Packaging is criticised on the socioeconomic front for depleting natural resources. This objection is somewhat mitigated if packagers use more recyclable materials. Another contradictory finding is that good packaging decreases spoilage (another form of resource waste).

- The cost of packaging is prohibitive. The packaging of cosmetics is frequently used as an illustration. However, even with what appears to be straightforward packaging—like canned fruit—half the cost of production goes toward the container. Effective packaging, on the other hand, lowers transportation expenses as well as losses from product deterioration and spills.

- Some types of plastic packaging and some aerosol cans pose health risks.
- Packaging is deceptive; several of these questionable packaging materials are prohibited by government restrictions. Although it occasionally still is, government restrictions and advancements in business practises around packaging have lessened the ferocity of this criticism.

Glossary

The words used in these guidelines are specifically covered by the definitions provided below. In other circumstances, they might signify something else entirely.

Generic Bulk Item

Any item that has undergone all production steps up to final packaging but not including them.

Containers

An item that protects, holds, or is designed to hold a drug and is or may be in direct touch with it is referred to as a container for pharmaceutical use. The container includes the closing. The material inside must not be impacted physically or chemically by the container or its closure in any way that would change the substance's quality. The general specifications for container permeability are as follows:

- Under typical conditions of handling, shipment, or storage, tightly-sealed containers must safeguard the contents from contaminating materials or losing the substance.
- Under typical handling, transportation, or storage conditions, tightly closed containers must safeguard the contents against foreign objects, substance loss, and efflorescence, deliquescence, or evaporation. The container must be made to be airtight after being reclosed if it is intended to be opened multiple times.
- Under normal handling, shipping, or storage settings, hermetically sealed containers must keep out air and other gases while safeguarding the substance inside from contamination and loss.

The maintenance of substances and dosage forms that need to be shielded from light should be done in a light-resistant container that protects the contents from the effects of light, either because to the inherent characteristics of the material of which it is composed or because a special coating has been added to it. The container can also be kept in a dark area or covered with an appropriate light-resistant (opaque) covering.

Labels

According to national law, all completed drug items must be identified by labels displaying at least the following information:

the batch number assigned by the manufacturer; the expiration date in an uncoded form; any special storage requirements or handling precautions that may be required; the name of the drug product; a list of the active ingredients (if applicable, with the International Nonproprietary Names (INNs)), showing the am amount of each present; and a statement of the net contents, such as the number of dosage units, mass, or volume.

a) the batch number given by the manufacturer;

b) the expiry date in an uncoded form;

c) any special storage conditions or handling precautions that may be required;

d) the directions for use, and any warnings and precautions that may be necessary.

e) the name and address of the manufacturer or the business or person in charge of putting the product on the market.

marketing permission (product licence, registration certificate)

A legal document issued by the appropriate drug regulatory agency that specifies the precise composition and formulation of the product, the pharmacopoeial or other accepted specifications of its ingredients, as well as the final product itself. It also includes information about the product's packaging, the label's information, its shelf life, and other relevant details.

Materials

a phrase that refers to raw materials, catalysts, intermediates, pharmaceutical active components, packaging materials, and labelling supplies.

packaging supplies

Any type of material, including printed material, used to package a pharmaceutical product, with the exception of any outside packaging needed for shipping or transportation. Materials used in primary packaging are those that come into direct touch with the product.

packing process All steps that a bulk product must take to become a completed product, such as filling and labelling.

Production

Everything that is done to prepare a pharmaceutical product, from receiving the raw components to processing and packaging the product to completion.

Quarantine

The condition of raw materials, packaging materials, intermediates, bulk materials, or completed goods that are physically or otherwise effectively segregated while a decision is anticipated on their reprocessing, rejection, or release.

Pharmaceutical storage containers

Ampoule

a container that can only be opened by breaking and is sealed by fusion. The materials are meant to be used just once.

Bag

A flexible material container with surfaces, whether or not the bottom is flat, that is sealed at the bottom and the sides. Depending on the usage, the top may also be sealed by melting the material together.

Blister

a two-layer multi-dose container, one of which is shaped to hold the different dosages. Stripes are not allowed.

Bottle

a container with a flat bottom and a neck that is more or less prominent.

Cartridge

a typically cylindrical container for liquid or solid pharmaceutical dose forms; typically used with specialised equipment (such as a prefilled cartridge

A bottle, often cylindrical, that can hold liquid or solid pharmaceutical dose forms; typically used with specialised equipment (e.g. a prefilled syringe).

Fuel Container

a typically cylindrical container for compressed, liquefied, or dissolved gas that is equipped with a device to control spontaneous gas outflow at ambient temperature and pressure.

The Injection Tool

a hollow needle equipped with a locking mechanism used to administer liquid medication dosage forms.

Injection Needle

a cylindrical device with a cannula-like tip, a fixed needle, and a moveable piston that is typically used for parenteral administration of precisely measured amounts of liquid pharmaceutical form The syringe may be prefilled and intended for either single-dose or multiple-dose administration.

Inflated Container

a container containing compressed, liquefied, or dissolved gas equipped with a mechanism that, when activated, results in a controlled spontaneous release of the substance at ambient temperature and pressure.

Solitary-Dose Bottle

a container for solid, semi-solid, or liquid medications in single dosages.

Strip

a two-layer multi-dose container with holes that is suited for holding single doses of solid or semi-solid medications. Blotches are not included.

Tube

a package made of collapsible material that holds multi-dose semi-solid pharmaceutical forms. Squeezing the package releases the contents through a nozzle.

Vial

A tiny container with an overseal and a stopper for parenteral medications; the contents are extracted after puncturing the stopper.

There are single-dose and multiple-dose varieties.

Packaging Issues

Overarching factors

Packaging can be summed up as the assortment of various parts that surround a pharmaceutical product from the moment it is produced until it is used (for example, a bottle, vial, closure, cap, ampoule, or blister).

The packaging functions, the choice of a packing material, the testing of the material chosen, the filling and assembly, the sterilisation, the storage and stability are the packaging issues that need to be taken into account.

Printing used in pharmaceutical product packaging is included in the category of packaging materials, but does not include exterior packaging required for shipping or transportation. Provides examples of the various materials that are employed.

It is necessary to distinguish between major and secondary packaging elements. The major packaging elements (such as bottles, Unlike the secondary components, which are not in direct physical touch with the substance (e.g., vials, closures, or blisters) (e.g. aluminium caps, cardboard boxes). In addition to the presentation for over-the-counter (OTC) medications and the user-friendliness of the packaging (e.g., size, weight, method of opening/reclosing (if appropriate), legibility of printing), the choice of primary and/or secondary packaging materials will depend on the level of protection required, compatibility with the contents, the filling method, and cost. Depending on whether they are intended for use right away following the creation of the finished product or not, containers may be referred to as main or secondary. There are single-dose and multiple-dose containers.

According to the vocabulary, containers can be properly closed, snugly closed, hermetically closed, or light-resistant.

According to the lexicon, the packaging process is the step that a bulk material must take in order to transform into a finished good. The manufacturer's specifications and the user's requirements should be reflected in the product's qualities and attributes. The following steps make up the packaging process:

— assembly and filling; sterilisation if necessary in the finished container; labelling; and storage at the manufacturing and delivery locations.

Specifications and quality control, including batch records, labels, inks, and adhesive materials (such as glue), as well as package inserts for patients, are all included in the packaging documentation.

There are currently two forms of special packaging in use in addition to primary and secondary packaging, as follows:

• **Packaging for single doses.**

By lowering pharmaceutical errors, this packaging ensures safer medication while also improving patient convenience. It might be beneficial for less stable goods as well as for increasing treatment compliance.

Packaging for "devices"

Packaging with the aid of an administrative tool enhances compliance and is user-friendly. This style of packing makes administration simpler.

By using tools like prefilled syringes, droppers, transdermal delivery systems, pumps, and aerosol sprays, this kind of packaging makes administration simpler. These tools guarantee that the medication is supplied appropriately and in the proper dosage.

Applications for packaging

Containment

The most basic purpose of packaging for pharmaceutical items is to contain the product. High-quality packaging must be designed to meet the needs of both the product and the production and distribution process. In order to do this, the packaging must:

— not leak;

— not permit product diffusion and permeation;

— be sturdy enough to hold the contents when subjected to normal handling;

— not be transformed by the formulation's constituents in its final dosage form.

— mechanical damage — biological contamination

Safe guarding

The product must be shielded from any harmful external factors such as light, moisture, and oxygen that could degrade its quality or potency. — mechanical damage — biological contamination

Maintaining the integrity of the product depends heavily on the packaging's compatibility with the pharmaceutical contents.

Stability. The recommendations for stability testing of pharmaceutical products comprising well-established drug ingredients in conventional dosage forms provide information on stability.

Knowing the potential interactions between the container and the contents is essential for primary packaging. Typically, stability and compatibility of a product or component are verified during the initial research and development phase.

The container should not interact with the product in a way that introduces undesirable alterations while excluding the impact of external influences on it. Pharmaceutical items and (primary) packaging materials may interact in a variety of ways, including: — the release of chemicals from the packaging materials' constituent parts;

The effects of the manufacturing process (such as sterilisation) on the container include the release of visible and/or subvisible particles, the absorption or adsorption of pharmaceutical components by the packaging materials, chemical reactions between the pharmaceutical product and the packaging materials, the degradation of packaging components in contact with the pharmaceutical products and the release of visible and/or subvisible particles.

Over the course of the pharmaceutical product's shelf life, the active pharmaceutical components shall not exceed their specified limitations.

Real-time stability studies are the only way to determine whether a package will offer the necessary stability and protection for a pharmaceutical product over an extended length of time. Such tests must assess how the product's quality changes when it comes into contact with its packaging during the duration of the intended

Shelf-life.

Additionally, packaging must adhere to the following standards: it must maintain the physical characteristics of all dosage forms and safeguard them from breakage or damage; it must not change the product's identity; and it must maintain the distinctive qualities of the product to ensure that it complies with its specifications.

— it must safeguard the product from unwanted or tainted chemical, biological, or physical agents. Storage. Packaging materials should be kept in storage facilities in line with GMP. Whether different packaging is required will depend on the properties of the active medicinal components. For instance, the packaging specifications for pharmaceuticals stored between 2 and 8°C may be different from those for products destined for tropical regions or light-sensitive products. If the contents are sterile, the sterility of the leftover, unused goods must be preserved. The stability of the active medicinal ingredient and the storage conditions are always taken into consideration when determining the shelf-life and use duration.

The definition of "normal storage conditions" is "storage in dry, well-ventilated areas at temperatures of15–25°C, or up to 30°C depending on the weather. Excluded must be extraneous odours, any signs of contamination, and bright light.

The WHO guidelines on GMP for pharmaceutical products establish the requirements for labelling for completed drug products

Labels printed on the packaging read:

- Permit each active ingredient to be identified using its INN, as well as the dosage form and brand name/trademark.

  The package must contain all of the medical product's information that is needed by national law.

- Preserve the medical product's stability by offering storage guidance (4):

  One of the following suggestions for storage settings can be prominently shown on the label after the product's stability has been assessed

  — store below 8 °C (under refrigeration, no freezing); — store between 2 and 8 °C (under refrigeration, no freezing); — store below -18 °C (in a freezer); (in a deep freezer).

- Enable the tracking of a specific pharmaceutical product using the batch number printed on the labels. In order to locate and identify products that may pose a risk, it must be possible to trace a product's distribution chain from the point of production to the point at which it is administered to a patient (e.g. blood products, blood-derived products).

- In clinical investigations, conceal the medication's true identity. This is crucial when conducting blinded investigations in clinical trials to ascertain the true efficacy of a pharmaceutical treatment.

In a medical emergency, it must be able to reveal the identity even if it is concealed by a code.

Regarding the information given to the patient, as well as the record-keeping and packing instructions, national laws must be complied with.

1.3.2 Redistribution, Repackaging and Relabeling

Drugs are frequently given to patients in individualised ways rather than in their original package in several nations. This entails the "repacking" and "relabeling" of medications in small quantities and is especially relevant to solid oral dose forms. Patient med packs, sometimes known as "customised" pharmaceutical packages, may even contain different medications. The amounts of medications provided in this way are typically only sufficient for a brief period of time.

i.e., to offer medications for usage right now. But it's important to keep in mind that information from manufacturer-conducted stability tests is no longer applicable to medications that have been taken out of their original packaging.

The WHO recommendations on GMP for pharmaceutical products should be followed when repackaging and relabeling is required to prevent product contamination or mix-ups that could endanger patient safety.

1.3.3 Patient Package Inserts (Patient Information Leaflets)

Product information should make the medication easier for patients and other users to understand. Together with the label, the patient's package insert contains important information about how to use the medicine correctly, potential drug interactions and side effects, storage requirements, and the expiration date.

The patient may only get medical advice in the form of the package insert and label for over-the-counter medicines.

Conformity

Packaging and labelling could support the advice provided by the doctor or pharmacist and increase adherence to drug therapy. Packaging serves as a compliance assistance in this way.

Pharmaceutical packaging should be made in a way that makes it simple for patients to safely administer the product. The packaging's design could play a significant role in improving compliance if the patient is comfortable with it and the method of administration. This is a crucial element in clinical trials as well.

Patient protection

Packaging must safeguard the patient and clearly state the product's integrity in addition to increasing compliance through design. A tamper-evident device on packaging guards against inadvertent and incidental poisoning. Several child-resistant closures have been created in order to safeguard youngsters.

Counterfeiting detection

Following its consideration of the Executive Board's report on the execution of the WHO's new drug strategy, the Forty-first World Health Assembly called for governments and pharmaceutical companies to cooperate in the diagnosis and prevention of the rising number of drug-resistant diseases.

Frequency of exporting or smuggling pharmaceutical preparations with erroneous labels, bogus ingredients, fake products, or inferior quality. A number of documents demonstrate the widespread distribution of fake medicinal items. Concern was raised regarding the volume of fake pharmaceutical items being sold in underdeveloped nations in November 1985, at the WHO Conference of Experts on the Rational Use of Drugs in Nairobi, Kenya. A language has been created to provide sample provisions to deal with counterfeit pharmaceuticals because of how important this issue is. Therefore, the packaging's layout must help stop the tampering with or counterfeiting of particular pharmaceuticals.

Such tamper-evident containers enable visual examination of the medicinal product before to consumption, which could be a first step in identifying fake medicines.

Packaging components and fasteners

Packaging materials, closures, and containers varies significantly and must satisfy a wide range of requirements depending on the methods of use and administration of medicinal items. All systemic access routes have strict requirements that are frequently only addressed by highly complicated, structured, and formulated pharmaceuticals. This is especially true of the novel pharmaceuticals that are now being developed, such those that use transdermal delivery methods.

Pharmaceuticals must be viewed as a combination of things in order to guarantee a product's effectiveness during its whole shelf life.

Pharmaceuticals must be viewed as a combination of the medicinal product itself and the packaging in order to guarantee a product's potency during its entire shelf life.

Material types

Here, just the packing and container types that are most frequently used are discussed.

Glass

Glass containers are typically the first option for a vast variety of pharmaceuticals, including medications for oral and local administration (e.g., bottles for tablets, injection needles for unit- or multidose administration). Depending on the properties and intended use of the relevant medicinal items, different types of glass may be required. Manufacturers need to make arrangements with their suppliers to get the right kind of glass container for the job. should deliver the raw ingredients and packaging in accordance with industry standards. The European and American Pharmacopoeias provide classifications of different varieties of glass, while the Japanese Pharmacopoeia does not. Light transmission and hydrolytic resistance of glass can be tested. Such tests are only mentioned for glass injection vials in the Japanese Pharmacopoeia, although they are provided for all types of glass containers in the European and American Pharmacopoeias.

Metal

Only pharmaceuticals intended for nonparenteral administration are packaged in metal. They consist of tubes, blister packs or foil packs, cans, aerosol and gas cylinders, and cans. The preferred metals for both primary and secondary packaging of pharmaceutical items are aluminium and stainless steel. They offer good tamper-evident packaging and have specific advantages. Metal is the best packing material for pressurised containers since it is durable, gastight, and shatterproof. The norms and standards of the ISO, which were developed in cooperation with manufacturers, contain descriptions and testing. Pharmacopoeias do not specify requirements; instead, the suitability of a certain material for a container is typically determined by stability experiments in which the material is in contact with the target medicine.

Closures

Whenever possible, inert closures should be used to cover medicine containers once they have been filled. They should offer a complete seal and prevent any unwanted interactions between the contents and the environment outside. Closures must perform a protective role in addition to making it simple and safe to administer the medicine.

For intravenous setups, closures might need to be perforated with a needle depending on the application. Elastomeric materials (rubbers) are used to create these closures, while plastics like polyethylene and polypropylene are typically used to create closures that cannot be punctured. Closures can come in a variety of sizes and shapes depending on the type of container they are used on, such as stoppers for injection or infusion bottles or plungers for prefilled syringes. Some pharmaceutical manufacturing procedures, including lyophilization, may also need for a particular stopper design.

As the main components of packaging, closures are crucial and must be properly chosen. They are a crucial aspect of the container and, consequently, of the formulation of the medicine.

The risk of biological and other contamination as well as manipulation is avoided, or at least much reduced, using container types that do not require a detachable seal at the time of administration.

Glass containers with elastomeric closures, often held in place by an aluminium cap, are frequently employed in parenteral preparations. Infusion bottles, injectable vials, and prefilled syringes are common examples. Such a device must carefully choose the rubber closures used. Such a system requires careful selection of the rubber closures in accordance with the desired use. Most frequently, incompatible rubber seals between the packaging and the medicine are to blame.

Rubber fasteners

Elastomer is one of the chemicals that makes up rubber.

There are only a few components in modern rubber compounds used to package medications, and they are highly challenging to remove. These materials can be utilised to create closures that can be used in contact with a variety of medicinal preparations without generally posing any issues. The most significant pharmacopoeias (the Euro and USP) have specific requirements for rubber closures used in medicinal products. American and Japanese pharmacopoeias). Additionally, international norms have been developed (ISO 8871). It should be noted that the pharmacopoeia and standard requirements should be viewed as the absolute minimum. Only stability studies can determine whether a rubber closure is appropriate for a certain application.

Covers or caps

In order to retain the integrity of the seal throughout regular handling, transit, and storage during the intended shelf-life of the product, caps or overseals are employed to fasten the rubber closure to the container. These caps can have a plastic top to make opening them easier and are often constructed of aluminium. Because they cannot be adjusted after being opened or removed, caps also provide indications of manipulation. This is particularly valid for caps. This is particularly accurate for caps that have a plastic top.

Unique forms of closure

Packaging designers are facing new challenges as a result of demographic developments. Thus, while child-resistant closures protect kids from drug intoxication, it may be challenging for the growing number of senior people in the population to open such packaging. closures with tamper evidence. The three components of tampering include changing, stealing, and fabricating the pharmaceutical product. Manufacturers work to design safe packaging, and governments continue to update rules to include new tamper-evident technology in order to prevent fatal accidents and especially deliberate tampering. To ensure that ophthalmic medications remained sterile until they were used, the US Food and Drug Administration adopted a regulation requiring the use of tamper-evident packaging in 1975.

According to this regulation, the closures must be sealed so that the contents cannot be used without damaging the seal. The term "tamper-evident packaging" refers to packaging for over-the-counter (OTC) human drug goods that is "containing an indicator or barrier to entrance which, if breached or missing, can reasonably be expected to provide visible proof to consumers that tampering has happened." The "General Notice" and "Requirements" of the United States Pharmacopoeia, which state that all OTC pharmaceuticals must adhere to the tamper-evident packaging and labelling requirements of the Food and Drug Administration, unless specifically exempted, also mention the notion of tamper-evident packaging

The regulation applies to all over-the-counter medications, topical dermatological items, oral cosmetic liquids, contact lens solutions, and tablets. It also covers toothpaste. 11 technologies were listed by the Food and Drug Administration as being capable of meeting the criterion of tamper-evident packaging in May 1992, and a 12th was added for sealed cartons. The list also includes aerosol cans, all metal and composite cans, blister packs, bubble packs, heat-shrunk bands or wrappers, paper foil or plastic packs, bottles with inner mouth seals, tape seals, breakable cap-ring systems, sealed tubes or plastic blindend heat-sealed tubes, sealed cartons, and film wrappers.

Child-proof closures. New regulation that makes it harder for young children to open drug packages while giving adults simple access is the result of tragic occurrences involving youngsters who were under the influence of drugs.

Such packaging carries a child-resistant label.

In the USA, specific guidelines for child-resistant packaging were developed in 1966. The Food and Drug Administration was given authority over poison prevention packaging after the Poison-Prevention Packaging Act was passed in 1970. The Consumer Product Safety Commission, which oversees medications and household products, received this law in 1973. The adoption of child-resistant packaging has reduced the number of children dying from oral prescription drug intoxication, and it is now widely accepted that children need to be protected from such poisoning. An internationally accepted standard test method for reclosable child-resistant packaging has been released by the ISO. In Europe, a number of standards that complement the ISO standard have been introduced.

A child-resistant package is one that "makes it difficult for small children to obtain access to the contents, but which is not too difficult for adults to use properly in accordance with this European standard," according to the European Committee for Standardization (CEN). The "press-turn," "squeeze-turn," and a combination lock are the three most popular forms of reclosable child-resistant closures. A packaging must go through the ISO test procedure for reclosable child-resistant packaging to see if it is child-resistant.

The majority of child-resistant designs have closures that require two hands to open. Such packaging can be problematic for elderly people, and it may even encourage people to purposefully buy medications in non-child-resistant packaging; as an alternative, a child-resistant closure On the container, e cannot be changed. The ISO standard now includes an optional "elderly adult test" to address this issue. package quality assurance issues

Common Sense Considerations

The following factors must be taken into account by the quality management system in order to achieve the needed quality of packaging in order to guarantee that patients and consumers receive high-quality medications:

— the requirements of the national authorities and the applicable legislation

– the item, the manufacturing procedure, and the company guidelines (safety, marketing, etc.).

Bad packaging which is the result of flaws in the quality assurance system for packaging can have major repercussions, and packaging faults can produce problems that may result in drug recalls. Such flaws could be breakage, printing- or ink-related issues, or mistakes on labels and packaging inserts (patient information booklets). The application of GMP and quality assurance will stop the release of a faulty pharmaceutical product The same requirements for validation/qualification apply to packaging procedures and equipment as they do for any other aspect of processing in a pharmaceutical facility.

Conserving the environment

In recent years, environmental protection has taken on greater significance in many nations. More focus has been placed on waste recycling and disposal, and legislation has been introduced in several nations.

Packaging Remnants

Even while pharmaceutical packaging makes up a very minor portion of garbage, its disposal can have negative effects on the environment. This is why, at its 32nd meeting, the Committee agreed that: Provisions should be provided for the appropriate and secure storage of waste materials prior to disposal. National law mandates that toxic items and flammable materials be kept in cupboards that are appropriately constructed, divided, and enclosed. Waste should not be let to build up. It should be gathered in appropriate containers, taken outside the buildings to collection points, and disposed of safely and hygienically at frequent and regular intervals.

Depending on the sort of packaging trash in question, the methods utilised for garbage disposal can cause environmental issues. Such trash could consist of:

Uncontaminated waste (assimilated to household waste: paper, cardboard, glass, plastic); contaminated waste (paper, cardboard, glass, plastic), such as waste that has come into touch with blood, blood-derived products, radioactive materials, or cytotoxic products.

Therefore, the method of disposal will differ, but it must always be in conformity with local laws. It's common practise to burn contaminated packaging.

WASTE DISPOSAL GUIDELINES

Waste is produced throughout the entire process of producing, supplying, and using a pharmaceutical product. The manufacturer or the end-user must consequently take care to protect the environment at every stage. Changes in the requirements for the licensing of medications have been made as a result of global environmental concerns. Therefore, in some instances, it may be necessary to conduct an environmental risk assessment in order to identify potential environmental problems associated with the storage, use, and disposal of pharmaceuticals. The pharmaceutical product as a whole may be the focus of the environmental risk assessment, thus it is important to take the adjuvants and excipients in addition to the active component into consideration the primary and secondary packaging, as well as the formulation. Another significant environmental issue affecting specific types of pharmaceutical products is the ozone layer threat posed by chlorofluorocarbon (CFC) propellants. On this topic, a European directive has been produced. Manufacturers are urged to recycle packaging debris in certain European nations where they must dispose of their drug waste or pay a specialist business to do it for them. Manufacturers and pharmacists have, respectively, created new guidelines and new process norms in response to this issue that:

- Packaging reduction. Efforts should be made to lessen the volume and weight of packaging materials as well as get rid of any packaging that isn't necessary to preserve the contents of pharmaceuticals.
- Packaging recycling and salvage. It is important to think about using environmentally friendly packaging, such as recyclable or biodegradable packaging. (For many years, valuable packaging materials like aluminium have been recycled widely. The list of recyclable packaging materials has recently expanded to include paper, glass, and plastic materials.) Materials that have come into contact with dangerous or highly potent medications, however, need to be given extra thought.
- Discarding and burning packaging. Some plastic products are burned because they can't be recycled. Polyvinyl chloride (PVC) burning is debatable since incomplete combustion could lead to an increase in the amount of dioxin in the environment. If the combustion heat generated by incineration may also be used for other reasons, it may be advised. Incinerators are frequently in short supply in developing nations. Nevertheless, this approach is thought to be the greatest one currently available for getting rid of contaminated packaging.

2.8 Product Management in Pharmaceutical Industry

The competitiveness of goods often entails any unique integral feature that highlights how they differ from those of a competitor and, consequently, influences how appealing they are to consumers. Competitiveness refers to both the important and substantial enough factors for the consumer's conditions of purchase and future usage of the goods, as well as merely qualitative aspects of the items. According to some authors, attempting to illustrate the competitiveness of products conceptually is akin to attempting to demonstrate the intricacy of the scheme and all the nuances of the market process. First and foremost, competitiveness is a way of working in the market that emphasises: - an awareness of customer wants and trends of change; Knowledge of the environment and its trends; the ability to develop such a product and deliver it to the consumer, giving him a competitive edge over rival products; and the ability to carry out all of these activities on a long-term, forward-looking basis.

According to research on consumer behaviour, consumers favour designing and choosing items that have the highest ratio of useful effect (E) to cost of acquisition and use (C) when compared to other comparable products. The following are the conditions for one product's benefits over all others:

$$k = \frac{E}{C} = MAX$$

The fundamental factor in a product's competitiveness is quality, which includes a variety of factors such as technical and economic quality indicators, manufacturing technology, and operational features. For instance, for medical products, the disintegration of tablet dosage forms, dispersion, uniformity of soft dosage forms, etc. should be considered.

- conformity of production to the legally required quality standards; special importance is now given in the majority of the world's nations to the quality standards that guarantee ecological cleanliness, a high degree of production unification, action of safety, and protection of human health; - ecological indicators that indicate whether a product complies with environmental protection laws and are based on ethical wildlife management;

- aesthetic indicators defining the external form and a kind of production, its design, appeal, expressiveness, an emotionality of influence on the consumer, etc.; - maintenance of patent cleanliness and patent protection of goods.

Ergonomic indicators are connected with considerations of properties and features of a human body and provide observance of hygienic, anthropometrical, physiological, psychological, and other norms.

The enterprise-manufacturer may typically only make it for sale at the domestic market in the event of a licencing agreement deciding to make production on the specified technology. Lack of patent purity renders production non-competitive in the relevant market and poses a significant barrier to the growth of export activity.

In addition to quality, competition includes marketing and commercial elements, which collectively have an impact on the price of sales or the cost of purchasing goods.

The marketing component reveals strengths and weaknesses in terms of product competitiveness based on the type and calibre of user research and market research, as well as the overall effectiveness of product development.

When compared to firms that are rivals, the commercial component of competitiveness attests to the quality of commercial work.

In addition to the aforementioned, economic factors such as the advantage or unprofitability of the offered items from the perspective of costs associated with their use or recycling also contribute to a product's competitiveness.

Image and prestige issues, as well as the authority of the nation where the items are created, have a place in the public eye. The price of consumption of goods, which includes ideas like the profitability of using the items while in service and the prestigiousness of its trade mark, is created by the sum of all the competitiveness factors mentioned above. A method of expert assessment, consumer research, and comparative estimates of important product parameters can all be used to estimate a product's competitiveness. The final method includes the following steps: market analysis; selection of the most competitive sample as a basis for comparison and definition of the level of offered goods' competitiveness; definition of a set of compared parameters for both goods; calculation of an integrated indicator of offered goods' competitiveness.

The term "goods quality management" refers to the processes that take place throughout production and as a product moves from the market to the consumer. Participants create a quality chain.

Chain of product quality

All phases of development, manufacture, distribution, consumption, and production recycling should be covered by the quality system. The operation of the quality system is governed by international standards ISO 9000, which place requirements on the marketing, supply, manufacture, and sale as well as the service policy and the quality system as a whole. Quality of production is established during a stage of marketing research. Based on the findings of the analysis of consumer inquiries, rival strategies, product advancement systems, etc., specifications for the quality criteria of the items are created.

The primary tool for ensuring the quality of a product is certification, which enables consumers to be objectively informed about its efficacy and safety. Both required and optional certification are possible. When it comes to meeting the requirements of the standard documents and the international (national) standards, installation of quality certification is a requirement.

Production is voluntarily certified in accordance with any standard papers that have been coordinated between the supplier and the client.

Standard documents that are used for production certification typically include specifications for: - technical or technological parameters, product quality, and testing conditions (methods, control rules, etc.); - production marks as well as the packaging, transportation, storage, and use of the product on direct appointment. The document that stands out for acknowledging conformance of certificated production to the defined requirements estimate and objectively attest to the consumer its safety and efficiency is the certificate of conformity of quality of production to operating standards. Both required and optional certification are possible. When it comes to meeting the requirements of the standard documents and the international (national) standards, installation of quality certification is a requirement. Production is voluntarily certified in accordance with any standard papers that have been coordinated between the supplier and the client. The majority of standard documents used for production certification include specifications for: - technical or technological parameters, product quality and testing conditions (methods, control procedures, etc.);

- manufacturing markings, its packaging, shipping, storage, and usage on negotiating directly.

The document that stands out for acknowledging compliance of certificated production with the stated requirement is the certificate of conformity of quality of production to operating standards.

Pharmaceutical companies' marketing strategies

Making decisions about the production of commodities should be based on a strategic strategy. It implies that any choice made in the relevant area should take the organization's long-term objectives into account. The term "marketing strategy" (strategy of coverage of the market) is defined by the businessman's encyclopaedic dictionary as "formation and realisation of purposes and problems of the enterprise-manufacturer and the exporter on each separate market (a market segment) and each good for the certain period of time (long-term, intermediate term) for realisation of industrial and commercial activity in full conformity with a market situation and opportunistic opportunities" (firm). The marketing strategy of a company is its plan for marketing activities in target markets, including fundamental choices for achieving marketing objectives.

The execution of a marketing strategy takes place within the constraints of a rapidly shifting business environment, which can only be taken into account in short-term plans, or "marketing technique" frameworks. On the basis of a marketing strategy and an assessment of the current state of the market, it also forms and manifests problems for the company in each of the distinct markets (segments) and with respect to each of the goods, but only in the short term and with constant problem-solving that takes into account shifting tactical and other factors. There are various methods for planning a strategy that are found in both marketing theory and practice. Ansoff's Product/Market Matrix,

Porter's Generic Strategies, a Matrix of Market Share/Growth (Boston Consulting Group Matrix), and other fundamental models of strategic decision-making

- General Electric Business Skin. The following types of strategies are included in Ansoff's Product/Market Matrix:

Market Infiltration. means raising sales through strategies including product promotion, brand positioning, and more. The product isn't changed, though, and we don't actively seek out new clients.

Market Expansion. Here, we introduce a new market to our current product lineup. This indicates that the product is promoted to a new market while remaining the same overall. One way to develop a market is to market the product abroad or in a new area.

Development of products. Our current clients will be promoted this new product. Here, we create and innovate fresh product lines to take the place of outdated ones. Then, we market these products to our current clientele.

Specialization. Here, we advertise brand-new goods to prospective customers. Diversification comes in two flavours: linked diversification and unconnected diversification. Remaining in a market or sector that we are familiar with is referred to as related diversification. Where we have no prior industry or market experience is with unrelated diversification. The business can use one of three major tactics when making its choice. The target market (within the entire area or distinct groups) and the strategic advantage are the two fundamental principles of marketing planning that are examined in strategic Porter's model (uniqueness or the price). Combining these two ideas, the Porter's model assigns such a fundamental approach to market coverage as:

- cost advantage (differentiated marketing is not differentiated); - differentiation (differentiated marketing is the marketing that is concentrated or targeted); An firm regards the whole market as a single given when it employs a market aggregation strategy, sometimes referred to as a mass market or an undifferentiated-market strategy. This unit is a single, collective market whose components are viewed as being similar in in all material ways. The management then creates a single marketing mix to reach the greatest number of consumers in this overall market. In other words, the business creates a single product for this large audience, creates a single pricing structure and distribution mechanism for its product, and utilises a single marketing campaign that targets the entire market.

A single homogenous segment of the overall market is chosen as the target market in a single-segment concentration approach. Then, a single marketing mix is created to target this particular segment. Instead of competing against numerous rivals in a large market, a small business might want to focus on a particular market sector. With the use of this tactic, a business can enter a niche market and establish a name for itself as an authority. They can enter this market even though they have few resources. Furthermore, as long as the market for the single sector is still limited, major competitors will probably avoid the single-segment expert.

In the multiple segmentation technique, two or more distinct target markets are recognised as prospective clients. The target market is divided into two or more distinct categories according to the multiple segmentation strategy. A corporation frequently creates a different version of the fundamental product for each category as part of the strategy of multiple segmentation. However, market segmentation can also be carried out without changing the product by using various marketing campaigns that are each specifically designed for a certain market niche Matrix BCG takes into account groupings of goods based on market growth rates, market share ratios for specific commodities to the corresponding share of the primary rival, amounts of investments made in the production of goods, earnings, etc. It divides the products into four categories: "stars," "cash cows," "problem children" or "question signs," "dogs," and corresponding marketing technique Dogs. These are goods having a small market share in a market with slow growth. They typically absorb cash instead of producing it for the business. Throw away these items. Money Makers. These are goods having a sizable market share in a setting of moderate growth. Overproducing cash cows return more on investment. So, for the time being, retain them in your product portfolio.

Problem Children.

These goods have a small market share in a sector that is expanding quickly. They use up resources while producing little in return. As you try to get more market share, they eat up the majority of your budget. Stars. These products have a substantial market share in markets that are experiencing rapid expansion. Stars typically bring in large sums of money Matrix BCG has received the further development in the model “attractiveness – competitiveness” offered by a consulting firm «MC Kinsey». Construction of this model is spent on two key parameters: attractiveness of branch and competitiveness or enterprise strengths. As indicators of appeal of the market (branch) can be used: market growth rates; profitability; competition level; market capacity; market state regulation; possibility of not price competition; concentration of consumers, etc. As indicators of competitiveness of the enterprise serve: market share; expenses; price level; appeal of assortment; image of firm. In construction process of a matrix for each of indicators weightiness is defined, the rank on the selected scale then the weighed estimation of an indicator taking into account the received estimation and factor of weightiness of an indicator is defined is appropriated. On the basis of the received values the matrix where it is allocated three zones for each indicator: high, average, low Keep your stars and expand them.

Table 2.1 Classification of a marketing plan.

Components that define strategy	Strategies and their characteristics, by kind
Market share	Assault the protective Distortion technique
Demand state of the market	Transformation Marketing Innovative and inventive marketing Provoking marketing rebranding Stabilizing or synchronising marketing Sheilding marketing "marketing in reverse Marketing retaliation
Commodity regulation	Distinctions Vertical blending Multifariousness specialised on a small number of commodities
Associated with product	Linear: When new products are continuations of products that have already been released and are based on a certain customer base. centered. When new purchasers are involved in the hunt for new products that, from a technological and market perspective, would be compatible with those previously produced. Conglomerate: When the introduction of new products that are unrelated to those that the company has already produced up to this point necessitates the creation of new technologies and markets.

The classification of a marketing plan might also depend on the state of the firm, the state of the market, and other criteria. The choosing of a marketing plan does not guarantee that the business will use it going forward. Strategy may change if certain conditions are met, including: - it hasn't consistently produced satisfactory indicators of sales volume and profit; - competitors' firms have drastically altered their strategies; - the external factors affecting a firm's operations haven't changed; - opportunities for accepting measures that can significantly increase a firm's profit have arisen; - customer preferences have changed or there are new tendencies to possible changes in this area have changed; - issues with the strategy have arisen.

CHAPTER 3

Promotion

Marketing, in other words, is communication, and vice versa. His succinct statement perfectly captures the essence of promotion as an explicit channel of interaction between a business and its surroundings. Since the environment tends to overlook and/or dismiss the contribution that marketing makes to all other company divisions and places an equation mark between promotional activities and marketing, promotion virtually competes with the idea of marketing itself. It goes without saying that the promotion function only makes sense and has the desired impact when used in conjunction with other marketing mix tools. In a straightforward communication model, the sender encodes specific information (the message's content) and sends it to the recipient through the proper channel. The recipient decodes the message to comprehend its content and provides the sender with the necessary feedback. The entire communication process is hampered by the presence of messages from other sources, as well as regulated and uncontrolled information that obstructs (or makes more difficult) the clear reception of the message. Noise is a general word for these communication-related elements.

Planning for marketing communications is based on a situational study of:

1. **The intended market:** Who the firm intends to appeal to, or who will be receiving its marketing message, is the main concern of the target market. In terms of purchasing motivations, value, frequency, and other factors, there is a key difference between the corporate market and the consumer market that sensible product selection and purchase practises dominate the business market. Despite the fact that pharmaceutical products are meant for individual consumers, unlike ethical products, the consumer cannot select the kind and brand of the product (s)he is about to use.

   This is carried out by the prescribing doctor, who is largely motivated by rational goals, and some characteristics of the pharmaceutical markets make them more similar to corporate markets than to consumer markets.

2. **The products:** While the stage of the product's lifecycle significantly influences the priorities and goals of communicating with the target market, the nature of the product dictates the capabilities and substance of marketing communication. According to what Brassington and Pettitt stated, an analysis of the as various marketing mix tools might influence the selection of the promotional mix, the full supply of values should be considered rather than the product as its component.
3. **The surroundings:** The possibilities for conducting marketing communication depend on a wide range of circumstances. Promotional efforts must, first and foremost, be socially acceptable and closely aligned with the culture of the target audience in terms of values, attitudes, and circumstances. Economic conditions affect the types of media that are accessible and the frequency of used marketing messaging. Legislation is the governing body that establishes the acceptable channels of marketing communication, and the pharmaceutical sector is a prime example of one with very severe regulations on advertising.

3.1 THE PROMOTION MIX

Advertising, personal selling, sales promotion, direct marketing and public relations are some of the promotional mix tools available to marketers. These initiatives are intended to achieve communication goals.

Advertising is a sort of mass communication that costs money and is impersonal since it uses mass media to address an audience. Institutional advertising refers to advertising that is targeted at a certain company or product. In the first scenario, the focus is on the product's demand, whereas institutional advertising aims to increase public awareness of the business and foster a favourable perception of it. The ability of advertising to inform, persuade, or remind message recipients consumers of the product, service, idea, organisation, or anything else that may be considered the object of exchange, with the ability to deliver values to consumers and meet a need is a point of agreement among most authors.

The ability of advertising to inform, persuade, or remind message recipients consumers of the product, service, idea, organisation, or anything else that may be considered the object of exchange, with the ability to deliver values to consumers and meet a need is a point of agreement among most authors. The appeal, or call to action, forms the core of every marketing message. It is "delivered" in the form of a message that is encoded in symbols that the medium allows for, such as words, images, sounds, etc. Without a doubt, television commercials are the most well-known type of advertising.

As different media forms increasingly specialise in serving the demands of more specialised target audiences, the contemporary media space (or media market) is characterised by both the proliferation and fragmentation of these media.

Marketers must be aware of the advantages of various media in relation to intended advertising effects, but also of those media's limits.

In order to reach certain sales and marketing goals, sales promotion is defined as "...a variety of marketing strategies established within a strategic marketing framework to add value to a product or service above and beyond the "regular" offering." His added value could be tactical in the short term or could be planned as part of a long-term franchise-building strategy. Activities for promoting sales may be directed at product customers or at wholesalers and retailers, who operate as middlemen in the marketing channel. All sales promotion efforts have one thing in common: they all depend on offering direct incentives to customers or other middlemen to make purchases. or purchase the item. Sales promotion is primarily linked with advertising into a single strategy and is rarely utilised independently. Personal selling is a sales representative's action carried out on behalf of the firm with the goal of achieving one of the communication objectives. Direct, face-to-face interaction between salespeople and customers is known as personal selling. Real-time feedback and message adaptation to circumstances and customer needs are made possible through two-way communication. In light of this, there are relatively few opportunities to influence the message that sales personnel communicate to customers. Companies make investments in professionalism and sales force training to offset this "loss".

3.2 PERSONAL SELLING

It requires a lot of labour and is therefore an expensive way to reach the target audience. Personal selling is more prevalent in complicated items with large unit values and high levels of risk (financial, functional, but also social), which makes its position in the major promotional mix for durable consumer goods. Customers rely on salespeople during the purchasing process so that the choice they make can be supported by as much information as feasible. The trust that customers place in sales reps is a direct result of their product competence and understanding. Prospecting, communicating information, persuading, installing, and/or demonstrating, coordinating activities with their own companies, staying in touch with clients, gathering information, and keeping an eye on competitors' activities are just a few of the duties assigned to sales representatives. Personal selling develops in line with the technology that is available.

Field work has been more efficient and effective thanks to portable electronics, and the advancement of communication technology has expanded the area of direct interaction with customers. Personal selling is no longer a concept that only operates in face-to-face interaction but also through other forms of communications in the "virtual world".

The Initiate for Public Relations (IPR) defines the field of public relations as "...the deliberate, planned, and continuous effort to institute and maintain mutual understanding between an organisation and its publics." (Institute for Public Relations website, viewed December 2008). The American Marketing Association's definition is more analytical and helps to define certain important characteristics and goals of public relations, whereas IPR's definition explicitly captures the essence of PR efforts. According to the AMA, PR is a type of communication management that aims to use publicity and other unpaid forms of promotion and information to sway consumers' feelings, opinions, or beliefs about a company, its goods or services, or about the worth of the goods or services or the operations of the organisation. The primary aspect of PR that the source authors concur on is that it is an activity that primarily uses mass media, addresses the general public, and aims to foster understanding between the business and the environment. Public relations is conceptualised as a "bridge of trust," suggesting that two-way communication is the foundation of PR activity. The media, government institutions and agencies, staff members, trade unions, various non-governmental groups and associations, buyers, suppliers, competitors, investors, shareholders, and most generally speaking, the target audience of PR efforts may be any of the aforementioned. In order to give the message or information the credibility of the media that transmits it, the majority of PR operations involve indirect modes of communication.

Boone and Kurtz's stance and AMA's definition both underline that this highlight that this message transmission is free, but Bearden et al. state that this is communication that is "not openly sponsored in the conventional advertising sense" which is more accurate. Public relations, according to Kotler and Armstrong, can significantly enhance a company's reputation and its acceptance in a certain community " at a substantially lesser cost than advertising." Since there are so many different types of activities, the financing methods, price, and level of control of transmitted information can only be taken into account in relation to particular situations.

Some authors differentiate marketing PR, which aims to achieve marketing objectives, from corporate marketing, which aims to achieve larger corporate objectives. Some authors separate marketing PR, which aims to achieve marketing objectives, from corporate PR, which aims to achieve larger corporate objectives. In light of the overabundance of advertising in the market and the growing importance of humanitarian, ethical, and environmental principles in many developed cultures, public relations assume special significance.

A direct relationship between a business and its clients can be established and strengthened through the use of direct marketing, which is defined as "...an interactive strategy of marketing that uses one or more advertising media to generate a measurable response at any location." The definition suggests a number of fundamental aspects of direct marketing:

a. Direct marketing uses a flexible, adaptable message to reach the conditionally "familiar" consumer.

b. Direct marketing is communication whose primary goal is to persuade customers to make an immediate purchase or request for information.

c. The result of direct marketing is explicitly measurable because there is a specific target audience and the response in the form of desired behaviour is directly tied to the moment of connection with the target customer. His method leads to the expansion of databases that contain data on customer behaviour. According to Baines et al. (2008), direct marketing has two objectives: first, to influence consumers' behaviour through targeted direct messages, and second, to obtain consumer data. It is essential to comprehend.

Direct marketing makes use of mass communication tools, but it only works effectively when consumer input and actions are taken in response, for example, by calling a call centre, clicking an online link, or mailing an order form.

The purpose of communication objectives is to achieve corporate goals, and they can be defined in a variety of ways. Connect communication goals to the necessity for the business to control the "scope of willingness to act" of the customers.

Every segment and/or combination of marketing communications aims to make customers aware of the presence of a product that can satisfy a particular need. Consumers who have access to updated information are more likely to be knowledgeable about the product, which is intended to result in favourable sentiments toward it.

This is how a business successfully cultivates customers' preferences for their goods and their confidence that they will live up to their expectations. Use a more detailed approach and separate the communication objectives into four categories. All marketing operations, including promotion, culminate at the point when the consumer decides to buy the company's goods.

Cognitive goals include defining consumers' needs, raising brand awareness, or increasing product knowledge.

Affective goals (focused on developing consumer preferences and a brand's or company's image);

Behavioural goals (encouraging consumers to seek out products and services); and Corporate objectives (corporate image, corporate relations, or the reputation of the company among the target public, etc.) are also important.

According to Boone and Kurtz, the main goals of marketing communication include educating consumers and other stakeholders, boosting demand, differentiating products, highlighting the benefits of the products, and stabilising sales. According to Bearden et al, the three primary objectives of marketing communication are to inform, persuade, and remind. Each marketing communication must have a clearly defined purpose, expressed as the desired response from the audience, from the perspective of the company that initiates it. Marketing communication is based on communicating a specific message or information to the target market or other stakeholders. Customers and/or other interested parties are a complicated group that is shaped by a variety of attitudes, ideas, intentions, and the very nature of interest in the business and/or its goods. In order to fully include the target population and satisfy all "information interests," different promotional mix instruments must be carefully combined. The majority of authors today talk about integrated marketing communication, which can be defined as "...strategic integration of multiple means of communicating with target market to form a comprehensive, consistent message" Reiterate that the integrated marketing communication process is centred on message recipients, i.e., consumers or clients, and that it is driven by their informational needs. All parties involved in the pharmaceutical sector have a need for information. The unique characteristics of pharmaceutical items can be seen in the applicability and relative weight of various marketing communication strategies.

3.3 THE PROMOTION OF PHARMACEUTICAL PRODUCTS

Advertisement regularly sparks debate. However, few industries' promotional efforts elicit such powerful emotions as those of the pharmaceutical industry. The controversy surrounding promotional practises in the pharmaceutical sector is nothing new and after more than 35 years of use, the same emotional charge still exists. This implies that the issue is unlikely to be solved anytime soon or for as long as there are insufficient resources to meet all needs.

The controversy and intense emotion have also led to tightly controlled pharmaceutical company promotional activities. The origins of such laws can also be seen in historical records, when unrestricted advertising in this industry led to the selling of pharmaceuticals under the slogan "one for man, one for all." two for the beast

In the absence of stringent regulations, "sometimes not labelled with their components, resulting in benign things as well as dangerous poisons being advertised as cure-alls containing "secret" ingredients." Although there is no concrete evidence, it was very unusual for certain preparations to worsen patients' conditions rather than improve them, including the sulphanilamide poisoning case, which claimed one live. A further tragedy occurred 30 years later in Europe when sedative use during pregnancy led to the birth of several children with birth defects.

These two isolated incidents influenced the pharmaceutical industry's tight regulation, which mandates that a drug's efficacy and safety be established before a selling licence is granted. Laws governing the packaging, labelling, and promotion of drugs were created at the same time. Legislation sets the parameters for what can be used to promote pharmaceutical items, however it would be incorrect to infer that this restricts promotional innovation. Pharmaceutical sector marketers have access to every promotional tool and all of its combinations. in order to reach the appropriate audience, using the tools at their disposal. Because of the nature of the product, regulatory requirements, and ethical standards, marketers must exercise above-average inventiveness and attention to the target demographic, message content, and selection of suitable communication channels in order for the message to have the desired effect. The marketing industry's promotional efforts for moral medications mostly target doctors who provide prescriptions. Since 1997, there has been a noticeable increase in the USA in the amount of money spent on ethical drug advertising messages directed to internal consumers and patients, or DTC (direct-to consumer).

Aside from this market, New Zealand is the only country where direct-to-consumer (DTC) medication promotion is legal. Medawar asserts that there has been demand from the pharmaceutical industry for DTC to be legalised in Europe as well, but other than talking about it, no action has been taken. Because OTC medications are prescribed for conditions where self-treatment is feasible, have relatively brief and clear box inserts, and are backed by significant amounts of information and extensive experience in their administration, OTC medications can be promoted to general consumers. The promotion of OTC items is analogous to the promotion of any other consumer good, and the existence of advertising in print and electronic media demonstrates the active promotion of OTC programmes by their creators. The crucial feature in this business is that the Direct customers are "returned" the decision of whether or not to buy a product, with doctors and pharmacists acting as advisors. Examine the variables that are affecting the pharmaceutical industry's increasing reliance on promotional activities. The complexity of the sector and its procedures makes it more difficult for regulatory organisations to oversee promotional activities:

1. **The growth of competition:** reduces the length of a product's exclusivity period and increases the availability of therapeutic alternatives, which causes pharmaceutical companies to make more efforts to differentiate their product from those of the competition.
2. **New pharmaceuticals:** as biotechnology advances, more alternative therapies are being developed, with personalised medicine as their ultimate goal. This will put current guidelines for judging the efficacy and safety of medications to the test. studies for medications meant for specific patients, or how to set rules.

   for marketing and labelling these medications? Contrasting opinions must be mentioned, as opposed to Morris and Pines opinion. The development of medications with minimal therapeutic benefit is due to the declining R&D activity in the traditional pharmaceutical business and the concentration on chronic illnesses in industrialised nations. Companies attempt to gain an advantage through marketing efforts in the lack of therapeutic benefits.
3. **Emerging media avenues:** Because the media landscape is fragmented and there are more points of contact between the industry and consumers and prescribing doctors, is it possible to adapt the message to each user and is their number heading toward "innumerable"? The context in which drug product promotion "operates" the availability to people of a geometrically expanding universe of health information via the internet as well as other, more and more diverse and specialised media channels.
4. **New knowledge needs:** as the involvement of other stakeholders in the healthcare system expands, so do information "appetites," and businesses now have to satisfy the various information needs of patients, payers, and prescribers. Because of medical specialisation, patients now consult multiple doctors for a single ailment, expanding the target market that pharmaceutical companies must target. The growth of recreational drugs is also accompanied by a need for specific information.

5. **Off-label use:** pharmaceutical corporations look for alternate uses for active ingredients as soon as they are developed, in addition to a drug's clearly indicated therapeutic uses. substance. These alternate uses cannot be promoted, but they do serve as the focus of peer-to-peer discussions and clinical trials. The issue of off-label use of pharmaceutical products is also highlighted by Sterling and Ravich. While many drugs have multiple therapeutic applications, the producers are required to complete a full cycle of clinical trials and submit applications for sales licences as if these products were completely new medications in order to demonstrate their safety and efficacy. Pharmaceutical corporations, which try to disseminate information on alternative applications of pharmaceuticals in other methods, are discouraged by the required cash, but also by the additional lost time.

His contentious practise is constrained by the legal prohibition on the promotion of such drug use and the requirement to give doctors access to all relevant information. Information that could be useful in choosing the optimal treatment option for patients. The moral/ethical aspect of Fox's popular TV series "Dr. House," in which the drug "Lupron" was used in such a way, with a critical question as to whether this was actually a promotion of the off-label use of this medication, exemplifies the delicate nature of the issue of the use of drugs for unapproved indications. Internationalization: In the truest meaning of the word, the pharmaceutical market is international; there is no uniform law for R&D, clinical trials, production, or marketing activities and media like the Internet transcend national boundaries. Where does the debate surrounding the promotion of pharmaceuticals come from products? The conflict between attitudes about pharmaceutical items and the rationale behind their creation or sale is what fuels the debate. What is the foundation for people's attitudes toward pharmaceuticals?

The clear beginning point is the nature of pharmaceutical items, which are meant to treat sick people and cause certain physical, biological, but more significantly, social and cultural phenomena (such as the feeling of empathy with the ill person). The fact that pharmaceuticals are complex substances with the potential to either benefit or harm the human body is the next important factor for the development of attitudes toward them (with a special emphasis on the fact that this attitude has three key components: cognitive, emotional, and native). The cost of pharmaceutical goods, which may restrict a drug's accessibility to those who need it, is the third characteristic. The economics behind the manufacture and distribution of medicinal products? Profits for a pharmaceutical company come from the selling of its goods. Every commercial organization's objective is to sell as many of its products as feasible, according to the economically rational assumption. The goal of every advertiser is to sell as much of their goods as they can while also achieving their corporate goals through education, persuasion, and reminders. The fact that the manufacture and consumption of medications combine a variety of interests often at odds with one another of multiple stakeholders on this complicated market adds another layer of complexity: prescribing doctors, lawmakers, payers, producers, consumers/patients, different socioeconomic groupings, and society at large. Peer-to-peer relationships are those between people in the same line of work or profession; in this instance, that would imply having a professional discussion between, say, two medical specialists.

3.4 DIRECT-TO-PHYSICIAN (DTP) MARKETING MIX

The primary goal of pharmaceutical promotion should not be to "sell a unit more of its product." The fact that "its product, message, promotional outlets, and even the audience are determined" by national regulatory agencies distinguishes the pharmaceutical sector from other professions. The main goal of pharmaceutical promotion is to deliver unbiased, fair information to the target audience. The promotional message provides the appropriate information that prescribers (as well as other stakeholders) need, and its Content becomes a fundamental component of

Fundamental basis of advertising messages in the pharmaceutical sector.

On clinical trials, the objectivity of the message is based. In the pharmaceutical industry, the promotional message and the scientific context are inextricably linked.

Promotional messages may only contain material that has been validated and proved in clinical research. His data comes from paperwork filed while requesting sale licences. A pharmaceutical product's promotional message must have an equal amount of positive (airmative) and negative information in order to comply with the balance of information rule. The only company mandated by law to list the negative aspects of its product is the pharmaceutical sector. The main issue is that it is difficult to distinguish between education and promotion. When it comes to pharmaceutical items, scientific (professional) communication and commercialization necessarily mix. Promotional actions that are based on clinical trial results disseminate scientific information, but a publication that comes from a clinical trial may also serve a promotional purpose. Additionally, we must reiterate the conflict between scientific and economic logic as it relates to R&D in the pharmaceutical industry. This information would be considered confidential in any other R&D-based industry. This knowledge must be disseminated to the expert public as part of the R&D process' scientific component in order for research to contribute appropriately to the body of knowledge about medicine, pharmacology, epidemiology, etc. On the other hand, regulation mandates that pharmaceutical firms adopt transparency in their R&D procedures, the components of their medicines, and other business practises. The outcomes of clinical studies. By drawing an analogy between Azoulay's viewpoint on technological innovation and the adoption of new knowledge, it is possible to conclude that the availability of pertinent information to prescribing physicians also contributes to the dissemination of new knowledge in medicine and pharmacological therapies. The time a physician finishes their undergraduate studies and throughout their whole professional career, they must innovate and keep up with new information. Given that "the body of knowledge regarding pharmaceutical goods is dynamic and increasing," a sizable amount of this body of knowledge is related to existing pharmacological treatments. The most significant information can be found in journals articles, seminars, conferences, and information sponsored by pharmaceutical corporations, among other information sources available to doctors. In light of "information overload," Lob and Kolassa (2005) wonder whether prescribing physicians are objectively capable of staying current on new material in the field of pharmacy. Prescribers' perceptions of various sources of information about pharmaceutical products are investigated by Gaither et al. The Physician's Desk Reference, medical books and textbooks, print media pieces, publications provided (sponsored) by medication producers, pharmaceutical company associates (sales force), other doctors (peer-to-peer), and pharmacists were among the information sources considered by the poll. The pharmaceutical sector has dominated tests. The pharmaceutical business now actively develops new pharmacological treatments and takes part in educating prescribing physicians about them. As professional decision-making in selecting moral medications for patients falls under the purview of the prescribing physician, the physician's goal is obviously to select the optimal treatment option for the patient. The interests of both parties in providing the necessary information have led to personal selling being the predominate method of pharmaceutical promotion.

Conferences and conventions have been "selected" as additional significant channels for disseminating information about pharmacological treatments due to the complicated nature of the goods and the specific target audience. The industry makes extensive use of specialised periodicals for knowledge distribution. new position

The growing role of patients as active participants in treatment has also sparked debates about marketing pharmaceuticals directly to internal consumers/patients and the benefits and/or drawbacks of this practise. The communication channel is not yet finished.

3.5 SELLING ON THE SIDE (DETAILING)

As the most effective component of the promotional mix, personal selling (detailing) dominates the pharmaceutical market. Information on the pharmaceutical business involves sales calls made to doctors in their offices by pharmaceutical sales representatives (PSR). The PSR speaks to the doctor about one or more of his company's goods during a call that lasts between 2 and 5 minutes, focusing mostly on the drug's composition, modes of action, therapeutic value, dosage, and probable side effects. Drug samples and some low-value gifts, typically memorabilia86 with the name of the business or the advertised drug, may be left by the PSR during the call. The doctors that PSRs visit are not chosen at random; instead, they choose the doctors. that are thought to be more inclined to recommend a medicine in their practise or to recommend it more frequently. By prescribing particular treatments, prescribing physicians are expected to create a specific demand for morally acceptable pharmaceuticals. The choice of a certain therapy is determined by a doctor under complex conditions that combine the knowledge and experience of the doctor with the information that is currently available:

The medical professional usually makes logical decisions. The doctor tries to provide the patient the treatment that is best for them under the circumstances.

The message's primary focus should be on its substance, which should emphasise the drug's indications, precautions, and side effects.

The message's substance is intricate and comprises professional information from a variety of fields (medicine, pharmacy, epidemiology, etc.), thus the sales person needs to be well-versed in the product, its mechanism of action, the advantages and disadvantages of the medication, etc.

Because of this, Serbian law stipulates that a sales representative According to Stout, Pizer sent physicians corporate gifts worth 86 million US dollars, principally pens, mugs, and umbrellas. A degree in medicine or pharmacy is required to work in detailing. According to survey results, sales personnel must provide customers with '...unbiased, evidence-based, scientific information about products, including head-to-head comparisons as well as risks and side/effects,' according to Mackintosh. The requirement for details to be precise is demonstrated by Smith and Youngers using the example of GlaxoSmithKline's Oxistat (oxiconazole), an antifungal medication for a number of epidermic illnesses. According to science. Promotional efforts are based on a comparison of all clinical studies of complementary and alternative therapies to determine the drug's key advantages clinical differentiation and are then followed by formal training for PSRs that covered skin anatomy, skin diseases, the drug's mechanism of action, therapeutic properties, and positioning in comparison to other treatments that are currently available.

The more unique a therapy is, the more information a doctor has to know, and the more difficult the job of the sales representative becomes. The reputation of a pharmaceutical company enjoys high levels of trust (and/or important, as is the PRS's reputation. In the aforementioned illustration, the authors of the promotional plan for Oxistat claim that the primary goal of educating sales representatives is to increase their technical product knowledge, as this will increase their credibility and confidence during "...interactions with physicians." Sales representatives' and prescribing doctors' interactions must be founded on a mutual respect for an acknowledgement of their respective specialties. By highlighting the contribution of pertinent information, Smith et al. Employ the idea of cognitive dissonance to support the use of direct-to-physician pharmaceutical marketing. Most of the time,

When prescribing a medication, a doctor has a number of options, and each one necessitates personal confirmation that the decision was taken in the best interests of the patient. benefit to the patient. The more options there are, the less attractive the alternative that is chosen, and the more severe the bad effects of the chosen alternative, the greater the cognitive dissonance. To the degree that they are educational and add to the doctor's overall body of knowledge, marketing initiatives for pharmaceutical items can effectively neutralise cognitive dissonance and make the process of selecting a course of treatment easier. The pharmaceutical industry's emphasis on details as the fundamental tool for promotion has resulted in a build-up of the sales force, or an increase in the number of sales representatives. According to Nickum and Kelly, the pharmaceutical corporations' "the more, the better" strategy has undermined the industry's reputation and "put a door in the face" of many sales representatives.

Prior to the calibre of these calls, PSRs' sales call. The theory behind the creation of blockbuster medications simply required a sales staff that could contact as many doctors as frequently as possible. Pizer, which is renowned for having the largest and greatest "army" of sales representatives, has recently tried to minimise costs by lowering their numbers as well. Pizer declared that its sales force would be reduced by 20% in the EU and US markets ('Pizer', Company Proile, Datamonitor). It should be noted that Pizer still views its sales force as one of its most significant competitive advantages despite the reductions in the sales force.

GlaxoSmithCline is also proud of its sales team, which is the second-largest in the sector. The corporation is currently not exploring further significant reorganisation as it has multiple "promising" compounds in development ('GlaxoSmithKline', Company Profile, Datamonitor). Datamonitor analysts suggest in their studies that sales force reductions are imminent for the majority of Big Pharma companies after AstraZeneca declared a reduction in sales force ('AstraZeneca', Company Proile, Datamonitor).

3.6 ONLINE PROMOTIONAL TECHNIQUES FOR OTC PRODUCTS

Sampling

PSRs may deliver product samples when they see prescribing doctors. "It is permissible to give one tiny packet of a newly launched drug, with a note on the packaging: Free sample, not for sale," in order to inform the expert public about the properties of the new drug (Law on Drugs and Medical Devices of the Republic of Serbia). According to Smith et al. Giving out samples is the ideal strategy to introduce prescribing physicians to the pharmacological characteristics of the medication because it will provide them the chance to assess the effects of the medication in a unique "personal clinical trial." The authors of the sauce typically compare providing samples to the chance to: give patients immediate access to treatment when it is unavailable at the time; give patients the chance to try a drug before buying enough of it to finish treatment (for acute diseases) or decide to begin treatment (for chronic conditions), with the potential for therapy adjustments; give patients short-term "financial aid" by giving them some of the medication for free.

According to Burns, PSRs frequently take the opportunity to distribute samples to gain access to physicians. The same author notes that this is a fairly constrained understanding of how samples are used in the pharmaceutical industry. To put it another way, businesses need to keep an eye on and and gauge how well doctors respond to samples by altering the way they typically prescribe pharmaceutical treatments.

According to a research cited by McGuire and published in the American Journal of Medicine, samples significantly alter how often doctors prescribe specific medications. When they run out of samples, they continue to prescribe this medication, hardly ever switching back to the medication they were previously prescribing or to an alternate kind of treatment. The study's findings indicate that the manufacturers' desire to use novel, expensive pharmaceuticals dominates the logic of samples, and that the short-term financial benefit to patients who receive them is minimal. The manner the samples are used is one of the definite issues discussed in the discussion. Yet another query The question of how to handle drug samples is raised in order to preserve their pharmacological efficacy and guard against potential abuse. According to Mizik and Jacobson, who used data from IMS Health, the detailing of pharmaceutical items in the USA cost roughly 5.8 billion dollars, with 11.5 billion dollars in free samples distributed. According to Buzzeo, the value of samples distributed on the same market in 2004 was close to 16 billion dollars.

Journals

The pharmaceutical industry is also represented in specialised journals, by funding studies whose findings are published in these publications, or by paid advertisements. The challenge of research is quite comparable to the challenge of planning scientific or business conferences. The issue of researchers' competing interests and research that values samples based on medicine retail pricing. Sponsors and the conundrum of whether a researcher's stance primarily serves the interest of the expert public (and the patients) rather than the commercial performance of a pharmaceutical product remains common issues. Sponsored research still maintains a veneer of objectivity that rests on knowledge and confidence in the researchers. The editors of these magazines work hard to uphold the Credibility of their magazines is maintained by editing the content that will be published, adding reviews, upholding high standards, and maintaining the proper balance between sponsored content and academic articles. A paid advertisement is only ever a paid advertisement. A sponsored advertisement surely delivers the message that it is paid promotion, leading to a loss of credibility and perception of the objectivity of the information supplied if pharmaceutical marketing is read primarily and its content is the major component. Due to an increasing preference for direct-to-consumer marketing (DTC), as well as the advent of other alternative media, the US market clearly demonstrates a decrease in the amount of money pharmaceutical companies spend on advertising in specialised periodicals. Dougherty, Kolber, and Mann contend in the issue of Medical Marketing & Media that are observing a change in the organisation of the pharmaceutical industry's spending on promotional efforts. The experts Levitt, O'Connor, Girondi, and Deal discuss the significant decline in the revenue from the sale of advertising space in general medical publications. This is the outcome of a decline in the R&D productivity of pharmaceutical corporations as well as the specialisation of media and pharmaceutical marketing on specialty markets driven by specific illness profiles (oncology, diabetes, cardiology, psychiatry, etc.). This pattern, which has been evident in pharmaceutical advertising for a while, confirms Henderson's assertion that the business is shifting toward specialised media with a focus on journals. Psychological, neurological, cardiovascular, etc.

Online promotional techniques for OTC Products

The Internet is a relatively recent addition to the mix of advertising media. This is a sophisticated medium that can convey a vast amount of information due to the fact that, unlike most other media, it allows for interaction with the user and flexibility, as well as the fact that the user chooses how to use the resources/information from web sites. According to objective standards, this media can be equally geared toward the general public and the expert public, including patients acting as internal consumers. Consumer, Patient, and Physician Focussed Web Initiatives, published by FGC Consulting, states that web-based solutions can take the form of branded or unbranded web pages (with or without a clear relationship with a pharmaceutical business), which are strategically oriented on: a particular product, therapeutic field, or disease state. Drummy identifies two crucial characteristics that make the Internet a successful medium for reaching the intended audience:

1. **Instant categorization:** The pharmaceutical company's website should be able to provide the information that different target groups need. Patients may look for information on how to maximise the effects of a therapy, the advantages of sticking with a therapy or the risks of stopping it; some people may be interested in information on disease prevention or diagnosis; prescribing doctors may look for information on the mechanism of action, contraindications or drug tolerance, taking therapy in combination with food and/or other drugs, etc. With the caveat that users cannot be "forced" to follow information paths they do not need to take or may find unsuitable, a web page must offer a natural, quick approach to the information requested. Time is a crucial component. The user is only 'engaged' in the content of the web page for a limited length of time; if the infrastructure of the web page is unable to guide the user to desired information within this incredibly short timeframe, the user will abandon the information search or turn to other sources.

2. **Synchronization:** The communication channels available to a firm as part of its promotional mix are numerous and complex, with the Internet being just one of them.

   Marketing professionals could create a synergy between "offline and online media," incorporating links to the internet into messages promoting traditional media (such TV and print media) and vice versa. A pharmaceutical company's website could make a great complement to personal websites. Selling, therefore some businesses, like Bristol and Merck, are augmenting frequently quick doctor visits with "e-detailing." They might, for instance, direct physicians to interactive websites that educate them about novel medications and that can be rapidly updated with the most recent clinical trial data to bolster their sales arguments.

3. **Involvement:** Pharmaceutical businesses should ensure that their target audience is sizable enough to be aware of a website's presence. The amount of information made available to different stakeholders on a website only makes sense in its entirety if it has contributed to the expansion of knowledge and/or information among a sizable enough population. Due to this, in the virtual world, luring the intended audience

to visit a website about a condition and/or For this purpose, in the virtual world, attracting the target audience to a web page about a disease and/or therapy is accomplished either by purchasing key words with major search engines (Google, Yahoo, MSN, etc.) or "catching" users who actively and intensively use the Internet but do not do so primarily in order to find health information, i.e. their access to social media. websites with pharmaceutical company sponsorships are the result of additional stimuli.

4. **Influence:** Future Internet infrastructure developments will enable more audio and visual content that is accompanied by animations, video, and other media. When it comes to marketing, Harrell cautions against adopting all of these new options "simply because they can, rather than because they are serving a specific marketing purpose or user need."

5. **Investment evaluation:** One of the common marketing challenges is evaluating the impact of spending money on promotional activities. Web-based advertising is quite simple to track, especially when it comes to the number of users who browsed various materials. However, the objective result won't become apparent until prescribers' or consumers' behaviour on the market changes. It calls for more intricate techniques for measuring effect. A company's relationships with its surroundings can be strengthened by having more channels for communication with stakeholders. In light of the fact that the prescriber demographic has changed, McGuire argues that the industry's "shit" toward the Internet and interactive promotional tools for prescribers needs to be understood. The older generation of doctors, who are resistant to information technology, are gradually leaving the profession, while the younger doctors, who were raised with computers, anticipate e-marketing strategies from the pharmaceutical sector. forecasts an increase in the use of the Internet for patient decision-making on health matters, particularly among the younger, more educated population who must make "a lifetime of healthcare decisions."

Ethical drug direct-to-consumer (DTC) promotion

In 1997, when the expense of connecting with internal consumers/patients increased exponentially in the US, the issue of direct-to-consumer (DTC) drug advertising gained steam. His method of promotion had previously been permitted by law, but it wasn't until the FDA, which oversees the world's largest pharmaceutical market in the United States, agreed to relax those restrictions that it could really be used. To be specific, the producers of these goods were given authority to "promote in the broadcast mass media without adding extensive or summary information on the usage, indications, and potential harmful effects of a drug."

Manufacturers were only required to list the most significant side effects, such as other media that provide comprehensive information (such as a website, patient hotlines, or print media) and a requirement, such as the direction to "contact their doctors/pharmacists," The premise that the physician has the necessary expertise to make a proper diagnosis and select the appropriate treatment option for the patient based on the information provided underlies the choice of an ethical drug for treating a patient's symptom and/or ailment. On the other hand, a patient who has determined that the "aberration from normal" in his or her condition is severe enough to need obtaining professional assistance in the field of socially recognised medical practise will delegate the option of the therapy that is best suited to his or her needs to a doctor. The doctor-patient relationship is built on mutual understanding of the rights and responsibilities that result from that relationship, as well as on trust. It is important to note that patient promotion is actually indirect, as its mechanism of operation assumes that a patient will influence a doctor who has undisputed final authority to prescribe a drug (or refuse to give it to the patient if it is inappropriate for the situation). Examining the viewpoints expressed by different authors, we can draw inferences about the benefits and drawbacks of DTC methods. The primary beneficial effect, in the opinion of many authors, is increasing patient information levels, which includes: enhancing the role of patients as active participants in their personal medical history; raising patient awareness of diseases, which helps patients recognise symptoms and receive more accurate and timely diagnosis and treatment (Dubois; Kavadas et al).

Raising awareness of therapeutic alternatives that are available, such as prevention and lifestyle changes (Buckley); hastening the dissemination of information on new therapies that are available; developing pharmaceutical brands; and having specialised knowledge in certain therapeutic areas and improving therapy outcomes through appropriate use of and adherence to treatment regimens. Claims that the best marketing strategy for pharmaceutical promotion involves "...evolving a dialogue with their patients to improve adoption, compliance and adherence."; making the most efficient use of doctors' time given that patients have a wealth of resources at their disposal for learning about their conditions, available treatments, and other information they may be interested.

When a physician's authority is undermined and (s) he becomes a provider catering to patients' desires, the doctor-patient relationship is disrupted, and the diagnosis and choice of therapy are given to the patient, pharmaceutical marketing's goal to "harmonise the needs and wishes in an efficient and efective manner" is challenged. Self-diagnosis is a unique issue that, It requires a significant amount of the doctor's time to discourage a patient who presents with his or her own, unsupported diagnosis.

How can a patient choose wisely when Smith et al., for example, identify four distinct producers who distinguish four distinct advantages of their hypertension therapies?;

There is pressure on doctors to recommend unnecessary or improper treatments that are based only on influence without knowledge;

- costs of therapy grow due to insistence on branded drugs when there is an appropriate generic parallel;
- there is a questionable ratio of positive and negative information in DTC promotion, where the authors agree that advertisers tend to overemphasize positives and play down negative effects).
- the issue of ethicality of influencing 'vulnerable and suggestible' audience

CHAPTER 4

Pharmaceutical Marketing Channels

Marketing requires a complicated web of connections and exchanges between many organisational divisions. Distribution demonstrates how this entire process may be handled to boost organisational effectiveness. The advantages a manufacturer has over his competitors and the advantages his customers can receive from his business are determined by the relationship he has with his suppliers. Depending on this relationship, distribution encompasses a variety of procedures and activities. It also involves the flow of a product inside and outside the company, in addition to the coordination of supply to the final consumers. In other terms, the phrase "Distribution" refers to all product motions. According to Mossman and Norton (1965), is the process that establishes time, place, and form utility by moving people and things across locations.

Distribution Management = Physical Distribution + Distribution Channel is an effective way to summarise this.

The idea of physical distribution has just recently become recognised as a distinct management function, around the past 20 years. The idea of physical distribution, like many other novel business concepts were developed in the US. It is based on the practical core tenet that the costs of storage and mobility are inextricably linked and that we can only fully utilise the possibilities of each by treating them as a single integrated activity. When it comes down to it, physical distribution focuses on the following seven R's: the Right product, for the right consumer at the right price, in the right amount, in the right quality, at the right time and place.

4.1 DEFINITIONS FROM VARIOUS AUTHORS

The word "Distribution" is used in a variety of contexts and ways. It can be interpreted to mean storage (warehousing) and movement of goods from the point of value addition to that of delivery to the final consumer when it is used to refer to the entire process of selling and transporting items to customers. Let's examine some of the term's technical definitions. Physical distribution, according to Charles A. Taff (1978), is the management of the flow of raw materials, processed commodities, and finished goods to and from the production line. It also includes inventory control, protection, and storage.

Physical distribution, according to the American Management Association (1960), is "Moving finished items from one end of a production line to clients," The obligation to design and manage a system to control the flow of raw materials and finished commodities is what David J. Bowersox (1968) refers to. The Council for Logistics, formerly known as the National Council of Physical Distribution Management (NCPDM), has provided the following definition of physical distribution: Physical distribution refers to a wide range of activities that are concerned with the effective movement of finished goods products from the end of the production line to the consumer. In some cases, physical distribution also involves the movement of raw materials from the source of supply to the start of the production line.

NCPDM concludes the definition with the following list of typical ancillary physical distribution functions: Transportation of freight, storage, material handling, protective packaging, inventory control, and choosing of plant and warehouse locations are some of these tasks. processing orders, predicting markets, and providing customer support. Consequently, it is proven that physical distribution refers to the actual transfer of commodities from the producer to the consumer. Here is an excerpt on physical distribution from John F. Magee (1960):

Distribution is a significant functional area in the majority of commercial organisations, whether they be retail, wholesale, or industrial units. Cost is only an issue in business once the customer has the goods in their hands. Two types of movement—the movement of people to goods and the movement of products to people—take place in order to complete this transfer. Additionally, before being delivered to the customer, the product may go through a lot of hands and be stored for a short while or a long time. Consequently, the physical distribution system's structural components includes

Material management, storage, transportation, and information processing.

Physical distribution management is one of the management topics that has garnered the most attention during the past ten years. According to some authors, physical distribution encompasses a wide variety of business operations that are concerned with the effective flow of products and raw materials from the production line to the consumer as well as internally to the site of manufacture. Others define physical distribution management as the area of management that is in charge of planning, implementing, and running a system that only controls the flow of processed items.

Therefore, physical distribution management is completed by meeting customer demand, excluding time and location and storage.

It is necessary to evaluate and plan modifications to an existing system before designing a new distribution system, which is more practical in practise.

Planning for operations and analysis. Managing and analysing distribution and logistics as an integrated activity (for instance, receiving, storage, distribution, and customer service acting together as a unified system rather than as self-contained microsystems unconnected to one another) is one of the guiding principles.

- Ensuring that distribution system operations are connected to the medical stores' and the larger public health system's overarching goals;
- Ensuring that the demands of the consumer are recognised and met.
- Finding a balance between cost and service trade-offs (for instance, while every hospital may like to have a medical store on its property, the resulting increases in inventory-holding and operational costs are make such a choice economical)
- Maintaining stock movement
- Cutting costs, lead times, and inventories
- Examining strategies to increase both effectiveness (such as reducing the number of warehouses, outsourcing transportation, and investing in new information systems) and efficiency (such as guaranteeing full transport loads, minimising inventory, mechanising materials handling, and automating order processing).
- Reducing the number of steps required for storage and handling, which lowers the risk of damage and loss

To make sure the system works as planned once it is installed, routine performance monitoring is required. The key design elements of a distribution network are just briefly described here; they are covered in more detail in following chapters.

4.2 PRIMARY DESIGN ELEMENTS

A distribution system's fundamental characteristics are the degree of centralization, the number of levels, and the geographic or demographic coverage. The difficulties in distributing anti-tuberculosis (TB) medications in Nepal's thinly populated, mountainous nation are highlighted in Country Study. Small island nations, like those in the Pacific, as well as geographically huge nations with sparse, mostly nomadic populations, like Mongolia, deal with comparable issues.

Pharmaceutical distribution and purchase are coordinated at the national level in a typical central supply strategy. The distribution of medications obtained at the central medical stores (CMS) to lower-level warehouses and then to the healthcare facilities. In a decentralised system, it is up to the districts or regions to receive, store and dispensing medications in accordance with their requirements; occasionally, they can also be in charge of procurement. various methods for distributing medications to the public sector are discussed. Some of these options call for in-house storage, while others do away with some or all of the need for public-sector supply system warehouses.

The following crucial actions must be followed while creating a distribution system or redesigning an existing system:

Determine the following:

1. The total number of storage levels in the system.
2. The locations of the storage sites.
3. Select the level of the supply chain at which order-related decisions will be made.
4. Establish order frequency or restock intervals.
5. Decide on a distribution or collection strategy for supplying medications to user units.
6. Pick a reliable method of transportation
7. Calculate the amount of inventory that needs to be held at each level of the system.
8. Develop a set of practical and cost-effective delivery routes, work out a workable delivery schedule, and choose the best modes of transportation to service these routes; decide whether it is more cost-effective to keep and maintain vehicles or contract out the delivery service.

9. Calculate the operational expenses and evaluate the cost-effectiveness of hiring outside help for transportation and storage at one or more levels.
10. Create a system for managing your warehouse that is based on a set of SOPs.

Network of distribution

A multi-layered structure of pharmacies, each serving a specific purpose, may be needed for a public pharmaceutical distribution system.

Purchases from a supplier are typically received by one or more principal stores, which typically service an entire nation or region and may or may not directly supply healthcare facilities. The regional or national demand for medications as well as the frequency of supply defines the physical size of the primary shops. With direct delivery from suppliers to intermediary stores, this level has been eliminated in certain nations. The distribution of medications occurs between the primary and intermediate stores. Their size is influenced by the demand from the local hospitals and the regularity of supplies from the grocery stores. Although they may be independent, intermediate stores are frequently located next to a regional or district hospital. Individual health institution stores receive drugs from intermediate stores. There would be four levels in this system.

It is occasionally necessary to have two layers of intermediate stores, with first-level intermediate stores feeding second-level intermediate stores. For instance, a regional retailer may provide district retailers. Each program's needs and resource limitations should be taken into account when determining the ideal number of levels, along with cost and benefit considerations. Some nations substitute direct delivery from suppliers or a principal distributor to facilities for both intermediate tiers of store.

Fewer warehouses improve control by reducing the possibility of losses. Geography, population, accessibility to storage space, staff, availability and cost of transportation, political and other resource constraints, and availability of staff are additional considerations to take into account when deciding the number of storage levels.

The three- and four-level systems are contrasted with regard to management complexity, setup costs, operating expenses, inventory costs, and applicability based on the location and density of healthcare institutions. Three-level systems are less complicated to handle and may cost less to set up and run. However, the four-level system may offer superior service and perhaps turn out to be less expensive to operate when all costs are taken into account when clinical facilities are widely spread and travel times are high.

As more levels are added, the quantity and, consequently, the value of stock stored in the system tends to increase. Provides examples of four alternative distribution networks. Be aware that there are not always direct correlations between costs and level count.

A CMS system with effective inventory management may have lower total inventory costs than a regional stores network with less effective inventory management. It is important to keep in mind that the relationships between costs and number of levels are not always as straightforward as depicted in the figure.

Although there is no surefire method for determining the ideal number of levels and facilities in the distribution system, the methods below could be helpful in determining the best hierarchy for a specific nation or programme:

1. Draw a diagram of the current supply chain hierarchy, including all clinical and storage facilities as well as the supply lines that link them.
2. Draw three or four workable alternative hierarchies, taking into account both patterns and links between the facilities already in place.
3. Estimate as precisely as you can the values for the elements specified for each of these options.

   To model these costs, total cost analysis is a helpful tool.
4. Draw a flowchart showing the information flows that are currently in place and those that are being considered.
5. Decide on and put into place the system that offers the greatest service possible for the money that is available.

   This methodical approach might reveal previously overlooked opportunities for distribution improvement.

Additionally, the data gathered can be used to support demands for increased funding from top officials or outside help organisations so that a more expensive but more successful plan can be implemented.

Push-and-pull mechanisms

Which tiers of the system place orders for medications and which, if any, passively accept medications provided from higher levels can be used to construct distribution systems. The two main options are—

1. ***Pull system*:** Each level of the system decides what kinds and amounts of medications are required, then places orders with the supply source (which might be a system warehouse or a private provider).

   An autonomous demand or requisition system is other names for this kind of system.

2. ***Push system*:** What kinds and amounts of medications will be given to lower levels in the system is determined by supply sources at some level in the system. At the start of a planning period, often a year, a delivery plan is developed, and the strategy calls for the delivery of the materials. This kind of arrangement is also referred to as an allocation or ration system; the ration kit system is the most well-known instance in pharmaceutical delivery.

Managers of operating units are supposed to determine their own demand forecasts and buffer supplies when employing a pull system, and then submit requisitions to central stores outlining their needs. In a push system, operational units are required to provide the supply source with specific stock and consumption data so that issuing officers can plan allocations.

When there is the ability to handle them properly, pull systems are recommended. A push system, however, can be helpful in some circumstances, such as during disaster relief efforts and when the supply pipeline isn't working.

A push system, however, can be helpful in some circumstances, such as during disaster relief efforts and when the supply pipeline does not operate properly across the system. Some nations employ a push-pull strategy where district and regional hospitals choose their own needs while consistently receiving primary health care medications in a kit. Although switching from a push to a pull system is preferable, doing so can be difficult and necessitate demanding modifications to distribution, warehouse operations, and inventory management. Tanzania is having difficulties when it switches from providing basic medication kits to a direct request method.

Push and pull distribution systems typically benefit from the following circumstances:

Circumstances that favour a pull system. A pull system of inventory management is advantageous when Lower-level staff employees are skilled at determining needs and managing goods.

- The supply sources have enough inventories to cover all programme requirements.
- A wide variety of items are handled.
- Field staff members receive routine supervision, and their performance is tracked.
- Decision-makers have access to reliable data.

Circumstances that favour a push mechanism.

- Lower-level staff members are inexperienced in inventory control, which is one of the conditions that support a push method of inventory management.
- Rationing is required because supply cannot keep up with demand.
- Only a few products are being handled.
- There is a need for disaster aid, or the circumstance necessitates a short-term supply via prepackaged kits.

Restocking interval

Deliveries to user units may be done quarterly, monthly, weekly, or at any other period depending on the resupply frequency. Weekly deliveries will result in average stock levels if below, stockout probabilities will be less likely, but transportation costs will be very high. Transport costs will be low if supplies are only made once a year, but average stock and storage expenses would be high. (and associated costs).

The ideal resupply interval should be determined to meet the requirements of each programme. The majority of public programmes use one- to three-month intervals. Before selecting a choice, it is wise to take the following into account:

- Availability, order size, carrying capacity, and transport costs
- Each level of the system's storage capacity
- Seasonal considerations that affect the dependability of transportation
- Staffing levels and staff competency at every level of the system
- Additional factors, such as expiration dates, protection against theft, cash flow, and other locally pertinent issues

Storage

Where medicines are required depends on the population and healthcare infrastructure distribution in a given area. In order to determine the kind and quantity of medications needed by each facility as well as the overall volume to be handled by the distribution system, storage planning first begins with an examination of current and future supply requirements. The central and intermediate stores' ideal locations and dimensions can then be established. It is important to choose store sites that make the best use of the current public and private transportation systems. Buildings can be constructed, bought, rented, or restored.

Huge storage structures should be designed with the need to efficiently move large amounts of material and the storage conditions needed for various items in mind. Health care institutions may have a modest storage with shelving for their stores. No matter how basic the shop, storage facilities should always have security measures in place to prevent theft and damage from water, vermin, or fire.

The regional cross-docking centre is another sort of facility that can contribute to the distribution system (or stockless distribution center). The centres do not hold or manage shares, as is obvious. They can primarily be used as data warehouses to gather, validate, and report on inventory and order data. Additionally, they get chosen and packaged.

Additionally, they get orders from the central supply that have been picked and packed for each health facility in the area, and they deliver the goods on time. A distribution system can only be successful with strategically placed stores. A flawless website does not, however, exist. Needs frequently clash with one another; for example, a location can be near a decent road but too far from the health clinics it must service. The logistics staff is in charge of balancing these needs. The decision-making process will be aided by the next several phases. A demand map for medications. Map the demand for pharmaceuticals by geographic region. Where can I find a hospital, a clinic, or an aid station? Whom do they most effectively serve? Calculate the annual pharmaceutical production volume and weight for each facility.

Utilizing morbidity statistics, medication requests, and delivery records, determine the annual volume and weight of pharmaceutical requirements for each facility. Prepare for growth.

Where are likely to find brand-new or expanded healthcare facilities? Will new public health initiatives be expanded? Are any of the prescribed treatments altering? How will these changes impact the location of current facilities and storage locations?

Find the points of supply entrance

The majority of nations only have a few entry points that can manage pharmaceutical imports. These include significant seaports, international airports, train stations, and border crossing customs offices. The logistics team should choose the locations and facilities that are most suitable for receiving pharmaceutical goods. The distribution of pharmaceuticals through more than one port to more than one principal shop may be effective in some nations when there are numerous suitable entrance sites for medications. In vast nations or when there are physical obstacles like mountain ranges or large rivers without bridges, multiple major storage places could be warranted.

It controls the flow of drugs into a nation's central supply by using regional warehouses as a point of aggregation. Utilizing a local distribution hub lowers the dangers associated with storing a lot of inventory, such as expiration, damage, and theft (SCMS 2010).

Choose primary storage locations

Examine the key stores' current locations and decide if they are effectively situated for both present and future demands. Geographical, societal, and communication variables influence where to locate a principal store. A location on the national transportation network concentrated in the area with the highest population density is a wise choice. Utilizing this site will assist in lowering total transportation expenses. The primary store does not necessarily need to be close to or in a major city. While administratively advantageous, a city site may be ineffective logistically. Store locations may vary depending on where local pharmaceutical manufacturers and suppliers are located. The transport component of pharmaceutical pricing can be decreased if stores are situated close to a significant concentration of local suppliers because medications received from those sources are typically delivered directly to primary or intermediate stores. Locate intermediate stores and plan major distribution routes. It is essential that there exist efficient transportation routes between the primary and intermediate stores (including any second-level intermediate stores). These routes must be dependable because they transport the most medications. Therefore, intermediate stores should be placed near railroad stations, bridges, or other navigable rivers, or on good, all-weather highways.

A supply route that serves two or more intermediate stores on a circuit is typically less expensive than one that serves just one, depending on the amount of medications to be delivered. However, lengthy primary delivery circuits must to be avoided in areas with poor roads, inadequate nightly security, or areas where prolonged exposure to unfavourable conditions may jeopardise the purity of medications. Create backup distribution routes. Health institutions are connected to intermediary stores via secondary distribution routes. Planning these routes necessitates in-depth familiarity with the state of rural roads, travel times, and available transportation. Local opinion is crucial. A convenient medical facility can be used to pick up prescription medications that can either be delivered from the intermediary store or collected from the intermediate store. The best option will differ depending on the medical facility.

The store sizes

The previous processes determine where additional stores are needed and which of the existing primary and intermediate stores are suitable locations (or cannot be relocated). It is possible to estimate the number of medications that should be kept in each store. The greatest amount that can be stored depends on how frequently medications are delivered; programmes that receive yearly delivery of medications need bigger primary stockpiles than those that receive them more regularly. The safety stock volume must be considered while estimating maximum stock levels. Although consumption is not always predictable and delivery are not always on time. The projected maximum stock holding should never exceed the available storage capacity to account for unforeseen circumstances and for each existing store's capacity has to be evaluated.

Five options are available if the current storage capacity is inadequate:

1. Rearrange the store by adding pallet racking, altering the shelves, or changing the layout.
2. Construct or lease more warehouse space. This choice involves capital expenditures for building a warehouse or ongoing expenses for renting a warehouse.
3. Possibly at some administrative expense rise, increase supply frequency to reduce the need for additional storage space. For deliveries that occur more frequently, suppliers might charge more. It might not be feasible to shorten the supply interval if it currently is.
4. Obtain higher-level status for one or more under utilised lower-level stores.
5. If there isn't enough room at the main level, think about holding larger equities at the intermediate level, assuming there is room for them. In most situations, it is best to avoid using a system that relies on routine stock transfers between stores at the same level because it might be challenging to track such movements. However, depending on the skills and motivation of the employees involved, some supply systems can handle redistribution.

Comparing delivery and collecting methods

Basically, there are two ways to get commodities from the warehouse to the receiving facility: delivery or collection.

With a collection system, obtaining supplies from the warehouse is the responsibility of the receiving facility. In a delivery system, the warehouse is in charge of providing supplies via internal transportation or a deal with the business sector, or maybe both. The costs of each hospital and health facility that sends workers to collect goods from a medical store depot or is in charge of distributing to lower levels should all be taken into account when building a public health distribution system, not just the expenditures borne by the medical store.

Before making any decisions, it is important to take into account the financial impact on hospitals or regional health authorities, even though changing the distribution systems of medical stores may result in cost savings.

Each approach has benefits and drawbacks; the selection should be based on the requirements and limitations of the specific programme. The general benefits and drawbacks of collection and delivery are illustrated.

Transport

Transport is typically the weakest link in the supply chain and a major source of dissatisfaction.

The choice of an acceptable mode of transportation, as well as the purchase and maintenance of automobiles or other modes of transportation, are necessary for transportation planning. Utilizing alternatives from the private sector; assessing fleet capacity; planning improvements to the transportation system; purchasing and disposing of vehicles; managing vehicle use; maintaining vehicles; and maintaining medicine quality while being transported are some of the matters to be taken into account.

Through careful route design, delivery scheduling, and consideration of private-sector options, transport managers should maximise the utilisation of available transportation.

Schedules for deliveries

To guarantee that supplies are delivered consistently and on time to each site, careful planning is necessary. For instance, an intermediate store may be in charge of forty clinical facilities with a one-month delivery window. The overall amount of time needed to provide all these facilities with the resources at hand cannot go beyond one month. The delivery schedule must be altered or more transport resources must be purchased if analysis indicates that a longer time frame is needed to supply all facilities.

The following criteria should be taken into account while choosing the right delivery intervals for each store and healthcare facility.

Primary, intermediate, and Hospital stores' total storage capacity: No store's holding capacity may be exceeded by deliveries. It is more likely that this condition will arise with irregular or infrequent deliveries. This problem can be solved by analysing product throughput and delivery frequency.

A rise in the cost of transportation per delivered unit to tiny, outlying facilities. Supplying these locations seldom is an apparent solution. The policy's drawback is that it raises the maximum stock levels at these facilities, which may also raise the danger of stock outs in areas where the environment makes long-term storage difficult or expensive.

Efficient use of the vehicle: If delivery intervals are too short, cars might travel with only half of their cargo. Large vehicles will be required if delivery intervals are lengthy. The health service may leave its vehicles idling for extended periods of time.

Climatic variables: Delivering to particular locations at specific times. of the year might not be feasible. Delivery volume and frequency must be planned to avoid disruptions brought on by wet weather or other recurring environmental factors.

Tools for managing distribution

Logistics supervisors

Transport and warehouse managers, as well as other officers in charge of logistics, usually had poor professional status under the traditional CMS supply paradigm, and their abilities and experience were generally devalued, if not ignored. But as the significance of pharmaceutical supply management to health programmes has grown, numerous nations are making significant reforms (such moving toward more autonomous, commercially oriented systems) and realising the necessity for qualified experts. Therefore, well-trained, seasoned personnel are managing logistics systems more frequently than they were in the past.

The operational planning, implementation, and monitoring of the duties mentioned in this chapter should be handled by qualified specialists. Regional cadres rather than a single group of national specialists may be more appropriate in large countries. The need of increasing medication accessibility and minimising delivery costs must be emphasised by logistics management. Technical support from expert suppliers may be beneficial when making important decisions.

In order to achieve successful administration and planning, The logistics management or planning team must have the authority to withstand political demands, such as refusing to establish a store where doing so would be against operational logic.

Workforce requirements to efficiently manage and run the pharmaceutical distribution system, the logistics managers must ascertain the necessary staffing numbers. Are there enough employees on hand? Are they properly educated? Are finances available to hire and train extra workers if needed?

Even the best distribution system won't function well if there aren't enough trained personnel to manage it.

Information technology

The coordination of the distribution network depends on accurate management information. Information about medication use travels up and down the network. The information system consists of forms and procedures to track pharmaceutical receipt and issue, cost and sale prices, and inventory levels. A manual, electronic, or hybrid system may be used.

The one-way flow of medications along the supply chain from CMS to district or regional stores and then to clinics, hospitals, and community health workers is simple to picture. The complementary flow of forms and reports required to organise pharmaceutical delivery is more challenging to comprehend and handle.

The primary components of the supply information system are forms, records, and reports. Forms are records that are sent from one unit to another and contain precise data concerning medical requirements, drug distribution, and related financial operations.

The audit trail used to track the movement of money and medications includes copies of forms that were filed at various locations throughout the distribution network. Records may be kept in ledgers, card files, databases, computer databases, or folders. The usage and cost of medicines should be summarised in reports that are issued on a regular basis. Local health care facilities are accountable to district offices, which are accountable to regional offices, which are accountable to the central office. Such reports are used to forecast medical needs, track usage patterns, update spending plans, and evaluate medical usage.

Any supply system can modify the forms to suit its needs. There may be forms that can be used as-is, forms that need to be modified, and additional forms that are needed to meet unique requirements.

A complete information system must be implemented whenever a new pharmaceutical supply programme is launched or an existing one is modified.

should be created as a part of the fundamental planning procedure. Before prescription drugs begin to circulate through the system, all required forms should be accessible, and all staff members should have received training in their use. Without such planning, the process of tracking medication usage and predicting medication needs quickly falters.

Communications

A pharmaceutical distribution system cannot function properly without effective communication. Staff frequently travels vast distances to deliver or collect reports and requisitions where trustworthy postal services and telephone networks are lacking, particularly in rural areas. If at all possible, these trips should be combined with supervision. Effective telecommunications decrease the need for travel, save staff time, boost security, and lessen vehicle wear and tear. The current telecommunications resources should be used to the fullest extent possible and suitable investments in communications technology should be made.

It would be possible to cut down on wasteful trip expenses by equipping a facility with a radio transmitter or a fax machine. Electronic communications are becoming more and more common, reducing resources and speeding up information delivery. Other technologies include mobile phone technology and VSAT (very small aperture terminal) satellite systems, which offer an affordable communication method even in remote places. In many locations, people report inventory data from the field using their mobile phones.

Products with higher market values are more vulnerable to theft and diversion than those with lower market values.

Distribution security will be more important since, for example, antiretroviral medications and combination therapies based on artemisin may be at greater risk. Without the driver's involvement, onboard computers in delivery vehicles can connect with a centralised location (like the CMS) via GPS, GSM, and SMS in order to track the location of the vehicle.

In order to control distribution and safeguard pharmaceutical supply systems, more people are using high-frequency radio and cellular telephones as alternative wireless communication methods with drivers.

Monitoring performance and analysing costs

Especially for evaluating the possible cost impact of different alternatives, gathering and analysing data on current operating expenses is essential when constructing or upgrading a distribution system. One technique for examining costs and modelling options in a supply system is total cost analysis. This section provides an overview of the variable costs that are relevant to the supply systems' distribution component.

Cost analysis is typically not a continuous process, and it should not be confused with performance monitoring which needs to be done on a regular basis using the right indicators to make sure that system performance is preserved.

Estimating costs

Calculating the internal costs of the distribution system and then estimating the costs of other alternatives for comparison are the initial steps in an option evaluation.

Storage space, store operations, inventory, employees, holding and transportation, administration and management, upgrades, and contracting out fees are all included in internal costs.

The annual amortised cost of the warehouses the health care provider owns as well as the rent paid to private warehouse owners are included in the cost of storage space.

Local property taxes and utility bills are part of the operational costs (electricity, gas, water, and insurance).

Annual amortised costs for equipment like forklifts, security equipment like fire alarms and fire extinguishers, specialty equipment like refrigerated rooms, and computer equipment are referred to as equipment costs. Finding other like items as well as in stock control. For things with an anticipated useful life of more than a year, costs should be amortised.

Costs associated with distribution personnel include overhead and compensation given to labourers, drivers, mechanics, and storekeepers.

The true cost of keeping stock in inventory is called holding stock.

In order to safeguard against stockouts and fully benefit from bulk purchase agreements, adequate inventory must be maintained. Too much stock keeps money locked up and drives up storage expenses; an effective distribution system strikes a balance between the two.

Transport fees encompass all distribution costs not covered by the supplier's contract, and delivery may be made to the client's warehouse, the factory gate, or the dockside

The following expenses may be incurred for transportation:

Transferring goods between modes of transportation

- Insurance
- Demurrage
- Port clearing
- Distribution of medications domestically
- Packing and unpacking.

The costs of using government vehicles for the distribution of medications include gasoline, repairs and maintenance, driver pay and daily expenses, and amortisation of the vehicles, Where accounting and financial management systems

Estimating the costs associated with the in-house service may be challenging if those systems are weak or poorly connected into the overall ministry of health accounting system. Transport expenses are more clear when parastatal or private carriers are engaged.

Most of the time, the pharmaceutical programme has little control over some costs (such insurance and port clearing fees). However, shipping costs are determined by the quantity, cost, and/or weight of the requested items as well as any fees levied by the shipping agent. When assessing pharmaceutical tenders, shipping costs are a crucial factor. When prices are listed as CIF (cost, insurance, and freight) or CIP (carriage and insurance paid), it is the simplest to compare pricing from different vendors.

All administrative expenses incurred by or charged to the distribution system are included in administrative overhead.

Direct costs associated with bad management include the following:

Stock theft, stock misdirection, unnecessary supplies in stock, and supplies that are damaged due to improper storage or transportation circumstances.

Stock shortages are another factor that raises costs. The majority of the time, emergency purchases results in additional expenses.

In the absence of medications, it may be essential to keep patients in the hospital for a longer amount of time, which will raise nursing costs and free up beds for other patients. Patients who are not given the required care could spread an infection to others. Although it is difficult to measure these indirect losses, cost-effectiveness analysis approaches can be used to estimate them.

An internal distribution system may need to be upgraded in order to reach a reasonable degree of efficiency. These expenses need to be tallied and added to other internal expenses for comparison with alternatives.

Contracting out entails costs for private distribution and storage, which should be calculated so that they may be compared to current costs? By evaluating the capability of the private sector and holding a non-binding tender to ascertain the costs of private-sector services, these costs can be determined.

Gathering and evaluating cost and performance information:

In order to precisely determine expenses, it is vital to gather information from internal accounting and reporting systems as well as from other sources in order to assess expenses accurately. Natural cost centres should be used to gather data; for instance, if the system is regionally organised, a study of the costs by area will show how each region is doing.

To plan and conduct out cost surveys, analyse data from survey questionnaires, and draw conclusions from incomplete data sets, qualified workers or consultants are required. The most insightful surveys gather field-based data from stock and vehicle maintenance records as well as from conversations with local workers. The same data should be gathered for monitoring schemes from many sources so that results may be cross-checked to evaluate the accuracy of current record-keeping and reporting systems.

The Definition of Marketing Channel

The idea of a marketing channel can be difficult to understand. Sometimes it is considered the path a product takes as it travels from the manufacturer to the consumer or another final recipient. user. Some people define it as the route taken by a product's title as it passes via different agencies. Others describe the marketing channel as a loose alliance of companies that have come together to conduct business.

It is likely that different perspectives or viewpoints are the cause of much of the confusion. The manufacturer, for instance, might concentrate on the many intermediates required to deliver things to customers and describe the marketing channel in terms of how the products are moved through these multiple intermediaries.

The passage of the title to the goods may be viewed as the correct delineator of the marketing channel by intermediaries like wholesalers or retailers that are expected to handle sizable inventories from multiple manufacturers and incur the risks connected with this activity. Customers may perceive the marketing channel as just "a lot of intermediaries" in their path to the product's manufacturer. The researcher may also describe the marketing channel in terms of its structural characteristics and operational effectiveness as they observe it functioning inside the economic system. It is impossible to establish a single definition of the marketing channel because of these divergent viewpoints. In this essay, we adopt a managerial decision-making perspective on the marketing channel as seen primarily through the eyes of marketing management, with a focus on producing and manufacturing businesses. As a result, one of the crucial areas for marketing decision-making that marketing management must handle is the marketing channel. The external contact organisation that management uses to accomplish its distribution goals is the marketing channel in this sense. The words "external," "contactual organisation," "operates," and "distribution aims" should be highlighted in this description.

The term "external" denotes the existence of a marketing channel outside of the company. It is not a part of a company's internal organisational structure, in other words.

It is not included in the internal organisational structure of a company. Thus, rather than intra organizational management, management of the marketing channel entails the use of inter organizational management (managing more than one firm) (managing one firm). It is crucial to remember this since a lot of the unique issues and peculiarities related to managing the marketing channel that are described later in the text are caused by this external (inter organizational) structure.

The phrase "contractual organisation" describes businesses or parties that engage in negotiations as a good or service flows from the maker to the final consumer.

The purchasing, selling, and transferring of title to goods or services are all examples of negotiation functions.

As a result, only businesses or parties that perform these tasks are considered marketing members. As a result, the marketing channel only includes businesses or parties that do these tasks. Other businesses that undertake tasks other than those of negotiators, such as transportation firms, public warehouses, banks, insurance providers, advertising agencies, and the like, are not included (and are typically referred to as facilitating agencies). It is not necessary to split scholarly hairs over this issue. The channel management issues that arise when dealing with companies or parties who engage in negotiation are frequently fundamentally different from those that arise when dealing with agencies that do not engage in negotiation. This will become clear throughout the narrative at various stages. The final term, operates, implies managerial engagement in the channel's operations.

This involvement may extend from the early stages of channel structure construction through day-to-day channel management. Management has decided not to leave the external contactual organisation to operate on its own when it is in operation. This does not imply that management has the ability to completely or even largely control the channel. This is not always achievable. On the other side, management is operating the channel in order to prevent the channel from unintentionally controlling its operations.

The fourth critical component in the definition, distribution objectives, signifies that management has specific distribution objectives in mind. These can be reached through the marketing route. Thus, the distribution goals of a company play a role in how the marketing channel is structured and managed. Variations in the outward contactual organisation and management's attempts to operate it can be anticipated to alter as these aims do.

The term "Channel Manager"

Throughout this article, we will often use the term "channel manager" to refer to someone working for a company or organisation who is responsible for making decisions about the marketing channels. In reality, very few businesses or organisations have a single senior role designated as channel manager. However, certain significant American companies, as depicted in Table 1, have executive positions with responsibilities similar to those of the channel manager as described here. At Compaq, for example

Table 4.1 Job Titles for Channel Management at Selected U.S. Companies.

Firm Name	Channel Management Job Title
American Cyanamid Co.	Business Development Manager
American Greeting Corp.	Team Marketing Manager Director
Bausch & Lomb Co. Borden, Inc.	Director, trade marketing
Borden, Inc.	Sales coordinator
Compaq Computer Corp. Coca	Director of channel management
Coca cola co.	Director, Customer Business Development
Duracell	Trade Marketing Manager
Ergodyne corp.	Market Team Adviser
Hewlett –packard co	Planning Manager, Channel Marketing
Johnson and Johnson	Trade Marketing Director
Leaf brands, inc	Vice President, Trade Marketing
Philip moris ,inc	Manager, Trade Relations
Polaroid corp	Trade Marketing Manager
Sandoz pharmaceutical corp	Director of National Affairs
Sara lee corp	Vice President, Customer Marketing
AOL Time warner, inc	Sales Development Director

The title of Director of Channel Management at Computer Corporation, which recently merged with Hewlett-Packard, is possibly the closest to the word "channel manager." Many different executives are typically involved in making channel decisions, depending on the sort of business or organisation and its scale. The vice president of marketing, general marketing manager, product manager, brand manager, and sales manager, for instance, may all be involved in large consumer products manufacturers. The top sales professional, such as the vice president of sales or general sales manager, may be the main channel decision maker in an industrial products company. A middle management executive known as the manager of franchisee relations occasionally performs a crucial position. In some franchise companies, which are typical in the fast-food and service industries, a middle management executive known as the manager of franchisee relations occasionally participates in key channel decision-making alongside the franchisor's top sales and marketing executives. Most channel decisions in smaller firms across a wide range of both consumer and industrial products companies will be made by the owner/manager.

We might have used a general phrase like decision maker or marketer when referring to a person making channel decisions given that so many different types and degrees of managers are involved in channel decision making and that there aren't many people who are officially recognised as channel managers. The phrase "channel manager" was instead chosen by us since it gives the discussion of the crucial function of channel decision making within the company some feeling of focus. Therefore, regardless of a person's real job title, when that person participates in channel decision-making, even if a formal channel manager position does not exist on the organisation chart of the company, that person is filling the role of a channel manager. In other words, everyone working for the company who decides which channels to use is a channel manager while doing so.

Channels for marketing and marketing management strategies

The well-known marketing mix strategy model offers the framework for evaluating the marketing channel from a marketing management viewpoint, as was hinted at in the discussion of Altoids at the beginning of this chapter. In case you forgot, the marketing mix model describes the marketing management process as a strategic blending of four controllable marketing variables (the marketing mix) to satisfy the demands of customers to whom the company wishes to appeal (the target markets) while taking into account internal and external uncontrollable variables. Product, price, promotion, and distribution make up the "four Ps," or basic marketing mix variables (place). The major environmental elements such as the economy, sociocultural patterns of consumer behaviour, competition, government, and others make up the external uncontrolled variables.

The business' non marketing activities make up internal, unpredictable variables. A common representation of the marketing mix strategy model. Finding potential target markets and creating suitable and coordinated plans for products, prices, promotions, and distribution to service those markets in a competitive and dynamic environment are the main duties of marketing management. The beer industry needs a promotion plan to establish and sustain brand recognition, primarily in the form of national brand advertising and point-of-sale promotion. However, Coors recognised that advertising is costly and has fleeting results as rivals fight for attention in a market that is becoming more crowded.

Coors came to the conclusion that emphasising channel strategy was its greatest chance for succeeding in the slow-growth, fiercely competitive beer industry given the constraints of the product, price, and promotion strategies of the marketing mix. In particular, Coors would forge closer ties with its independent beer distributors than did its main rivals.

Coors' decision to prioritise channel strategy as the primary means of attaining a long-term competitive edge in the competitive beer market is not a new one.

One of the key strategic spheres of marketing management is marketing channel strategy, which falls under the distribution (location) variable of the marketing mix. To satisfy the needs of the firm's target audiences, management must design and manage its marketing channels in a way that complements and strengthens the other strategic components of the marketing mix.

Coors Brewing Company developments show how channel strategy relates to other strategic factors in the marketing mix and the growing importance of the variable for channel strategy. After Miller Brewing Company and Anheuser-Busch Inc., which is best known for producing Budweiser beer, Coors Brewing Company is the third-largest brewery in the country. From being primarily a regional brewery, Coors has expanded to have full national distribution in all 50 states. However, Coors faces formidable obstacles as a key player in the very competitive national beer market. Due to anti-drinking initiatives and shifting consumer preferences, the consumption of beer has decreased as more consumers have moved to nonalcoholic beverages. Due to the main breweries' aggressive competition for market share, competition has become extremely intense. Microbreweries, which have grown in popularity in recent years, and overseas brands have brought still another level of competition to the battle.

Coors Brewing Company is adapting to this intensely competitive climate. Coors has thoroughly considered all of the strategic elements of the marketing mix to address this extremely competitive climate. Due to high rates of new product failure, short product life cycles, and competitors' ability to swiftly provide similar items, it is difficult to establish and maintain a competitive advantage in the field of product strategy. Coors made the decision not to base its business strategy primarily on new product development.

Coors came to the conclusion that pricing strategy faced significant challenges for maintaining a competitive advantage. The increasing focus on price strategy in the beer market has resulted in aggressive price reductions and the so-called "beer wars." 30% to 50% of all beer was sold at beer was offered at a discount, and in some states the percentage reached 60%.

It is not intended to imply that Coors' choice to emphasise channel strategy as the primary element in attaining a sustainable competitive advantage in the competitive beer market overrides the significance of product, price, and promotion tactics. On the contrary, they are also crucial because, obviously, no company can hope to be successful for very long without decent items that are attractively priced and well-promoted. However, a channel strategy that aims to forge a solid bond between the manufacturer and its channel partners can be very successful from the perspective of creating a competitive advantage with long-term survival. Why? because rivals would find it difficult to replicate such a relationship. It is impossible to swiftly replicate using technology, a temporary cost advantage, or a brilliant idea. It cannot be rapidly replicated using technology, a temporary cost advantage, or a brilliant idea, which are frequently the foundation of competitive advantages based on product, pricing, and promotional methods. Instead, a channel approach that fosters close bonds between channel participants, what in recent years has increasingly been referred to as partnerships or strategic alliances is built on assurance, trust, and the strength of the channel's members. In other words, a strong channel relationship's higher performance is likely to be a result of the strengths of the individuals inside the various channel members' businesses and their propensity to provide superior performance focused at attaining mutually beneficial goals.

Coors, the third-place finisher in the very competitive beer industry, has relied heavily on its independent beer distributors to remain competitive against its bigger competitors. Strong distributor supports also enabled Coors to increase its earnings despite the recession that occurred in the first year of the new century, which was quite an accomplishment given the brutal competition the two larger firms engaged in to win shelf space in beer distributors.

Although Coors' choice to prioritise channel strategy was made in the beer sector, many companies across a wide range of sectors, including automotive, high-tech devices, consumer packaged products, fashion, industrial machinery and equipment and many more, are taking similar moves.

4.3 CHANNEL ORGANIZATION

In the marketing literature, the concept of channel structure is one that is frequently not stated precisely.

The length, or the number of tiers of intermediaries in the channel, is perhaps the dimension that receives the most attention.

Diagrams are widely used to depict channel structure. Symbolic notations such as the ones below may also be utilised.

M →C (two-level)

M →R→ C (three-level)

M →W →R →C (four-level)

M →A →W →R →C (five-level)

These methods give a rough sense of the many types of marketing channel players and the levels at which they exist, but they do not describe the channel structure precisely.

Additionally, they omit to mention the connection between channel management and channel structure. By defining channel structure as the collection of channel members to which a set of distribution duties have been assigned, our definition adopts a managerial viewpoint. According to this definition, the channel manager must make an allocation decision while creating channel structure. This means that, given a list of distribution tasks that must be completed in order to meet a firm's distribution goals, the manager must choose how to divide or organise the jobs. As a result, the channel's organisational structure will demonstrate how he or she divided up these tasks among the channel's participants. For instance, if the channel structure looks like M→ W →R→ C following the allocation decision, this indicates that the channel manager has decided to distribute the tasks among his or her own company, wholesalers, retailers, and customers.

The phrase "multi-channel strategy" has become more commonplace in recent years. This merely indicates that the business has opted to use multiple channels to communicate with its clients. Because distribution tasks have been divided across many channel structures, a multi-channel marketing strategy inevitably leads to a multi-channel structure. In the latter few years of the 20th century, when E-commerce and online sales began to take off, several businesses created multi-channel systems that incorporate internet channels. For instance, sales through the multi-channel structure employed for Polo by Ralph Lauren clothing include.

The company sells its products in high-end department stores, specialty shops, company-owned stores.

In both the consumer and corporate industries, using various channel topologies to reach clients is not at all uncommon. Today, businesses that only offer their products through a single channel are the exception rather than the rule. The majority of businesses either use or will soon employ a multi-channel strategy, and many of them are utilising e-commerce technologies to include internet sales into their multi-channel frameworks.

As was previously said, specialisation, the division of labour, and contact efficiency are the main paradigms for making such allocation decisions. The channel manager would prefer to have complete control over how distribution duties are distributed so that they can be given to the specific companies or parties that are most qualified to do them. The channel manager, however, does not always have complete control over the division of distribution tasks because the channel has members that are independent enterprises and because the channel is subject to environmental restrictions. We will address the challenges and limitations the channel manager faces while seeking to create an ideal channel topology.

Antecedent Structure

Since only individuals who engage in the negotiation-related activities of buying, selling, and transferring title are included in our definition of the marketing channel, those who do not engage in these activities are not included in the channel structure. These nonmember participants or facilitating organisations will be regarded as a part of the marketing channel's auxiliary structure. We specify accessory structure as follows: the collective of organisations (facilitating agencies) that helps channel participants with distribution-related activities. The channel manager must make an effort to assign distribution responsibilities to individuals who are best qualified to complete them. This is the fundamental choice that must be made while trying to construct auxiliary structure. However, because the channel manager is interacting with nonmember channel participants, it is likely that the issues encountered when creating (and managing) ancillary structures will be less complicated. This is due to the fact that channel decisions, which ultimately determine how goods and services are distributed to their target markets, are not affected by facilitating enterprises. Instead, after the fundamental channel decisions have been taken, the job of the facilitating agencies that make up the ancillary structure is to offer services to the channel members. We will use the Black & Decker Corporation (B&D), one of the top power tool producers in the world, as an example. Many of the industrial power tools that B&D sells are distributed via independent wholesalers (industrial distributors), who in turn in order to reach manufacturers, contractors, repair shops, schools, government organisations, and other industrial market groups, B&D sells many of its industrial power tools through independent wholesalers (industrial distributors). Retailers like hardware stores, home centres, mass merchandisers, automotive stores, and others sell B&D's consumer power tools by purchasing them directly from the manufacturer or from wholesalers.

A multitude of non-negotiable tasks, including transportation, storage, insurance, finance, and advertising, must be completed for these marketing channels to function effectively. B&D, as well as its distributors and dealers, sometimes find it more beneficial to "farm out" certain responsibilities to supporting organisations (the supplementary structure) than to carry them out themselves.

For instance, rather of maintaining its own fleet of vehicles, B&D employs common carriers to deliver its power tools to industrial distributors. Similarly, rather than aiming to self-insure, it relies on commercial insurance providers to guard against hazards while the products are in transit. As an alternative to creating all of its advertising in-house, B&D occasionally works with independent advertising companies to advertise its products. B&D power tool wholesalers and dealers also work with facilitating organisations to complete some of these responsibilities rather than going it alone. The channel manager interacts with facilitating agencies that are outside of the channel decision-making process and who construct the ancillary structure to carry out these activities. . The comparatively easy process of moving the goods from point A to point B is all that the trucking firm is concerned with when it transfers a load of power tools from a B&D manufacturing facility to an independent industrial distributor. Additionally, the channel manager is not required to bargain with them or treat them similarly to other channel members. For instance, convincing independent industrial distributors (channel members) to stock and passionately promote its DeWalt line of power tools in the face of competition from rival companies like Porter-Cable, Makita, or Ryobi is a difficult undertaking for B&D. B&D must also consider challenging questions like how to select channel members and how big of a role each member will play while creating channel structure. The extent to which each will influence decision-making, the means by which control will be applied, the standards by which performance will be judged, and a host of other topics have been covered.

Two broad categories can be used to classify pharmaceutical products:

1) Prescription medication
2) OTC goods

Whether a product is promoted to consumers or medical experts is the determining factor in this category. Drugs that the FDA has approved for marketing are divided into groups based on how a patient can lawfully receive them.

Definition of Prescription

A prescription is a crucial piece of legal documentation. It is a prescription for medication given to a patient by a trained doctor, dentist, veterinarian, or other registered medical professional. By giving the patient the medications listed on the prescription, the pharmacist complies with the order.

OTC medications or non-prescription medications

Drugs judged safe enough for the general public to self-treat minor ailments for which professional medical assistance is not typically sought after. Without a doctor's prescription, over-the-counter (OTC) medications are sold. Direct consumer sales are made of these medications. They are applied to manage mild illnesses. OTC medications that are directly marketed include anti-cold remedies, analgesics, and antipyretics. OTC medications are covered under direct marketing since the customer has the power to buy the brand of their choosing from the pharmacy. Media advertising is necessary for OTC medicine direct marketing.

Prescription medicines

Drugs on prescription are those that can only be obtained with a doctor's prescription. These are the approved medications that are governed by law. Without a prescription from a doctor, chemists are unable to sell these to patients. Typically, "Rx" is frequently utilised as a shorthand for prescription medications.

Only on the prescription of a qualified medical professional are prescription medications made available that are thought to be beneficial only after expert diagnosis or too harmful for use in self-medication. The majority of medications sold solely by prescription are vital, including anti-HIV, anti-cancer, anti-cancer, and antibiotics.

In addition to the allopathic or modern medical system, there are numerous other medical systems that are frequently referred to as traditional, alternative, or complementary systems. Different medical systems are practised and their medications are available in India.

Allopathic (modern medicine), Ayurvedic, Siddha, Unani, and homoeopathy are the accepted medical systems in India. The majority of these may typically be easily differentiated by reading the label.

The Indian market offers about 80,000 brands of different medications. On the other hand, the WHO identifies a little over 270 medications that can address the vast majority (more than 95%) of a nation's health issues. Most of the 80,000 or so goods that are said to be on the market are dangerous, absurd, or useless.

Prescription chain process and product chain procedure:

The consultation process typically culminates with the prescription of medicine. When a patient visits a doctor, they anticipate that the doctor will take action to address their issue. The majority of the time, medicine prescriptions are involved. Therefore, the patients anticipate some concrete advantages from the doctor's service. The doctor must meet the patient's expectations by taking the appropriate action to reduce the patient's symptoms at the conclusion of the visit.

The public's awareness of pharmacological treatments and ailments has raised their expectations for the care they receive from their doctors.

The Supply Chain

The choice of molecules is the first step, and the patient's hands are the last. This process chain is quite labor-intensive because it begins with the selection of molecules, is followed by their critical screening, by the identification of the raw material source, by the beginning of the pilot batch manufacturing process, and by the planning of clinical trials. When the pilot batch is successful, the drug's commercialization process begins. The medicine is now in the distribution process and on its way to stores after promotional and price tactics have been decided upon. Following the doctor's diagnosis, the patient purchases the medication from the chemist.

The chain of pharmacies

The expertise provided to doctors by medical representatives of pharmaceutical companies is the first step in the prescription chain procedure. They distribute the material in a variety of ways, including through out-of-clinic promotional initiatives. The patient then buys the medication once the doctor, if pleased, has prescribed it. The prescription chain and the product chain are both connected to the fundamental marketing goal.

The vital function of medical representatives in the promotion of pharmaceuticals

Individuals who visit a doctor, dentist, pharmacist, or nurse with the intent of persuading these healthcare providers to purchase, suggest, or prescribe a product.

Medical Representatives (MR), Pharmaceutical Sales Representatives (PSR), and Pharmaceutical Company Representatives are the names given to them (PCR). The key channel of contact between the drug producer and the public is the medical rep.

The key channel of contact between the drug maker and the medical community is the medical representative. He is the most trustworthy source of information regarding client perception, sales methods, and what is happening to a company's goods in the cutthroat market. Medical representatives serve as a conduit between a business, stockists, and customers, ensuring the efficient operation of the entire network.

Medical representatives actively participate in information dissemination, inventory management, delivery of goods, returns of goods, the introduction of new products, and assistance for the pharmacy. They also actively participate in the physical distribution of drugs across channels. The pharmaceutical missionary salesperson is known as the medical representative.

Healthcare professionals are aware that these individuals are being dispatched when they see the medical representatives. to persuade them to use, prescribe, and advocate their goods. Koekmoer (1987) asserts that the primary goals of medical representatives are either to reinforce an already positive opinion towards a pharmaceutical medicine among prescribing doctors or to change that attitude. "Like television and radio are to consumer products, medical representatives are to ethical products".

Through its medical professionals, the pharmaceutical industry primarily promotes its products. There is limited room for error in the doctor and representative meetings. Reps have a big impact on how a doctor writes prescriptions. They have been properly referred to as medical "stealth bombers." Prescribe my medicine is their slogan.

Doctor: Medical Representatives are always courteous and have some level of expertise. They research a doctor's prescribing practises before to their appointment using data acquired from neighbourhood pharmacies and a sneak peek at some of the patients' prescriptions. Additionally, they learn a little bit about the doctor's interests in social activities, his or her family, and likes and dislikes in general.

The medical representative is the primary resource for putting marketing plans into action for its most crucial client, the patient. The fieldwork plan calls for frequent doctor visits to remind him of the brand and persuade him to recommend all promoted products. It is believed that convincing a practitioner to change their approach takes between one and two years.

The prescriptions are what primarily drive the big pharmaceutical business. Doctors' prescriptions are the primary factor driving the big pharmaceutical business. As a result, the competence and efficiency of the pharmaceutical companies' medical representatives are crucial to their success. The medical representative should obtain the most recent knowledge, scientific data, and technical advancements about the product, in line with the majority of doctors' emphasis on the value of routine visits.

Science graduates are primarily recruited as medical representatives through a competitive process. After being hired, they underwent a structured training course that taught them how to monitor and evaluate doctors' personalities and preferences in addition to teaching them technical information about pertinent items. The medical reps refer to this process of gathering personal data on doctors—such as their family and lifestyle facts, hobbies, and personal interests—as "history taking."

The pharmaceutical company's internal training department offers 2-4 weeks of instruction on the fundamental knowledge that serves as the foundation of facts for the details. A trained medical representative will be more efficient with appropriate industrial and clinical knowledge, which will expand access and provide the busy physician with higher value.

To learn more about the technical aspects of prescription medications, doctors frequently consult with medical representatives. The medical representatives are instructed to serve as a tool to help the companies increase their market share by developing a personal rapport with the doctors, attending to their wants and expectations, whether or not they are expressed, and meeting their own personal goals. Some businesses use young reps whose sole responsibilities are dropping out samples and keeping up with connections, leaving the important interactions to more experienced salespeople.

Medical representatives are essential to implementing the company's agenda, cultivating relationships with specific doctors, and settling disputes with pharmacies. Rep's inability to satisfy doctors' needs: Pharma corporations have employed huge armies of field employees, frequently ignoring the need for appropriate certification and competence, as a result of little product differentiation, fierce competition, and great market potential. Companies acknowledge recruiting individuals with backgrounds outside of science to fill open positions.

Only 1/6th of all field employees currently hold marketing degrees in addition to post-graduate degrees in pharmacy.

A sizable group of salespeople are needed as treatments get more intricate and medications become more specialised. The field employees have been dissatisfied by their companies' slow adoption of digital technologies. According to studies, the majority of Representatives in India lack closed-loop marketing solutions, meeting schedules, CRM systems, and digital medical material.

In contrast to the Certified Medical Representatives (CMR) Institute in the US, there aren't many institutions in India that offer medical representative's official training and certification. Some of the leading pharmaceutical companies in India employ a field force of about 5000 people and allocate up to 20% of their overall budget on recruiting and educating new employees. Field force activities receive a staggering 60% of the overall promotional budget. The pharmaceutical sector employs 1, 40,000 medical representatives in India, according to estimates.

Some doctors disagree with the idea of medical representatives pushing medications to licensed physicians.

They claim that the term "medical representative" is inaccurate. They contend that medical reps are not professionals in medicine. They lack any qualifications. They don't have any medical training, and neither do they speak for any medical professionals or organisations. They are merely compensated workers employed by a pharmaceutical business to persuade doctors to prescribe the company's goods using any legal or illegal means, hence boosting the firm's revenues. Giving doctors medical information by so-called medical representatives is just incorrect. It is unfortunate that doctors elevate salespeople to the rank of professors. With the use of the internet, doctors must learn medicine through medical professors, books, and journals.

We can infer that the bulk of doctors and pharmacists get their knowledge from medical reps.

Medical representatives play a part in educating doctors about the pharmaceuticals that are sold on the market and their prices. The practitioner must employ reps while being careful not to be excessively swayed by their pitch.

Direct selling to doctors:

One of the most significant marketing strategies employed by the pharmaceutical business worldwide is direct marketing to physicians. Reps who visit doctors armed with presents like pens, cups, and samples have a high success rate in persuading doctors to write prescriptions for their products. The interaction between the doctor and the pharmaceutical business is seen as positive.

Selling on the side

Personal selling is described as "the process of person-to-person conversation between a salesperson and a prospective customer, in which the latter strives to meet the latter's requirements by providing the latter with the chance to purchase something of value, such as a good or service."

The phrase can also be used to describe a scenario in which a business relies heavily on its sales team to interact with customers. "Personal engagement with prescribers is a vital success factor in the sector given the nature of pharmaceutical products" (Corstjens, 1991). According to Corstjens (1991), the strength of the pharmaceutical company's sales staff is the most important component for successful product penetration and profitability, along with the quality of the pharmaceutical products.

As opposed to the predefined message delivered by other promotional techniques, personal selling enables the pharmaceutical representative to customise the message to particular doctors. The best strategy to market medications to doctors has been shown to be one-on-one interactions because reps may tailor their approach to the individual they are selling to by determining their primary drivers and decision-making processes.

"I naturally grow fond of the representatives who come to see me frequently. I then attempt to recommend two or three of his products. I believe that most physicians share my sentiments. - A medical specialist.

The World Health Organization member nations passed a resolution in May 2007 to establish or enforce legislation against the "inaccurate, deceptive, or unethical promotion of pharmaceuticals" in response to the rising opposition to "irresponsible" marketing techniques.

Providing specifics and a reminder of the brand

For the past 50 years, medical representatives have accounted for 60% of all sales and marketing expenses and have been the primary means of "detailing" marketing material to physicians.

The most crucial aspect that a representative must complete is the detailing. The only method to boost prescription generation is by effective details supported by a suitable visual aid, according to ethical standards.

The sales representatives emphasise the USPs of their brand of the drug during the detailing process by using a variety of detailing and visual aids to demonstrate its superior benefits, increased efficacy, improved cost-effectiveness, and improved safety when compared to the products of their rivals. Simple pamphlets to elaborate presentations on Digital Video Disc (DVD) players can be used as detailed aids.

Sales representatives will present a little product-advertising gift, such a ballpoint pen imprinted with the brand name, at the conclusion of the detailed procedure. It is customary to provide the doctor with enough samples of the medication and an informational booklet.

In many impoverished countries, the detailing is still an essential means of communication. In China, for instance, conferences and visits with sales representatives account for about three-quarters of the information doctors receive about new medications. It is a proven truth that Indian doctors receive lower-quality drug information than their western counterparts. While numerous studies have demonstrated the value and calibre of the promotional information provided to doctors in India, little is known about promotional practises in general.

When flip charts were first proposed by Glaxo in 1972, the company's revenues increased by a factor of two in just one year. While earlier doctors would receive a "detail card" offering in-depth details on the medication's advantages and disadvantages, some advocates claimed that doctor.

The corporation removes the confidential volumes and flip charts every two to three months and destroys them.

Many times, according to certain reps, there were discrepancies between what they had been instructed to tell the doctor, what was written on the flip charts, and what was contained in the comprehensive literature. Representatives claimed that their training on pharmacological information was rudimentary and that their primary presentation tool was a flip chart.

The majority of doctors think that visits from representatives who utilise flip charts for this purpose led to them learning about new medications. These flipcharts demonstrate the advantages of their medications over those of.

They also offer the outcomes of studies they've conducted on the effectiveness of the medicine. Some doctors claimed that while representatives infrequently brought up drug interactions and bad effects, they were typically happy with the information given and understood the representative's duty. Everything is explained clearly, and the medical reps are knowledgeable about their products and able to respond to the doctor's inquiries.

According to studies, decision-making by physicians will be impacted by restrictions placed on the flow of pertinent medical information from any channel unless those restrictions can be easily overcome by another channel. Drug sales agents give doctors and nurses with controlled, timely, and practical clinical information.

Supporting the requirement for knowledge to be freely shared with the medical community, The US Supreme Court recently found that a Vermont law that restricts detailing to physicians is unconstitutional because it prevents pharmaceutical companies and sales personnel from providing doctors with information about prescription drugs. The decision was reached by a 6/3 majority. In addition, the majority ruling of the Court stated: "If pharmaceutical marketing influences treatment choices, it does so because physicians find it convincing. Since it enables detailers to tailor their messages to each doctor's practise, the record does indeed show that some

Vermont doctors find customised detailing based on prescriber-identifying information to be "extremely beneficial."

The pharmaceutical industry and advertising

There is a dated marketing joke. "I know some of my advertising is effective, but not all of it." The Latin word "advertere," which meaning "to turn towards," is the root of the English word "advertise." The majority of the top pharmaceutical corporations currently invest more in marketing than in R&D. Despite the fact that modern pharmaceutical marketing techniques are sometimes mistaken for contemporary phenomena, they are actually a direct descendant of 19th-century patent medicine advertising. The top spenders and primary creators of the printed advertising approach were known as "Nostrum-mongers." The first trademarks and distinctive packaging, as well as "pull" or demand stimulation methods, were used by Nostrum sellers.

In general, advertising is seen as a valid strategy for promoting the competitiveness that powers a free market economic system. The benefit to the consumers is the moral justification. Because advertising aims to increase consumer choice and chances of receiving the best value for their money, consumers are assumed to gain from it. Consumer satisfaction-driven businesses will outperform those that don't.

However, advertising have a potential for deceit by virtue of their very existence. Any advertisement has the potential to be deceptive. No company would invest money unless it was certain it would receive something in return. Many people waste a lot of time and money if the advertisement is ineffective. The WHO has ruled that "pharmaceutical product advertisements should be accurate. Regarding its contents and their percentage, nothing should be said incorrectly. The dosage form, mode of administration, proprietary name as well as the generic name, side effects and treatment of toxic effects, precautions, and contraindications should all be well described. The aforementioned claims ought to be true, accurate from a scientific standpoint, and supported.

Although there are many limits, the goal of advertising in the market for ethical pharmaceuticals is the same as it is for any other product. Without a valid prescription from a doctor, a patient cannot utilise a medicine. The Drugs and Magic Remedies (Objectionable Advertisement) Acts of 1954 and 1955 prohibit direct advertising of pharmaceutical products, the majority of which are morally acceptable goods. However, non-prescription items like pain relievers, inhalers, antiseptic creams, and other items can be advertised directly through well-known media because they are available over-the-counter.

Branding

Any name, word, sign, symbol, design, or combination thereof that serves to distinguish the products or services of one seller from those of their rivals is referred to as a brand (Kotler, 1980).

A brand is defined by a distinctive name, visual mark, trademark, and copyright that work together to give a product a distinctive look and personality. Additionally, the brand is made to "contain" a distinctive informational content that clearly identifies the product qualities, benefits, values, and users through a consistent, meticulous, and expensive branding effort. Brand equity, which includes awareness, acceptability, loyalty, preference, price premium, and unit volume, is a measure of a brand's capacity to compete.

Pharmaceutical products may genuinely provide value to the consumer because branding, which essential to consumer goods is positioning, is also applicable to them. A pharmaceutical branding strategy can directly benefit the product's maker, payer, prescriber, and patients.

Direct-to-consumer (DTC)

The other major kind of advertising is direct-to-consumer (DTC) pharma marketing artillery's main weapon. just two nations Currently, businesses can operate in the US and New Zealand. They sell their medications directly to patients.

Pharma companies spend the most on DTC marketing. 5 billion US dollars, or 14% of their whole marketing budget budget. But DTC fell short of meeting the industry's expectations.

expected. The US House of Representatives passed the the Committee on Energy and Commerce began an looking into the false and deceptive advertising after many egregious instances of drug abuse, rules.

Free offerings

Free product samples are an extremely effective marketing tool. tools. Almost all medical professionals that obtain samples from Patients will receive them from reps.

When free samples ultimately run out and a prescription is required, doctors frequently write the same medication even though they may have genuinely considered a different medication.

Presentations as a reminder

The relationship between the drug rep and the physician has become so important to the drug company's marketing strategy that gifts are frequently not recognised as such. Dr. Ashley Wazana discovered that the practise is widespread and extremely effective after reviewing all the papers that had been written about the effect of gifts from pharmaceutical companies on physician behaviour.

Two strategies were employed by the pharmaceutical corporations to provide presents. Each month, several small gifts and free samples of were given to the doctors as part of the proactive strategy. During routine promotional visits by the reps, various small gifts and free drug samples were delivered to the doctors each month as part of the proactive approach. Usually, brand names were written on these presents to serve as reminders for the doctors.

Over time, it seems that gifts have become more expensive and more obviously incentivized than tokens. To encourage doctors to write prescriptions, gifts are frequently utilised as marketing techniques, from stationery to home goods to international trips for conferences.

Accepting these presents, especially the pricey ones, makes them obligated to repay the favour by altering accepted prescription norms and boosting sales.

Representatives were supposed to offer doctors with tiny gifts in order to keep their brand in their minds. These "brand reminders" included prescription pads in addition to desktop accessories and small medical supplies. It was also claimed that certain businesses hired marketing experts to

The alternative strategy entailed giving doctors incentives depending on their requests, or "anything she/he wants as gifts." Even the family members of doctors, particularly the younger members, are subject to this culture of seduction.

Gifts that are more overtly incentives to prescribe are given as well as tokens like brand reminders to foster the doctor-drug company relationship. In order to get them to recommend their company's medications, medical reps presented presents to doctors, and many of them appear to accept these rewards. By remembering special days like birthdays, you can establish a personal connection with the doctor. In their promotional techniques, pharmaceutical corporations did not distinguish between qualified and unqualified physicians.

Doctors and medical representatives agreed that gifts with greater value than stationery were increasingly replacing brand reminders. These include everything from jewels to electronics to cars. Despite the fact that "brand reminders" are supposed to influence doctors' prescribing practises, the majority of doctors had no issues with them. Many medical professionals believed that pricey presents were acceptable.

It's interesting to note that none of the doctors thought their decisions were influenced by incentives, but they all acknowledged that their peers had. This is known as the "illusion of unique invulnerability."

The type, volume, and quality of the incentives provided to doctors depend on their ability to write prescriptions. With few exceptions, doctors join the system whether they want to or not. Although the unethical marketing strategy is started by the pharmaceutical industry, doctors are ultimately responsible for its continuation. The makers claimed that although novel treatments were pushed on the basis of their scientific relevance, "me too" drugs, or modifications of currently available drugs, required vigorous promotion. They claimed that physicians were more inclined to demand rewards for prescribing the first option.

Katz et al. claim that friendship, flattery, and food are all effective persuasion strategies, especially when used together.

E-pharmaceutical marketing with contemporary marketing communications methods

Alterations in the pharmaceutical industry's doctors' purchasing patterns The pharmaceutical market is experiencing changes in doctors' purchasing patterns, necessitating the employment of new marketing communications strategies. Growing interest in e-marketing strategies as a tool for supporting both marketing communications and gaining market share in the prescription drug market is being driven by the changing role of medical representatives and legal regulations aimed at restricting direct contacts between representatives and doctors.

Doctors today have access to a wealth of online tools for learning about novel medications. 51% of doctors claimed they are already aware of the drug information that representatives provide in the e-Pharma Physicians Annual Study. They now anticipate that reps will go above and beyond the norm and add more value to their business.

Pharma marketing needs to change in order to survive by adopting a "fish where the fish are" mentality. Digital communications are more than simply a medium; they represent a completely new method of conducting business that has an impact on everything from developing strategic insights to carrying out tactical plans. A coordinated strategy is necessary, and digital is the bridge between all parties. To be fully effective, digital media that is paid, owned, and earned must be balanced. At every opportunity, the goal is to directly address the audiences with important messages. The ID model is an additional illustration of how pharmaceutical marketers are embracing fresh approaches to connecting with physicians on their terms.

Physicians are changing their media consumption habits and utilising social media and mobile devices like everyone else, which is prompting marketers and sales representatives to change their promotion techniques. For the past 50 years, sales representatives have accounted for 60% of all sales and marketing expenses, serving as the primary conduit for "detailing" marketing information to physicians. ZS Associates, a consulting company that keeps a database tracking physician appointments with salespeople, reports a 20% reduction in the number of doctors ready to visit reps since 2008.

Interest in the possibilities of e-detailing is continuing to increase as the amount of money spent on face-to-face promotion is becoming increasingly disproportionate to the return on investment.

Digital or virtual detailing was first used in the early 1990s and was pioneered by pharma giants like Merck. It is now more advanced, efficient, and widely accepted.

E-detailing will eventually develop to include more interactive features like videos, web chats, and information from key opinion leaders as a cost-efficient and growth-intensive strategy, aiding in the advancement of the shifting pharma sales and marketing landscape. With the help of real-time patient-level data, the new innovative platform Instinctive Data (ID) aims to improve healthcare professional education based on speciality and patient demographic while providing pharma marketers with unmatched access to a healthcare practitioner's practise.

The most valuable resource for everyone is time, and modern healthcare providers are no exception. Every day, tens of thousands of healthcare professionals from various disciplines conduct business through MD On-Line (MDOL). Pharma businesses are able to effortlessly integrate sponsored, sophisticated, and targeted communications into the daily workflow of healthcare providers thanks to ID, a feature found on the provider's MDOL online portal.

The material provided is useful, significant, and easy to share. With the touch of a button, tools like "Forward to a Friend" enable health care professionals to email interesting and pertinent content to colleagues, converting paid media into earned through word-of-mouth and potential internet buzz.

Health care practitioners are able to take quick action with their patient group to promote behaviour change thanks to additional capabilities like "Search for Patients" and "Print a Reminder for Patient's Chart." These tools aid in encouraging the healthcare professional to discuss important information with patients during visits, hence maximising ID's potential for earned publicity. These marketing strategies not only aim to raise the standard of care and strengthen the doctor-patient bond, but they also have the potential to improve how healthcare professionals view the pharmaceutical sector in the long run.

The medical representatives themselves are a dissatisfied group since they are living in uncertain times and worry about losing their jobs or becoming irrelevant in the industry. A medical representative's friend, not enemy, is digitization!

In truth, digitization makes it possible for patients to have more rewarding encounters with clinicians by empowering them with analytical insights. Digital platforms that are impartial, like Docplexus, assist pharmaceutical businesses in "listening" to doctors' unbiased comments and maintaining ongoing interaction. However, the Indian pharmaceutical sector lags well behind its western counterparts in implementing digital solutions, according to Indegene's Digital Savvy Healthcare Sales Rep 2017 Report.

Some pharmaceutical marketers erroneously conflate digitization and edetailing. E-detailing is but one component of a larger, all-encompassing digital approach. For digital to effectively enhance the connection between pharmaceutical companies and physicians, it must permeate all departments and hierarchies. The efforts have been aided by Docplexus' digital marketing solutions, which include product releases, webinars, and CME programmes. s of the field force of its clients.

While the medical community has gotten accustomed to using digital technologies, many pharmaceutical corporations have yet to develop a thorough digital strategy that incorporates field force activities. Doctors are quite dissatisfied with this.

The function of electronic details as a technique for communication in the promotion mix:

E-Pharma marketing is a term that has evolved in recent years to describe online communications that are entirely virtual. E-detailing is a versatile instrument that offers limitless possibilities for developing the promotional message and at a very modest cost makes it possible to reach a large audience of doctors with a compelling and appealing message. The addition of e-detailing to pharmaceutical companies' marketing strategies entails utilising a visually appealing mode of communication that allows users to customise the marketing message in a variety of ways and appeal to most of the senses and emotions with the help of flash animations, 3D presentations, or video webcasts. The message and interaction are more effective because doctors are involved.

E- Detailing is a process of communicating via online interactive multimedia presentations that highlight the features and benefits of a certain pharmaceutical medication.

A presentation like that ought to influence physicians' viewpoints and choices on the prescribing of particular medicines. Due to the concurrent use of interactive promotional activities (providing marketing and substantive material) and access, this is made possible. access to analytical data, which allows for swift communication strategy changes after studying a particular doctor's behaviour. When a drug is first introduced, it can be used to enhance doctor awareness; when a product matures and grows, it can support conventional marketing strategies and broaden market penetration.

Along with doctors' increasing interest in having online access to medical information, the e-detailing tool is becoming more and more well-liked. According to research, 47% of doctors are open to the idea of e-detailing, and around 88% of doctors are interested in such access.

whereas around 50% think that this is effective promotion depends on integrating it with conventional methods.

Visits from medical professionals

The principle of Closed Loop forms the foundation of e-detailing.

Marketing and focuses a focus on research in particular. the doctor's requirements, goals, and perspectives on communication, i.e. the doctor's participation in the message being delivered.

CLM is already well-known overseas.

Factors supporting e-crucial detailing are function in business

Internet marketing's increasing importance

Communications in the drug industry can include

Due to the following elements:

The pursuit of alternate communication methods

More stringent regulations for pharmaceutical advertising

An increasing number of different online promotional initiatives

Online advertising has more trust compared to additional types.

Marketing agencies are becoming more specialised

Tools used in e-pharma marketing often include:

Websites (including product cards, thematic portals, and medical portals), databases, and databases (medical registers)

Emailing, which makes it possible to use viral marketing strategies.

Online PR (press coverage on the Internet, word-of-mouth advertising), e-knowledge (e-learning, e-CME), and

Internet communities (web 2.0, web 3.0)

Advertising games

Visual conferences

SEO and SEM (Search Engine Marketing) (Search Engine Optimization)

CLM, e-detailing (Closed Loop Marketing)

Benefits of electronic detailing:

- The possibility to personalise the session's message; The chance to learn about the product and the therapy at a time that is convenient for the doctor (i.e., on the doctor's terms);
- Lower costs for audience outreach compared to other forms of marketing communication
- Finding out more about the preferences of the physicians and pharmacists
- E-detailing presentations may include: A multimedia presentation to improve the calibre and appeal of medical representatives' visits.
- Video demonstration
- Static presentation with a component of interaction

E-Pharma marketing initiatives

The emergence of broadband Internet has also influenced new media, giving marketers the chance to incorporate eye-catching audiovisual effects in their advertising. Thanks to advancements in technology, mobile devices like phones can now be used in marketing communications. Modern communications are fundamentally characterised by mobile marketing, which makes it possible to communicate with the recipient, increase client loyalty, and create social networks centred around a brand. The prescription drug section of the pharmaceutical business is where cutting-edge technology are used in marketing communications most frequently.

Face-to-face contacts with medical representatives are strengthened by e-Pharma marketing initiatives.

the fact that they are becoming more accessible, more widely accepted by the medical and pharmaceutical community, and acknowledged by pharmaceutical corporations' corporate and anti-corruption policies, however, progressively renders such gatherings obsolete.
They don't interfere with doctors' scheduled appointments.

Sites for e-pharmaceutical marketing

The development of online communities is especially important for marketing communications. General Websites, such as those of medication manufacturers and news portals, are crucial instruments for universal e-pharma marketing because they are targeted at both patients and doctors and pharmacists. They receive a considerable amount of traffic from people looking for information or assistance. Patients utilise the internet to find knowledge about a particular topic in order to solve their problems.

Instead of specific medications or information on where to buy them, include information about a certain illness, potential therapies, and dietary recommendations.

Websites provide a platform for promotional operations that use unconventional promotional techniques to enhance the message. These websites are broken down into general medical portals (including Eskulap, Medycyna Praktyczna, Lekarze.com, Res Medica, and MedSerwis) and specialised portals for particular medical issues and treatments. Doctors are using the internet more and more frequently, building their own online communities, and being involved in their practise.

Medical Continuing Education (CME)

Continuous medical education or yearly recertification is not mandated by law in India. The doctor's only source of information on the most recent advancements in medicines is frequently medical representatives. A marketing strategy used to raise money for conferences and educational activities is called continuing medical education. Drug firms frequently covered the costs of conference fees, lodging, and travel for specific doctors. Most doctors indicated they could not otherwise afford these meetings, which they viewed as educational, but had no objections to such help. Drug Corporation's claim that since conferences went outside, financing medical conferences had become less cost-effective from lecture halls of academic colleges to five-star hotels. Things have advanced to the point where physicians are now requesting corporate support.

Future Prospectives of Professional Sales Representatives

Pharmaceutical field forces continue to play a crucial role, and this is likely to be the case for the foreseeable future. Instead of opposing the idea, we should concentrate on giving this field army next-generation capabilities. This entails creating a more comprehensive model of reaction and concentrating on how we might capitalise on modifications to our selling encounters.

By forecasting and predicting resource needs based on customer journeys, giving on-demand access to information, and engaging SMEs during customer engagements, the next-generation capabilities for medical sales representatives will let businesses engage with their customers in new ways.

In this approach, we examine the future of medical sales agents They have the ability to transcend beyond conventional selling encounters, in our opinion (such as product detailing). In fact, the field force becomes a formidable competitor in the fight to promote new pharmaceutical goods when it is combined with the newest technology in pharma marketing.

Digital engagements seem to work best when facilitated by a friendly and knowledgeable person who can tailor the information and the conversation to the doctor. There was a time when the industry worried that digital would eventually replace the medical sales representative, but it now seems that this is not the case. There doesn't seem to be a substitute for face-to-face communication in Pharma. Why should it, too?

In the pharmaceutical industry, digitalizing a person's approach is more important than replacing a person with a computer. The sales role is becoming more difficult. The greatest value that pharma once had was medical knowledge, which is now much more readily available. Simply telling doctors about a product no longer works to pique their interest in the Indian market, which is dominated by generic drugs with little to no uniqueness.

Mehul Shukla, Director, Marketing Excellence at Cipla, questions why established businesses are still failing to go past the awareness or interest stages and are instead stuck there instead of moving on to the purchase or recommendation stages.

Medical sales representatives will soon be expected to balance selling their products with providing services that doctors will value in order to establish their own practises. Care for patients and fostering relationships may fall under this. The profession of a medical sales representative will become incredibly fulfilling as a result of services, which will not only strengthen distinctiveness but also make the position much more patient- and relationship-centric than it was previously.

K. Satya Mahesh, a former head of business excellence at Emcure, elaborated on the idea, saying, "We all recognise that most partnerships are based on value exchange. The value provided must, nevertheless, be regarded as valuable.

Knowledge, Attitude, Skill, and Habits (KASH) of the field associates, complemented by distinctive services provided by the business, are essential.

The least understood pharma growth lever, treatment adherence is undoubtedly helped by initiatives like patient services. Better illness outcomes are produced by these services. As a result, the effect will persist a long time because better patient health outcomes are in both parties' best interests.

The organisations and medical professionals who recognise the need for such patient- and knowledge-centered services will be the ones who will lead us into the future. For improved business and health outcomes, this does in fact suit the interests of the pharmaceutical company, the medical representative, and the doctor.

Numerous avenues for outreach

A brand must compete fiercely to be at the top of doctors' minds in the generic industry. Medical sales staff must find opportunities to visit doctors and "remind" them of their brands in order for this to happen. This frequently has an overwhelming effect and irritates customers, producing the reverse of the desired result. Sales calls are a huge drain on resources for the organisation because they are expensive. As an alternative, a number of digital players have arisen with programmes to help pharmaceutical firms establish "multi-channel interaction." In addition to the work of the medical sales person, this encompasses marketing via emails, websites, webinars, and WhatsApp/SMS.

Building different channels for reaching out to doctors identified as the most crucial skill that would support the future job of the medical sales representative in the MedicinMan poll.

Comprehensive View of Customer Needs

As previously stated, we think that the pharmaceutical industry needs to transition from focusing on product sales to developing partnerships through services. If so, it would be incredibly challenging to assist someone we know so little about. Consequently, giving the pharmaceutical sales force a complete picture of consumer wants will be one of their future talents. Since they are the ones who know their clients best, medical sales professionals typically act in this way naturally.

However, the use of sophisticated analytical tools and a central data repository can offer considerably superior insights to support the work of the field team. This metric was ranked as the second-most crucial future capacity in the MedicinMan poll.

Individualised in-clinic content

Pharma has typically used data to analyse go-to-market strategy rather than the content used to promote products. Brand-specific requirements have spurred content development. The function of personalised content will be crucial both now and in the future. Relevance is the key characteristic that fosters engagement, and there is ample data to support the claim that personalization fosters relevance. No physical encounter or multi-channel campaign will elicit the necessary response from physicians without involvement. Therefore, it was quite unexpected to see that this characteristic came in third among the list of four potential skills.

Superior sales calls

The commercial excellence division has been concentrating on raising the calibre of our sales calls for years. More than ever, data pouring from doctor calls is making it simpler to figure out how to raise the call quality. Companies who employed closed-loop marketing platforms and used the data to inform subsequent calls during the pandemic observed an improvement in average call times from 0–3 minutes (2019–20) to 18–22 minutes (2020-21). What sustainable methods can we use here? Will this still be the case when doctors and medical sales personnel interact virtually instead of in person?

As the fourth future skill that field troops would need to master, this would be a crucial skill to debate and discuss.

We can refine, elucidate, augment, and personalise content that is valuable to clients if we have a clear grasp of their needs. This guarantees calls of higher quality, Satya continued.

Mehul Shukla states, "We marketers need to discover our digital golf course," indicate that businesses must engage online just as CEOs of various firms do on golf courses.

To boost sales, the pharmaceutical sector is moving away from a mass market strategy and towards a target market strategy. The pharmaceutical sector is no longer rewarded for me-too goods, incremental innovation, and pill sales. Pharma needs to concentrate on explaining how their brand benefits

CHAPTER 5

Pricing

Pharmaceutical pricing policies are a set of written guidelines or standards that have been accepted or implemented by a public entity (such as the government), a collection of buying organisations, or a specific health service in order to manage the costs of pharmaceutical products. The overall goals of pricing policies should be to maintain supply security of high-quality products while also ensuring that consumers and health systems have access to affordable and equitable pharmaceutical products with guaranteed quality. These policies should also ensure value for money based on improved health outcomes at the population level.

It has long been understood how crucial it is to get inexpensive access to pharmaceutical items in the global movement towards universal health coverage. Sustainable Development Group (SDG) Target 3.8 was most recently established by the United Nations as "financial risk protection, access to quality essential health-care services, and access to safe, effective, quality, and affordable essential medicines and vaccinations for all" (emphasis added). By extension, all levels of governments in Member States and the international community are accountable for fulfilling this Goal.

It is good that there is a commitment to provide affordable access to critical pharmaceutical items worldwide. Nonetheless, despite this commitment, high pharmaceutical product prices continue to provide considerable obstacles in both high- and low-income countries. It is generally known that many healthcare systems struggle to give access to all patients due to the high cost of pharmaceutical items. Patients and their families frequently endure severe, if not catastrophic, financial hardship when in need of pharmaceutical supplies when there is no insurance coverage. People without any financial resources might not even be allowed access to effective medicinal treatments. In contrast, low pricing could produce profit margins that are judged insufficient to satisfy the expectations of commercial actors for preserving the extent and scope of business operation. This might disrupt the operations of the healthcare system and have a negative impact on patient health by making some medications unavailable, causing supply disruptions, or creating a scarcity of such medications.

By combining sound pharmaceutical pricing strategies with other system-strengthening measures, health systems may be better able to increase access to inexpensive pharmaceuticals while preserving supply stability.

5.1 DEFINITION OF PRICE

Price is the term used to describe the cost of any commodity or service. One of the key components of the marketing mix is price. This is also how each company organisation makes its money. Hence, the price of goods determines whether a corporate organisation makes a profit or loses money. Pricing is another way to convey a product's or good's quality. In general, high grade products cost more money than low quality ones. Consumers choose products based on price in accordance with their purchasing power. No trade of any commodities or services is possible without a set price.

- Price is typically expressed in money. Price has been defined by a variety of authors and authorities.
- Here are a few crucial examples: Prof. William J. Stanton stated that "price is the quantity of money and/or other useful stuff needed to purchase a product.
- Prof. Philip Kotler asserts that only the price factor of the marketing mix generates income; all other components just generate costs. "Price is the traded value of the product or service stated in terms of money," says David J. Schwartz.

Pricing Definition

Price refers to the process of choosing the pricing objectives, identifying the potential price range, devising price strategies, deciding on the ultimate price, and putting that decision into action and maintaining control over it. All parties engaged in the creation, transfer, and consumption of goods are impacted by the vital and highly significant decision of price.

Pricing is a source of revenue for distributors and has an impact on both the volume of production and the amount of profit.

- Pricing, in the words of M.J. Jones and S.W. Jetty, "begins with an understanding of the corporate mission, target markets, and the marketing objectives; then pricing objectives are developed; next management estimates as to extent of flexibility in establishing prices by studying costs and profits internally and demand and competition externally; prices are then set between these two extreme ends by deciding price strategies in the light of objectives so set; specific methodologies are then used to determine prices between these two extreme ends.

"Pricing is the function of determining the products value in monetary terms," claims W.J. Stanon. Pricing is the process by which a business determines the price at which it will sell its goods and services, and it may be a part of the business's marketing strategy. When determining prices, the business will take into account the cost of production, the market, its competitors, its environment, its brand and the quality of the product.

Objectives of pricing

1. **Goals pertaining to profits:** Profit has continued to be the primary goal of corporate endeavours.

   The firm's pricing policies and tactics are intended to achieve the following profit-related goals:

   i. **Maximum Current Profit:** Increasing current profits is one of the pricing goals in order to make as much money as possible.

      The business seeks to establish its price such that it can generate more immediate profits. Company, however, is not permitted to raise prices above the cap. But it focuses on making the most money possible.

   ii. **Target Return on Investment:** The majority of businesses aim to generate a respectable rate of return on their investments.

   The target return could be

   A set percentage of sales,

   A certain ROI, or a set amount of rupees.

   The business designs its pricing strategies and policies such that sales income finally produces an average return on total investment.

   For instance, a corporation wishes to get a 20% return on its $3 crore total investment. It needs to establish the product's price so that it can make 60 lakh rupees.

2. **Goals pertaining to sales**

   i. **Sales Growth:** The company wants to expand sales volume, therefore it sets its prices to allow for continuous growth in sales. It is presumable that increasing sales will directly increase earnings. Hence, pricing adjustments are made so that sales volume can be increased.

   A corporation designs its pricing strategies with the goal of reaching or maintaining the target market share. Price selections are made in a way that allows the business to capture the desired market share. Market share is a specified dollar amount of sales calculated in relation to the total industry sales. For instance, a corporation can aim for a 25% market share in the concerned sector.

Increase in Market Share: Price and pricing are occasionally used as a technique to increase a company's market share. When a business expects that its market share is lower than anticipated, it can increase it by setting prices appropriately; pricing is intended to increase market share.

3. **Goals for the competition:** Every company strives to respond to the competitors by using the right business tactics, which is why competition is such a strong influence determining marketing effectiveness.

   The following competition-related goals may be prioritised with regard to price:

   i. **To Meet Competition:** The company sets and alters its pricing strategies in order to respond forcefully to the competitors. Pricing is the main worry with facing competition in today's market.

      Price is a popular strategy used by many businesses to respond to the degree and ferocity of competition.

   ii. **To Discourage Competitors:** One of the primary goals of pricing may be to keep competitors out. The adage "prevention is better than cure" also applies in this situation. No need to engage in combat with competitors if they are kept at bay. To accomplish the goal, a business keeps its pricing as low as it can to reduce the profit appeal of its items. In some instances, a business will behave aggressively to block the arrival of rivals by selling products even at a loss.

   iii. **Price is Another Means of Achieving Quality Leadership:** Pricing is Another Means of Achieving Quality Leadership. Buyers typically associate a high price with a high-quality product, according to the quality leadership. The corporation creates its pricing strategies in order to convey to customers that its products are on par with or better than those of its direct rivals. The pricing methods and policies are intended to drive competitors out of the market.

   iv. **To Eliminate Competitors from the Market:** This can be accomplished by sacrificing current earnings by keeping prices as low as possible in order to maximise future profits by charging a high price after eliminating competitors from the market.

4. **Customer-related Objectives:** Every marketing choice is based on the needs of the customer. The company seeks to accomplish the following goals with the appropriate pricing policies and practises:

   i. **Gaining the Trust of Customers:** Serving customers is the goal. The goal of the company's pricing strategies is to gain the trust of the target market. Customers' trust that the price being charged for the product is reasonable can be established, maintained, or even strengthened by the company through suitable pricing practises. Consumers are given the impression that they are not being duped.

ii. **To Please Customers:** The main goal of any marketing initiatives is to satisfy customers. Pricing is also not an exception. A corporation should plan pricing in such a way that results in maximum consumer happiness. A company sets, adjusts, and readjusts its pricing to satisfy its target customers.

5. **Further Goals:** Beyond the goals we've just outlined, the corporation has other goals it hopes to accomplish through price. They are listed below:

   i. **Market Penetration:** This purpose asks for providing the lowest price to attract price-sensitive clients and involves penetrating the market deeply to draw in the greatest number of customers.

   ii. **Marketing a New Product:** To successfully advertise a new product, the company initially sets a low price for its items to encourage trial and repeat purchases. The corporation may debut a new product successfully with the help of sound pricing.

   iii **Sustaining Image and Reputation in the Market:** The company's efficient pricing practises have a favourable effect on its image and reputation in the market. By setting appropriate prices, stabilising prices, or maintaining steady prices, a company can build a positive reputation and image in the eyes of its target market.

   iv. **To Skim the Cream from the Market:** This purpose is to make the most money possible in the early stages of a product's life cycle. A corporation can charge a relatively high price for a new product since it offers unique and superior advantages. Certain market segments will nevertheless purchase the product at a premium price.

   v. **Concerning price stability:** Pricing plans and approaches are developed by companies to prevent seasonal and cyclical swings, which helps them achieve price stability and a top ranking in the market. The buyers are positively impacted by price stability. Frequent price fluctuations have a negative impact on the company's reputation.

   vi. **Survival and Growth:** Lastly, pricing aims to ensure the ongoing success of a company's business ventures and operations. It serves as a fundamental pricing goal. Price strategies are chosen so as not to jeopardise the viability of the business.

The Value of Price

Priority for the economy

I **Factors that determine Demand and Supply:**Price is crucial in influencing the volume of demand since the cost of goods directly influences demand. Price has so been acknowledged as a fundamental component. In other words, as price falls, demand increases, and when price increases, demand reduces, therefore the low of demand applies. If the price is raised but the quality of the product remains the same, then demand for the products decreases, and if the price is lowered, demand increases. In this approach, the amount of supply and demand is dependent on price; pricing can be considered a determinant of supply and demand.

ii **Impact on the Production Factors:** The cost of goods is crucial to the economy and business. Wages, rent, interest rates, and earnings are all directly impacted. The factors and means of venture productions include capital, labour, land, and venture. It is appropriate to share wages for work, land rent, interest on capital, and acceptable profits from business ventures. Demand and supply are influenced by the factors and methods of production (land, labour, capital, and entrepreneur). Wage rates draw in workers, but high interest rates draw in capital. Price so significantly influences the ingredients and means of manufacturing.

iii **Impact on Investment and Savings:** Inflation may be impacted by set/fixed prices for the intended market. This suggests that rising prices of goods are a result of inflation. Customers experience challenges if the cost of goods or services rises. Investment is discouraged when the cost of goods falls, while investment increases when the cost of goods falls and saving increases. This circumstance aids in the growth of the community and the country.

2. **Organizational Importance:** Price management is a very challenging issue for profit-making firms, so sensible decisions should be made for pricing management. Price is an important aspect or factor of the marketing mix. It is possible to compete successfully in the market, but the only way to make money is by charging more. The following topics are covered to clarify the significance of price:

i **Sales and Profits:** Pricing is crucial in determining an organization's revenue and profit. By multiplying the per-unit price by the number of units sold, the total revenue can be calculated. When sales volume stays the same but prices drop, income likewise drops. Income increases if the price is raised while the quantity of sales stays the same. By deducting total costs from total revenues, one can also calculate or determine profit. Hence, by raising or lowering the price of goods, profit can be increased or lowered. Nonetheless, the company would suffer from the rapid changes in prices and revenue.

ii **Competence:** Competition is something that every business organisation must deal with as new rivals enter the market. Without a doubt, it must contend with price competition. The business can draw in more clients by lowering the price if market competition for the already established pricing increases. As a result, the production cost is reduced and sales volume is increased.

iii **Product Line Expansion:** The ability of a company to increase its target markets and product offerings is directly impacted by price. Pricing plays a role in determining whether to expand a product or add a new line to an existing one. Comparing the production cost and the price can help determine this. The choice to expand should be made if profit appears assured. Yet, if there is a direct contradiction, Therefore, the decision should not be made to increase the product line if there is no chance of profit and just loss.

3. **Relevance to the Clientele:** Price determination needs to be supported by valid justifications. Price determination that is rational benefits general consumers. To further clarify their significance for regular clients, the following aspects can be discussed:

(i) **The significance of the product choice:** Most buyers prioritise pricing and carefully consider it. They strive to choose products while taking prices into account. These clients downplay utility and quality. People have the option of choosing to purchase goods with affordable costs.

(ii) **Significance of the Quality Perception:** Prices play a crucial part in satisfying customers' needs and wants. In a similar vein, reassuring them of the products' calibre is also beneficial. If customers know that high-priced goods and services are of high quality and that low-priced goods are of low quality.

(iii) **The significance of customer benefits:** Cost of goods has an impact on customers' advantages. Customers still purchase low-cost goods and services even though their revenue sources are declining. When money rises, demand for goods remains constant regardless of how expensive they are. Customers who are price-sensitive may decide to purchase goods when the price has reduced or a reduction is offered. Some clients place a premium on their social regard, satisfaction, and dignity.

Marketing Techniques

1. **Penetration Pricing:** In order to increase market share, prices for goods and services are artificially kept low. The cost is raised after this is accomplished. This strategy was employed by Sky TV and France Telecom. These businesses must sign up a sizable number of customers in order for their efforts to be profitable, therefore they entice individuals to sign up for their services by providing free phones or satellite dishes at deeply discounted prices. Once there are many subscribers, prices start to progressively rise. When there is a premium movie or athletic event, for

example, Sky TV or any cable or satellite company shifts from a penetration approach to more of a skimming/premium pricing approach.

2. **Cost-effectiveness:** This is a straightforward cheap cost. A product is marketed and promoted for the least amount of money possible. Supermarkets frequently carry budget brands like soup, spaghetti, etc. The practise of reducing overhead costs as low as possible while charging customers a comparably less expensive rate to load an aircraft is known as budget flying.

   The first few seats on a flight are offered for a very low price (almost a promotional price), the middle portion are economy seats, and the final few seats on a flight are the most expensive (which would be a premium pricing strategy). Although recessions increase sales, economy pricing is not the same as a value pricing approach.

3. **Price Snatching:** Price skimming occurs when a business raises its pricing because it has a significant competitive advantage. Yet, the benefit usually does not last. Because more businesses enter the market as a result of the high price, the price inevitably decreases as a result of the increasing supply. In the 1970s, makers of digital timepieces adopted a skimming strategy. Further marketing tactics and price plans are put into place once additional manufacturers were lured into the market and the watches were made at a cheaper unit cost. As a result of the creation of new items, the watch industry became known for its inventiveness.

4. **Premium Costs:** A premium pricing approach sets a price that is higher than that of the opposition. It's a tactic that can be employed successfully when the product has a distinguishing feature or is the first of its kind and the company has a clear competitive advantage. For businesses entering a new market and looking to maximise profits in the early phases of the product life cycle, premium pricing can be a good approach.

Table 5.1 Pricing stratergy matrix.

PRICE (LOW → HIGH)	LOW	QUALITY
LOW	ECONOMY	PENETRATION
HIGH	SKIMMING	PREMIUM

The four primary pricing policies/strategies—premium pricing, penetration pricing, economy pricing, and price skimming—are represented in the diagram. They serve as the exercise's foundation. However, there are several significant approaches to pricing, including the following:

1. **Psychology of Pricing:** This strategy is applied when the marketer wants the customer to react emotionally rather than logically.
2. **Price by Product Line:** When there is a variety of goods or services, the prices reflect the advantages of particular selections. Although product lines offer a range of costs that consumers view as being reasonable progressively - over the range - they rarely represent the cost of producing the product. Although they are priced across the entire range, it can be advantageous for the manufacturer to offer them separately in terms of profit margin. Profit is made on the range as opposed to individual items.
3. **Product Options Price:** As soon as clients start to purchase, businesses will make an effort to boost their spending. Optional "extras" raise the cost of the good or service overall.
4. **Captive Product Pricing:** Companies will charge a higher price when a product has a complement because the consumer has no other options. Another instance is when printer manufacturers offer you an inkjet printer at a low price, knowing full well that you will need to purchase additional ink, which is usually quite pricey, as soon as the consumable ink runs out. Again, there is no other option because the cartridges are not interchangeable.
5. **Price for Product Bundles:** Here, vendors package a number of things together. This helps move out-of-date inventory as well. Moreover, product bundle pricing may be seen when items are sold at auction, where a desirable item may be bundled with a box of less desirable items so that you must bid for the entire lot. It effectively moves sluggish-moving goods and, in a sense, is another sort of promotional pricing.
6. **Discounted Prices:** Price is frequently used to advertise a product. There are numerous instances of promotional pricing, including BOGOF (Buy One Get One Free), money-off coupons, and discounts. Promotional pricing is frequently the focus of debate. Many nations have rules that specify how long a product must be offered for sale at its full price before being reduced.

   Sales are extravagant displays of discounted prices! Location-Based Pricing Geographic pricing accounts for price differences around the globe. For instance, rarity value or an area where shipping costs affect price. There is more than in others.

7. **Location-Based Pricing:** Geographic pricing accounts for price differences around the globe. For instance, rarity value or an area where shipping costs affect price. Some nations impose higher taxes on specific product categories, increasing or decreasing their cost, while others have laws that restrict the number of products that can be imported, further driving up costs. When you travel abroad, you'll notice that sometimes products are lot cheaper, or obviously much more expensive. This is because certain countries tax inelastic goods like alcohol or gasoline in order to raise income.
8. **Price Points:** This strategy is employed when external forces, such as the recession or increased competition, push businesses to offer value-added goods and services in order to maintain sales, such as value meals at McDonald's and other fast-food establishments.

Value pricing, which is comparable to economy pricing in many aspects, refers to prices that give you a feeling of receiving a lot of stuff for your money. One must not fall into the trap of believing that the good or service has additional worth. Usually, lowering the price does not raise the value. See also international marketing pricing and eMarketing price.

Our financial goals in terms of price will be safeguarded by how much cash we expect to generate from a product, how much we can sell, and what market share we will gain in comparison to rivals. While choosing the best pricing strategy for your mix, you must take into account goals like these and how a company produces profit relative to its cost of production.

The marketer must be conscious of its position in relation to competitors. The marketing mix should consider what clients anticipate to pay. There are numerous approaches to product pricing. Let's examine a few of them to try to determine the best course of action or strategy in varied.

Guidelines for developing and putting into practise pharmaceutical pricing plans

WHO advises that while developing and implementing pricing regulations for pharmaceutical items, countries follow eight guiding principles.

i. **A specific goal:** The overall goals of pricing policies should be to maintain supply security of high-quality products while also ensuring that consumers and health systems have access to affordable and equitable pharmaceutical products with guaranteed quality. These policies should also ensure value for money based on improved health outcomes at the population level.
ii. **Context-specificity:** The backdrop of the local health system, including its structure, as well as the supply and demand of pharmaceutical

products, should be carefully taken into account when choosing pricing strategies.

iii. **Coherence of policy:** For managing prices along the supply chain, pricing strategies should be utilized in conjunction with a comprehensive set of technical requirements.

Price rules should be used in conjunction with a logical set of technical requirements to manage prices at various stages of a product's life cycle and along the supply and distribution chain. Since the pharmaceutical industry in a nation interacts with the health industry and other sectors, it is important to identify broader principles and take them into account when deciding which course of action to take.

4. **A comprehensive foundation:** With a view to generating a supportive environment for policy implementation, pricing policies should be integrated with the legal framework of the health sector and other associated sectors, administrative structures, and technical capabilities.

i **Transparency:** Transparent communication with important stakeholders, such as suppliers and customers, is required for adopting price policies, including the procedures, technical approaches, decisions, and results.

ii. **Monitoring and review to ensure policy relevance:** Regular monitoring and evaluations of the degree to which the policies have achieved their goals—not just with regard to prices but also with regard to their impact on other outcomes like out-of-pocket costs and the accessibility of essential medications—are necessary to maintain the relevance of pricing policies. Where necessary, facts and experiences must be used to guide changes to the pricing policies.

iii. **Adherence and monitoring:** When pricing laws or policy recommendations are implemented, compliance should be prompted by suitable incentives, monitored by routine data and information collection, and enforced by proportionate penalties to deter policy violations.

iv. **Cooperation:** Collaboration with stakeholders and other health systems, including information and skill sharing about policies, the pharmaceutical market, and impacts on price and access, strengthens the effectiveness of national pricing strategies.

Definition, design and policy rationale

External reference pricing

The technique of using the price of a pharmaceutical product in one or more jurisdictions to derive a benchmark or reference price is referred to as external reference pricing (also known as international reference pricing). Pay attention to the fact that jurisdictions can refer to nations, areas, or other formalised purchasing authorities.

In order to determine or negotiate the price of the pharmaceutical product in a particular jurisdiction, external reference pricing evaluates the suitability of pharmaceutical product prices based on the chosen benchmark prices. External reference pricing may apply to both single-source and multisource supply products, but it has been used most often to set the price for single-source, on-patent pharmaceuticals. External reference price, depending on the policy's design, aims to prevent a jurisdiction from paying more than other comparable jurisdictions or less when the country has a lower revenue. Pricing obtained from outside reference pricing could not be within a jurisdiction's budget.

One of the key phases in implementing external reference pricing is choosing relevant and comparable national standards. Geographical closeness, national income, the accessibility of medications, country of origin, and market size may all be considered as selection criteria. At frequent locations in the supply chain, like ex-manufacturer price, prices would be compared. Many nations that use external reference pricing have different formulas for calculating the conversion of benchmark prices into the final price. They include the lowest price, the average price, the average of the lowest prices, and prices that have been modified for market elements like purchasing power parity and market size. Products with a single source of supply or items with a less typical mix of sources of supply may be subject to external reference pricing.

Many European nations, as well as high- and middle-income nations from other areas (such as Brazil, Egypt, Saudi Arabia, Thailand, Turkey, and the United Arab Emirates), have embraced the concept of external reference pricing. Several nations are contemplating implementing foreign reference pricing as well.

The following elements should be taken into account for external reference pricing policy operating effectiveness:

An international collaborative network that encourages price sharing and skill transfers;

a. sufficient technical capacity; database management; monitoring and evaluation;

b. a governance structure supported by transparent legislation and appeals process;

c. overall system readiness, including gaining political support. The following elements should be taken into account in external reference pricing methodology:

The number of jurisdictions included to obtain reference prices;

a. The comparability of referenced jurisdictions, such as market sizes, national income, and purchasing power; the comparability of price types along the supply and distribution chain (i.e., ex-manufacturer, ex-wholesaler, pharmacy, and consumers);
b. the quantity of jurisdictions used to obtain reference prices;
c. the comparability of referenced jurisdictions, including market sizes, national income, and purchasing power;
d. legislative measures and operational procedures for methodologically challenging situations, including the availability of data only from non-comparable jurisdictions, missing data, and currency fluctuations; and
e. use for products with insufficient competition (to which external reference pricing is most applicable).

Internal reference pricing

Internal reference pricing is the technique of creating a benchmark or reference price from the prices of a group of pharmaceutical goods that are interchangeable and therapeutically related in order to set or negotiate a product's price or reimbursement rate. The Anatomical Therapeutic Chemical Classification System (ATC) classifies therapeutic comparability and interchangeability either by chemical entity and pharmacological class or by therapeutic indication.

Internal reference pricing aims to reduce price variation among comparable products by coordinating the costs of goods with the same or similar therapeutic effects. Moreover, it might promote rivalry amongst goods that have equivalent or comparable therapeutic effects.

The selection of groups of interchangeable and therapeutically equivalent items is a key step in implementing internal reference pricing so that prices may be compared. In cases when multiple products' active pharmaceutical ingredients share a chemical compound, a reference pricing may be established through ATC 5th Level taking into account elements like dose and pack size. Assessment of clinical trial evidence of non-inferiority and therapeutically-equivalent dose could be taken into account for therapeutic equivalence at ATC 4th Level for the purpose of setting the reference price, with consideration given to elements like frequency of dose administration.

Prices for various goods would be compared, established in accordance with evidence of equivalentity, and applied at common distribution sites.

Many nations use internal reference pricing to link the costs of medicines that are (closely) substitutable, such as generic, biosimilar, or therapeutically identical pharmaceuticals. Internal reference pricing has been used to set reimbursement rates for nearly comparable items in healthcare systems with public pharmaceutical insurance or when payments from private insurers are subject to regulation, in addition to setting prices. For instance, patients who choose a branded product would pay the price premium between the branded and lowest-priced product or reference generic.

Strong national regulatory agencies to ensure

a. the quality of generic and biosimilar medications, including established post-market surveillance;
b. concurrent implementation of policies to promote the use of quality-assured generic and biosimilar medications, including but not limited to the policy.
c. A clear understanding of the supply chain incentives, including financial incentives to service providers, that may moderate or enhance the overall effects of internal reference pricing;
d. Forward-looking policy design in anticipation of growing demand for biosimilar medicines with market characteristics likely to mirror;
e. public health campaigns for patients and providers with respect to use of generic medicines, with a view to building trust and acceptance;

The following elements should be taken into account by internal reference pricing methodology and processes.

a. Therapeutic equivalency is determined for therapeutic reference price using recognized scientific procedures (e.g. supporting evidence from pharmacokinetic and pharmacodynamic studies).
b. When appropriate (for example, in health care systems with reimbursement), methodology, policy, and legislative processes should be clearly defined for particular situations (e.g. when considering the delisting of a product that does not comply with internal reference pricing or when authorizing the use of products priced higher than the internally referenced price because of specific patient clinical needs).
c. In order to inform pricing based on production costs, the prices of generic medications could be compared to the costs of raw ingredients.

Value-based pricing

The goal of value-based pricing is to base pharmaceutical product costs on the measurable and quantifiable "value"13 that patients and healthcare systems place on those medications.

According to theoretical justifications, value-based pricing may inspire profit-maximizing businesses to develop and create medications with the qualities that society and governments value most. It is crucial to remember that a variety of governmental initiatives, including investments in R&D infrastructure and staff, tax breaks or reductions, and regulatory flexibility, have been put in place to promote innovation.

Value assessment can be carried out through **Health Technology Assessment** (HTA), which is the process of systematically assessing the characteristics, affects, and/or outcomes of health technology a multidisciplinary approach to assessing the social, political, organisational, and moral implications of a health intervention or health technology in order to assist policy decision-making. When establishing the price, the technical methodology frequently places restrictions on the "value" and, consequently, the price, such as an explicit or implicit budget or willingness-to-pay threshold (e.g., the United Kingdom) or a frontier for efficiency optimization (e.g. Germany).

Most frequently used in conjunction with other pricing regulations in nations, such as negotiation and reference pricing, HTA-informed value-based pricing is most frequently used to advise the pricing of pharmaceuticals that are on patent or that are sourced from a single source. It is important to note that HTA has been utilised for more than only determining drug prices. A budget impact analysis is frequently included in HTAs in order to better understand the complete opportunity costs of financing decisions (i.e., "value" from a system viewpoint), which goes beyond economic evaluation of health technology (i.e., cost-effectiveness analysis). Broad health system reform and divestment decisions have been based on HTAs.

In order to inform coverage of health technologies, including their prices and amounts of reimbursement according to the value of the health technologies, many countries around the world have initiated or established formal or informal processes or dedicated agencies for undertaking HTAs. These efforts have been made in collaboration with professional organisations or networks. Yet, only a few high-income nations (such as the U.S. and the U.K.) consistently and explicitly relate coverage decisions to value-based pricing that is guided by HTA. Australia, the United Kingdom, and the Republic of Korea are just a few examples of high-income nations (e.g. Thailand). This illustrates the substantial financial and human resources needed for its implementation.

The following criteria should be taken into account for value-based pricing utilising HTA to operate well.

a. In order to maximise health outcomes, value-based pricing should be used (see also different conceptualizations of "value" such as innovativeness, industry development, and public expectation).

b. In order to take into account local decision-making structures and technical capacity, countries should think about value-based pricing and HTA techniques.

c. Nations should work together to encourage information sharing and, if necessary, to establish standard guidelines for value-based pricing utilising HTA.

d. Developing legislative and technological capacity to fully capitalise on the potential benefits of value-based pricing utilising HTA in pharmaceutical price setting might be done in stages by various nations.

   The decision-making process, as well as the roles and duties of decision-makers and other stakeholders, should be clearly defined in the legal and administrative framework for value-based pricing using HTA.

f. Horizon scanning may be undertaken in anticipation of future medications and technologies.

- Value-based pricing utilising HTA may take into consideration the following approaches and methodologies, especially those anticipated to have substantial public health implications.

a. Reviewing reports from other nations with comparable health system settings and only applying the methodology and findings if they are applicable to the health system settings under consideration;

b. Reviewing reports on value-based pricing using HTA submitted by companies with consideration to applicability to the local context; Evaluating the availability and completeness of the evidence on the new technology;

c. performing a value assessment that considers the availability and completeness of the available evidence regarding the new medication and any accompanying technologies; and

d. implementing value-based pricing using HTA based on local information (such as clinical service and financing models) and data (e.g. demographic structure, costs).

Mark-up control in the entire supply and distribution chain of pharmaceuticals

A markup is the term used to describe the additional fees and costs that are added to the price of an item to pay for distribution costs, overhead costs, and profit or surplus. Policies may regulate wholesale and retail markups as well as pharmaceutical compensation in the context of the pharmaceutical supply chain.

By establishing defined pricing guidelines, mark-up regulation seeks to limit the volatility of prices along the supply and distribution chains. This may improve price transparency for patients and healthcare systems and increase spending management predictability. If the markup levels closely match the costs, well-designed markup restrictions may increase efficiency and encourage the supply of some products (such as low-volume products). if the markup percentages nearly match the expected costs and profits.

Anyone in the supply chain could specify a fixed or % markup (e.g. mark-up at ex-factory price level; and incorporating fee-for-service remuneration into the mark-up, such as fees for dispensing or meeting a pre-specified service quality standard). In order to designate the maximum prices, also known as price caps or price ceilings, other methods of price regulation, such as direct price controls, may be implemented at any stage of the supply chain.

By establishing pricing and markup levels throughout the pharmaceutical supply and distribution chain, several health care systems have managed the cost of pharmaceutical products. There are policies that stipulate a maximum markup for medications provided by privately owned retail pharmacies (e.g., Kuwait, Oman), a maximum markup for medications provided by public facilities (e.g., China, Kuwait), a fixed or percentage markup for the majority of distribution stages (e.g., Australia, Brazil, Jordan, Lebanon, Mozambique, Syrian Arab Republic, and Tunisia), fixed or maximum fees or prices, or a combination policy (For instance, consider the regulations in South Africa that include a single exit price at the ex-factory level with annual adjustment, a prohibition on volume discounts or bonuses, a maximum dispensing fee based on regressive margins for pharmacists, and a separate maximum dispensing fee for non-pharmacist licenced dispensing practitioners) .

Considerations for Implementation

- The following is necessary for mark-up restrictions to operate effectively in the supply and distribution chain:

a. sufficient expertise to manage the operation, including statistical expertise to gather and analyse price data, clinical expertise to assess the effects on rational use of medicines, and economic expertise to ensure that policy design balances the supply chain's incentives and maintains overall financial sustainability;

b. a mechanism for monitoring medicine prices, use, and sales, supported by adequate information technology infrastructure, and arrangements for seeking out and addressing any problems that may arise;

c. taking into account potential effects on unregulated goods; d. taking into account both potential adverse and advantageous effects on the operational revenue of healthcare services as a result of mark-up legislation adjustments.

- The following elements should be taken into account when developing mark-up restrictions along the supply and distribution chain:

The following factors should be considered when applying mark-ups:

a. the point or points along the supply and distribution chain (e.g., ex-factory, ex-wholesaler, ex-pharmacy) at which mark-ups should be applied;

b. the magnitude of mark-ups at each point on the supply and distribution chain, price level, product type, and facility type, where appropriate;

c. design of the regressive markup structure, which can be expressed as fixed or percentage markups;

d. techniques for gathering information and calculating markup percentages (such as financial impact modelling).

e. non-price-related actions, such defining a dispensing charge and offering performance bonuses.

f. non-price-related actions, such defining a dispensing charge and offering performance bonuses.

Encourage pricing transparency

In order to ensure accountability, price transparency refers to the sharing, disclosure, and distribution of information about pharmaceutical product pricing to relevant parties and the general public. Complete pricing transparency entails publishing prices for all price tiers (such as ex-factory prices and retail prices at pharmacies), as well as disclosing the net transaction prices between suppliers (such as manufacturers and service providers) and payers/consumers (governments, consumers).

The sharing and publication of the pricing methodology, including a description of the basis for and scope of reimbursement rates, as well as price components where appropriate, constitutes the transparency of pricing policies (e.g. production costs, R&D costs, added therapeutic value, profit margin). Also, the information contained in pricing agreements including managed-entry contracts, patent status, and licencing agreements must be shared and made public.

Pricing policies must be designed and implemented with consideration for cost and pricing transparency. The values of good governance can be harmed by opaque drug pricing, and transparent accountability can be weakened by secret deals. 2019 saw the adoption of resolution WHA72.8 on enhancing the openness of the markets for pharmaceuticals, vaccines, and other healthcare products by the 72nd World Health Assembly. This resolution calls on Member States to take the necessary actions, including disclosing information on the net prices of health items, in a public forum.

By either voluntary or required agreements, some countries have, to varying degrees, shared pricing and price information about pharmaceutical items. The Transparency Directive of the European Union requires the release of the list prices.

The Transparency Directive (70) in the European Union requires the publishing of the list costs of all reimbursable medications. When sharing information with the public, it is typically published on websites or gazettes, although the information frequently pertains to list prices that do not take discounts and rebates into account (e.g. Australia, Denmark). In some nations, the information is not made public and is only given to the authorities of specific jurisdictions. There is a severe lack of market transparency in nations where medications are not delivered through a national publicly-funded or publicly-regulated programme (i.e., an uncontrolled private sector).

A number of nations have put policies into place to encourage price transparency. Examples include the Single Exit Price policy in South Africa, which requires the disclosure of the weighted average of all net sales prices for each medicine on a government website, in order to clarify to logistics service providers or medicine dispensers at what price a manufacturer may sell a pharmaceutical product. Both of these policies are implemented to protect the public health.

The Price Disclosure Policy in Australia requires manufacturers to reveal to the government authority the sales revenue and the volume sold in units of brand (including any discounts, rebates, and bonus stocks), for products with multiple brands as Manufacturers distributed these goods to wholesalers and pharmacists.

With the use of this policy, the government hopes to ensure that the prices it charges for goods sold under various brand names, as well as the reimbursements it provides for the delivery of those goods, are reasonable.

However it has been commonly observed that there is a widespread lack of price transparency. Also, there are several secretive agreements on discounts and rebates that are intended to speed up access to expensive medications with debatable therapeutic benefits. Market transparency, especially the degree of price competition, has been obscured by these agreements.

Considerations for implementation

- The following elements must be taken into account for policies to encourage price and pricing transparency to be effective at the national level.

a. The creation and execution of national rules that are pertinent to the openness of the markets for health products, including the publication of pricing along the supply and distribution chain and, where appropriate, reimbursement rates and amounts.

b. Standardization of communication and decision-making processes among government entities to ease reporting

c. Cooperation to enhance providers of registered health goods' reporting of data, including reports on sales revenues, pricing, units supplied, marketing expenses, and subsidies and incentives.

d. Usage of performance-based managed-entry agreements (such as risk-sharing agreements, coverage with evidence development, and flat discounts) and financial-based managed-entry agreements (such as price-volume agreements, capping) only in the event that such agreements:

    ✓ promote early access to innovative medications at reasonable costs;

    ✓ address product performance uncertainties (such as clinical efficacy and cost-effectiveness);

    ✓ maximise the usage of the product in the population most likely to benefit;

    ✓ set a budget limit;

    ✓ are on non-confidential terms;

are operationally controllable without requiring an excessive amount of resources to handle complicated monitoring and contract administration.

e. Clarification of the scope of disclosure that must be made in accordance with national legal frameworks, including any confidentiality agreements that may already be in place.

f. Adoption of legislation, rules, or regulations to compel transparent pricing and price reporting, where necessary.

- **The following elements should be taken into account when implementing policies to encourage price and pricing transparency on a global scale.**

a. The accessibility of global data platforms (such databases) and discussion boards for the exchange of knowledge on prices and pricing strategies.

b. Creating data standards for pricing information to improve data interoperability across jurisdictions, taking into account current frameworks (such as International Commercial Terms (Incoterms) and the United Nations Statistical Commission's data interoperability guide) as well as potential links with information on other related metrics (e.g. Product Quality Review).

c. A clarification of the scope of disclosure that is necessary or allowed by current confidentiality agreements as well as foreign legal frameworks.

Negotiation and tendering

Definition, layout, and justification for policy

In this section, two approaches that share the common goal of controlling drug costs by fostering competition are simultaneously discussed. Tendering is any formal and competitive procurement process whereby offers (tenders) are requested, received, and reviewed for the purchase of drugs and vaccines, with the goal of awarding the contract to the tenderer with the best offer. Discussions aimed at coming to an arrangement with potential suppliers are referred to as negotiating. The results of tendering and negotiating may include particular price reductions through discounts and rebates in addition to acceptable general terms and conditions.

In a formal procedure known as tendering, potential tenderers are encouraged to compete for the contract. Favorable tenders are chosen based on objective, pre-established criteria such as price, product quality, and value for money. Negotiation is typically used to resolve any outstanding differences over the terms and conditions of an offer or to define the terms and conditions on various procurement issues (such as price, quality, risk, and payment schedule) between the negotiating parties.

The stages involved in conducting formal tendering are well-documented in the literature (e.g., , and they include establishing pertinent legislation, defining the scope by choosing pharmaceutical goods inside the tender, and creating and publicising tender documents to solicit proposals. collecting bids from prospective bidders, evaluating proposals and choosing suppliers in advance of granting the contract, keeping track of suppliers' performance, and, if required, enforcing contract requirements.

The negotiating process is typically less formal and depends on a variety of elements, such as the scope and complexity of the contract, the parties involved, their prior interactions, and other business, legal, regulatory, and medical needs. Tendering and negotiating have been used separately, jointly, or in conjunction with other pricing policies, depending on the situation.

One of the primary methods of procurement that are frequently employed in many nations is tendering and negotiation, particularly in lower-income nations or when foreign organisations are making purchases on their behalf. Tendering has been employed mostly in medical settings and public services, like pandemic planning and human papillomavirus vaccinations, in higher-income countries. considerations for implementation

The World Health Organization advises users of this guideline to refer to the operational principles for good pharmaceutical procurement, which are thematically reproduced below together with additional points brought up by the GDG (Guideline Development Group).

- **The following aspects need to be taken into account for tendering and negotiation to be effective.**

a. Various offices, committees, and people, each with the right knowledge and resources for the relevant purpose, should divide up the various procurement functions and responsibilities (selection, quantification, product definition, pre-selection of suppliers, and adjudication of tenders).

b. Contract award procedures should be based on clear criteria and follow formal documented procedures at all stages of the process.

c. Proper planning and regular monitoring of procurement performance are essential. The latter should include an annual external audit and be capable of identifying potential supply disruptions.

d. Systems for ensuring dependable financing for procurement should be put in place. To get the most out of your financial resources, you should practise good financial management.

a. Every measures should be taken to ensure that the drugs being purchased are of the highest quality. The national regulatory authorities and procurement agencies should work closely together to accomplish this.

f. Members of the purchasing groups must buy all items on contract from the supplier(s) that are in possession of the contract.

g. Selected suppliers should be monitored through a process that takes into account product quality, service reliability, delivery time, and financial viability. Potential suppliers should be pre-qualified.

h. Buying groups should build and improve their ability and skills in negotiations.

- **Methodology of procurement through tendering and negotiation should take into account the following criteria**

a. national or local formulary list should be the only list used for public sector purchases.

b. Medicines should be listed in procurement and tender papers using their generic or international nonproprietary names.

c. An accurate assessment of the real need should serve as the basis for order quantities.

d. In order to obtain economies of scale, procurement should be carried out in the greatest number of units possible; both centralised and decentralised systems should follow this rule.

e. Potential tender structure options should be investigated in order to maximise market size, purchasing power, and supply security (e.g. single vs split tender).

f. The length of agreements is related to the frequency of requests for proposals.

g. A clear minimum set of information is required to start a tendering process.

h. In order to determine the relative merits of tendering and negotiating, it is important to evaluate the status of the patent and the number of supply sources.

i. Clearly stated standards should be upheld in order to discourage and punish unethical or illegal behaviour, including the purposeful withholding of items or the purposeful giving of products of subpar quality.

Promoting the Use of Generic and Biosimilar Medications With Quality Assurance

Definition, layout, and justification for policy

This policy relates to initiatives to promote the use of quality-assured generic medications or comparable biological medications that are directed towards patients, prescribers, or pharmacists (i.e. biosimilar medicines).

Although it does not directly affect how much pharmaceutical products cost, using more quality-assured generic and biosimilar drugs would have an impact on those costs, both because they are more affordable than brand-name drugs before they lose their market exclusivity and because of increased price competition. How is the policy put into practise? Governments have put in place a number of demand- and supply-side policies. the use of voluntary licences, the removal of regulatory restrictions, When appropriate, patented medicines may be subject to voluntary licence agreements or World Trade

Organization (WTO) Trade-Related Aspects of Intellectual Property Rights (TRIPS) flexibilities; generic medications may be subject to specific pricing and purchasing policies, such as internal reference pricing.

Governments have also introduced additional measures to affect demand, such as required substitutes, preferential co-payment schemes for generic medications, or public awareness-raising efforts about the efficacy and safety of generic medications.

Albeit to a lesser extent, similar measures have been utilised to encourage the use of biosimilar medications.

During the 1990s, encouraging the use of generic medications with quality assurance has been a significant public health policy worldwide.

Considerations for Implementation

- The following elements should be taken into account when operating policies that encourage the use of generic and biosimilar medications with quality assurance.

a. Law authorizing dispenser substitution and, if applicable, specifying the requirements for required substitution.

b. Development of a national prescription replacement standard for generic and biosimilar drugs.

c. Teaching medical professionals and drugstore staff on proper substitution.

d. Creating a monitoring and process strategy for particular situations, such as when there are instances of products that don't satisfy quality requirements and market anticompetitive behaviour.

e. The implementation of additional policies to improve price competitiveness, such as the use of voluntary licencing agreements, the application of WTO TRIPS flexibilities for patented medicines, and other supply-side actions like encouraging local manufactures, where necessary.

f. Nations with weaker regulatory capacities may take into account using data from the WHO prequalification programme or data from other recognised regulatory bodies.

Promoting the use of generic and biosimilar medications with quality assurance.

- The following elements should be taken into account when formulating policies to encourage the use of quality-assured generic and biosimilar medications.

To simplify the market entry of generic and biosimilar medicines, a clear definition of evidence is required to show bioequivalence and therapeutic equivalence, taking into account the following recommendations

- ✓ Guidelines on the evaluation of monoclonal antibodies as similar biotherapeutic products (SBPs):
- ✓ Guidelines on the quality, safety, and efficacy of biotherapeutic protein products prepared by recombinant DNA technology.
- ✓ Multisource (generic) pharmaceutical products: guidelines on registration requirements to establish interchangeability.

b. There are detailed technical specifications provided for quality control.

c. The use of internal reference pricing policies (Section 3.2) to standardise the costs of generic and biosimilar medications (branded or not), unless there are certain pre-defined circumstances (e.g. specific clinical needs, product characteristics).

d. Making sure that generic and biosimilar medications are introduced to the market at a reasonable cost (e.g. where possible, informed by the differences between generic ex-manufacturer prices and the estimated cost of production).

Pooled purchasing

Definition, layout and justification for policy

A formal agreement wherein financial and non-financial resources from numerous purchasing authorities are pooled to form a single entity for the purpose of acquiring health products (such as medications) on behalf of individual purchasing authorities is referred to as a "pooled procurement."

Pooled procurement has been put into place to increase efficiency by sharing human resources (such as knowledge and workload) and possibly expediting the procurement process, as well as to increase purchasing power through economies of scale and scope.

In general, there are four pooled procurement models that represent various degrees of integration and collaboration: coordinated informed buying through collaborative market information exchange for price and supplier information.

Group contracting through cooperative negotiation; informed purchasing through the exchange of supplier and price information; coordinated informed buying through joint market research; and central contracting and procurement through a seasoned procurement agent.

At various levels of administrative jurisdiction, pooled procurement has been widely adopted. The "high-cost medicines E2 access programme" for medications for rare diseases and complex conditions in Thailand is one example of centralised procurement systems for public hospitals implemented at the national and subnational levels. Other examples include specialised national programmes (for example, for tuberculosis, vector-borne diseases, and HIV/AIDS) in India.

Examples of international initiatives include the Organization of Eastern Caribbean States' Pharmaceutical Procurement Services, the Southern African Development Community's pooled procurement services, the Beneluxa Initiative's joint HTA/reimbursement and pricing negotiations, pilot projects among Valletta Declaration signatories, and the Gulf Cooperation Council's group purchasing programme.

The Global Fund to Fight AIDS, Tuberculosis and Malaria (the Global Fund), the Stop TB Partnership Global Drug Facility, and the Pan American Health Organization (PAHO) Regional Revolving Fund for Strategic Public Health Supplies are just a few of the organisations that have managed pooled procurement. the Pan American Health Organization (PAHO) Regional Revolving Fund for Strategic Public Health Supplies; the Global Fund to Combat AIDS, Tuberculosis, and Malaria (the Global Fund); the Stop TB Partnership Global Medication Facility.

Considerations for Implementation

- **The following elements should be taken into account throughout pooled procurement preparation and operation.**

a. From the beginning, the terms of international agreements must be specified, including shared goals, compatible laws, administrative frameworks, and deadlines and milestones.

b. Both established and new groups are seen to benefit from sharing knowledge and experiences through cross-training, study tours, or twinning in order to spread lessons acquired. Political and technical levels should be used to facilitate this kind of cooperation.

c. For regional pooled procurement, the creation of databases on topics including cost, patent status, supplier qualification, and registration of medications can be beneficial and, in certain situations, essential.

d. At the national and regional levels, capacity building based on best practises should be carried out while taking into account the unique requirements of member nations.

e. Regional pooled procurement can help local production by promoting fair competition (as defined by competition laws) and creating good manufacturing practises.

f. In especially for international pooled procurement, a third party can be considered to assist nations with harmonising points for pooled procurement, such as legislation, rules, economic variables, and administrative processes.

- **The following elements should be taken into account in pooled procurement methodology.**

a. small list of products may be used to start a pooled procurement (e.g. high cost medicines).

b. Long-term agreements in pooled procurement demonstrate a commitment to purchasing and should be taken into account to assure reliable sources of supply and permit favourable manufacturer prices.

c. The final arrangement should take into account variables unique to the different categories of pharmaceutical items (e.g. storage and supply requirements for vaccines and volume forecast for medicines for rare diseases).

Setting the price of pharmaceutical products via cost plus pricing

Definition, layout, and justification for policy

Cost-plus pricing is a pricing strategy for determining the price19 of pharmaceutical products that takes into account the costs of production, the costs of R&D, the costs of regulatory processes and compliance, overhead and other operational costs, and a profit.

The concept of cost-plus pricing has been praised for its clarity and justification of price laws, which offer some degree of stability for budgetary planning and profitability for the suppliers.

A few nations, including Australia's "cost-plus technique", Japan's "cost accounting system," and the United States, have acknowledged cost-plus pricing as a component of national pharmaceutical pricing policies with no equivalent goods.

The scope of actual application and the specifics are not well recognised, though. Costs are frequently the only factor considered when negotiating prices (e.g., in Europe). This is probably a result of the practical difficulties in acquiring trustworthy information about direct material costs, direct labour costs, overhead expenses related to R&D and manufacturing, regulatory processes and compliance, and other operating costs from suppliers. Determining the final price could also be difficult since suppliers and the pricing authority would need to agree on a profit margin above and above the expected costs based on a mutually accepted level and structure (for example, a percentage or a fixed amount).

How frequently is this policy applied? It has not been common practise to establish drug prices at the ex-manufacturer or ex-wholesaler levels using cost-plus pricing.

Considerations for Implementation

- Those nations that wish to replace or supplement their cost-plus pricing approach with other policies, such as those covered in this recommendation, such as using cost of production to determine the price of generic and biosimilar medications, should take into consideration their current cost-plus pricing approach.
- When contemplating cost-plus pricing (in the context of price transparency), national policymakers must take into account the limits of price data provided by manufacturers and create a system for appropriately verifying the data.

Pharmaceutical products are exempt from taxes or have their taxes reduced.

Definition, layout, and justification for policy

Taxes are forced financial transfers from private citizens, institutions, or organisations to the government. Direct taxes, which are imposed by governments on the earnings of people and businesses, and indirect taxes, which are included in the cost of products and services, are the two primary types of taxes. In high-income countries, direct taxes and social security levies typically account for around two-thirds of all government revenue. Indirect taxes on foreign trade or on the purchase of goods and services are important sources of income for governments in low-income nations.

Medicines may be excluded from taxes, such as sales or value-added taxes, or their taxes may be reduced as part of policies pertaining to pharmaceutical items.

Tariffs and levies may act as trade obstacles, which could impede access and market competitiveness. It is also possible that the patients may bear an unfair share of the tax burden (also known as tax incidence), which will diminish affordability.

The Treasury or Ministry of Finance typically oversees the policy through incorporation into the larger taxation system.

Many nations, especially those with high incomes, have done away with customs taxes on pharmaceutical goods. These include parties to the 1995

Mutual Agreement on the Elimination of Tariffs on Pharmaceuticals of the World Trade Organization, often known as the Zero-for-Zero programme.

Yet, many low-income nations continue to impose import levies on pharmaceuticals of up to 10%. Pharmaceutical products are now more frequently subject to value-added tax, which can be up to 25%. Yet, some nations apply a lower rate than the regular tax rates for all pharmaceutical products or specific medicines (such as medicines that have been reimbursed).

Considerations for Implementation

- Mark-up laws might be combined with tax exemptions or reductions, and they could apply to certain groups of medications or active pharmaceutical ingredients, such as those in patient access programmes or active pharmaceutical ingredients used in local production.

However, the potential effects on equality, the viability of implementation, and administrative costs would need to be taken into account when applying tax policies selectively.

5.2 INDIA'S HISTORY OF PRICE CONTROLS

The Pharmaceutical Prices (Display & Control) Order of 1966 allowed for limited price hikes for drugs with the government's previous consent. Yet, the government lacked the authority to lower the cost of any medications. A 1968 amendment gave businesses the ability to set the price of new medications with previous government approval. However, no rules were laid forth, so producers were essentially free to set the prices of new products as they pleased, just as there was no price regulation. The government originally gained control over setting the maximum selling prices of bulk medications under the Drug Prices Control Order (DPCO), which was passed in 1970. The government set rates for 18 bulk medications and frozen prices for other medications. Government set pricing for 18 bulk pharmaceuticals and frozen prices for additional bulk drugs; prices could not be raised without government consent. For formulations, a mechanism for determining prices based on material costs, conversion costs, and packaging fees was announced. A selective strategy has been used since DPCO, 1979, as opposed to DPCO, 1970, which essentially encompassed the whole drug sector. Between 1979 and 2013, the DPCOs' fundamental design remained mostly unaltered. The primary differences between the DPCOs relate to the number of scheduled pharmaceuticals (i.e., those included in the DPCO for price control purposes), the amount of markup over cost permissible for formulation pricing, and the rate of return permitted for bulk-drug pricing. Over the years, the range of oversight has been reduced while the degree of markups and the rate of return permitted have increased. The cost of formulations that fall under bulk pharmaceuticals were fixed under DPCO-1995. The prices of formulations (final medications) were established using a cost- 1 based formula, whereas the prices of bulk drugs (74 in total) were fixed using real costs plus a markup.

(RP = (1 + MAPE/100) + ED x (MC + CC + PM + PC))

In the DPCO-1995, the essentiality of medications was taken into account rather than the financial factors of drug turnover, manufacturer count, and market share. Hence, from 142 under DPCO-1987 to 347 under DPCO-1979 to 74 under DPCO-1995, the number of bulk pharmaceuticals fell. In an effort to further liberalise price control, the proposed Pharmaceutical Policy, 2002 sought to cut the number of medications to under 35. (Selvaraj et al. 2012). The government was urged by the Supreme Court to "formulate adequate criteria for guaranteeing that vital and life-saving pharmaceuticals do not fall out of price control" after the court rejected this programme. The National Pharmaceuticals Pricing Policy (NPPP)- 2012, which was subsequently released by the government, included three significant modifications to the pricing control laws:

1) The essentiality of the pharmaceuticals under price control, not economic factors, should be used to determine their price. For this, the National List of Essential Medicines, 2011 (NLEM) should be consulted.
2) The pricing of bulk medications will not be restricted; only the prices of formulations will beMarket-based pricing, as opposed to the previous "cost-based pricing," will be used to control formulation prices.

   To implement the NPPP-2012 policy, the government unveiled DPCO-2013, which has the following two provisions:

1) The 348 medications (only formulations) specified in the NLEM will have their ceiling costs fixed by the government. The market-based data provided by IMS Health, a private sector market research firm, will be used to determine the ceiling prices.
2) The simple average of the prices of all the brands having a market share of 1% or more will serve as the ceiling pricing. The calculation of market share will be based on changing annual turnover.
3) Depending on changes in the Wholesale Price Index, the ceiling prices will be subject to annual adjustment.

Marketing tactics are frequently a challenge for businesses. Although most people believe that marketing is a simple concept, the strategy must be appropriate for the particular organization and the target market. There are many strategies that can be used in an effort to draw in the proper clientele and increase revenues. Both horizontal and vertical marketing strategies are among them. Although they are both marketing methods, they take different approaches to the market.

Vertical Marketing System: What is it?

This marketing strategy tries to draw in and connect with companies in the same sector. The manufacturer, wholesaler, and retailer are the three parts of the vertical marketing system, and the wholesaler's job is to buy the goods from the producer and give them to the retailer. These three collaborate with the goal of maximising profit.

The segments of the vertical marketing system are:

- Corporate vertical marketing system: Under this system, one distributor controls all aspects of production and distribution and hence owns all distributors. Amway is one of the examples. An American marketing firm creates goods for the home, body, and health. The brand sells goods only through its authorised outlets, making it a part of a corporate vertical marketing structure. As a result, the business functions as both a manufacturer and a distributor of its products.
- Contractual vertical marketing system marketing: This system, which is common in franchising, allows each member to work autonomously while contractually integrating operations. As a result, profits are made while working alone. An instance of a contractual kind is working with a franchise. People need to buy a licence in order to open one of these shops or cafés. They must, however, adhere to a franchisor's standards, procedures, and rules. Franchises like Pizza Hut, Domino's, and McDonald's are well-known examples.
- Managed vertical marketing system - Members' strength and size have an impact on the activities. The strong member thereby controls the other members' activity. Procter & Gamble, as an illustration. High levels of collaboration are expected from this consumer goods company.

Horizontal Marketing Systems: What Are They?

With this marketing strategy, comparable-sized companies band together to benefit from economies of scale. In an effort to increase their profits, the businesses pool resources like marketing, distribution, production, and even human resources. This marketing strategy has recently grown in favour due to rising market competitiveness.

Manufacturers, distributors, and retailers may work together to create a horizontal marketing system. Johnson & Johnson and Google are two examples of businesses using a horizontal marketing strategy. The two have partnered to develop a robotic surgery platform. The horizontal marketing system has the benefit of concentrating on larger audiences rather than narrow niches. It saves time by taking less time.

Horizontal Integration Types

Mergers, acquisitions, and internal expansions are the main types of horizontal integration.

Merger

When two businesses combine, two independent entities become a new, combined organisation. Although the activities and people are divided between the two prior independent companies, the brand of one of those two businesses is typically kept. Also, both businesses' product lines are frequently comparable and equally competitive on the market.

Both businesses are aiming to increase their position in their current markets through a merger. The majority of mergers include organisations that are comparable to one another, making it possible for the two businesses to integrate easily because of how similarly they once operated.

Acquisition

An acquisition happens when one firm completely takes over the activities of another company, much like a merger does. Despite the fact that the two businesses formally merge, only one company retains leadership. While the resources of the acquired company are integrated as management deems appropriate, the staff, executives, and operations of the acquiring company frequently remain in place.

Acquisitions are frequently sought after by businesses looking for a specific item. For instance, Microsoft aimed to strengthen its position in the video gaming industry. Activision Blizzard was so purchased in January 2022 as a result. This acquisition illustration illustrates a frequently intentional strategy for a certain industry in which a corporation aims to accomplish a very specific goal.

Internal Growth

Businesses can potentially start the process of horizontal integration by more carefully allocating internal capital. A business simply decides to alter direction and allocate more resources in a new way through internal expansion. For instance, a restaurant might decide to add catering services, or a beverage company might start producing food items.

In these instances, a business continues to run as it always has. But, it decides to use those resources internally to train people, buy equipment, make capital investments, and expand a new branch of operations on its own rather than investing money to buy an outside company or merge with another firm.

5.3 RURAL MARKETING

It can be difficult to advertise a product in the current, cutthroat environment. Businesses compete fiercely with one another to advertise the products. Finding new markets has become essential for the development and growth of every organisation. Markets are categorised. the two markets, urban and rural. Urban markets have now reached a point of saturation and increased competition. There is a lot of business opportunity in rural marketplaces.

Most people reside in rural areas in both developed and developing countries. As a result, there is a huge opportunity for product marketing in rural areas. Today's businesses have mostly understood the possibilities of rural markets. Hence, they begin to concentrate on rural markets. Analysis of rural markets is the main focus of the current subject, "Rural Marketing." In this section, the nature of the rural market and the traits of rural consumers are discussed.

Rural Economy

India is a very populous nation. Rural areas are home to the majority of Indians. In recent years, the purchasing power of rural residents has dramatically expanded. Also considerably increased was public awareness of rural residents. Businesses that concentrate on the rural market can flourish for sure. Real marketing now includes rural areas. India has a rural economy compared to other countries. India lives in rural areas, as Gandhiji famously remarked. Rural marketing in India offers a tonne of promise.

The majority of India's population lives in rural areas. The unusually high percentage of India's population that resides in rural areas reflects the nation's economy, which is primarily agrarian:

The rural sector and the urban sector can be considered to make up India's two primary economic sectors. The agricultural sub-sector and the non-agricultural sub-sector are the two main subsectors that make up the rural sector.

Features of the Rural Economy

In India, there are 6.27 lakh villages. In villages with a population of 1,000 to 5,000, 50% of the rural population resides. 10% of the rural population lives in villages with a population of more than 5,000. 20% of rural residents reside in communities with less than 500 residents. Following are some key aspects of the rural economy:

1. **The Indian Family System:** Family is a significant social control mechanism. In villages, the joint family structure is used by the majority of families. The ties that bind families together in rural settings are

particularly strong. Marriage is viewed as a religious requirement. In rural community, divorce is unusual and not encouraged.

2. **Women's Issues:** In comparison to men, women do not enjoy favourable standing. Rural places offer less independence for women. Men rule, and they frequently make choices without consulting their life partners. Yet, the situation of women in the rural economy has significantly improved recently.
3. **Pattern of Occupations:** The primary industry in the rural economy is agriculture. Traditionally, agricultural work has been done in villages. Several rural residents also engage in activities that support agriculture. In most cases, both men and women work in agriculture.
4. **Revenue Creation:** People in rural areas primarily rely on agriculture and other associated industries to generate money. Agriculture generates seasonal income. They get more money during harvest season and spend it on numerous products. Other times of the year, rural residents limit their purchases and may even borrow money from banks and moneylenders.

   Although there is no guaranteed income in agriculture, a huge number of rural residents are currently moving to metropolitan regions.
5. **Literacy Rate Rural residents have a low literacy rate:** Particularly in rural areas, women have very low literacy rates. Many copycat businesses easily sell their items in the rural market due to the low literacy rate. The rural areas are the scene of many exploitations. It is crucial to raise awareness among rural residents.

Market differences between rural and urban areas

Rural markets differ significantly from urban markets due to their many distinctive characteristics. This section discusses the importance differences between rural and urban marketplaces.

1. **Density of the Population:** In the rural market, it is low. In the urban region, there is a significant population density. Many rural residents are moving to metropolitan areas today. Thus, the urban regions' population density is constantly rising.
2. **Profession:** Agriculture is the primary industry in rural areas. In rural areas, agriculture is seen as a key source of income. Contrarily, in metropolitan areas, trade, industry, and service are thought to be the predominant occupations.
3. **Economy:** In contrast to the open and commercialised urban economy, the rural economy is closed and less so.

4. **Infrastructure:** The remote areas' infrastructure amenities are subpar and unreliable. The importance of infrastructure facilities in rural areas is the lowest given by governments. Infrastructure facilities are better in urban regions. Urban areas are increasingly populated today. Governments must therefore make comparable improvements to the infrastructure facilities.
5. **Modernization-friendly Mindset:** Rural residents' views on modernity have always been fixed. Urban residents are more exposed. They are prepared for change and adaptation.
6. **Family Organization:** People in rural areas adhere to the joint family arrangement. The nuclear family concept is practised in cities The joint family structure in rural marketplaces is significantly impacted by the urban family system.
7. **Possession of Personal Property:** In rural markets, it's low. The ownership of household assets is high in urban marketplaces.
8. **Movement:** Individuals in rural areas continue to work at their regular jobs. As a result, there is little movement in rural markets. Urban areas have a high level of mobility. The idea of lifetime employment is no longer prevalent in private businesses. Individuals frequently switch employers. As a result, urban mobility is continually improving.
9. **Literacy:** Low levels of literacy are present in the rural market. The literacy rate is high in metropolitan areas.
10. **Exposition:** Those in the rural market have little exposure to it. as they pursue education. Due to their poor level of education, individuals have fewer opportunities to be exposed. Urban residents are highly exposed.

    They have more of a chance to obtain good exposure thanks to their high literacy rate and access to a variety of media.
11. **Life's outlook:** Individuals in rural marketplaces tend to be fatalistic. People in metropolitan markets have a more rational mindset.
12. **Production Activity:** In the rural markets, it is low. There are several manufacturing operations taking place in the metropolitan marketplaces.
13. **Outlets for Distribution:** There are fewer outlets in rural marketplaces compared to metropolitan markets.

Pharmaceutical costs make up 43.16% of all out-of-pocket health expenses. This makes it the single largest category under OOPE, followed by spending on general practitioners, government hospitals, medical diagnostics, private hospitals, and so on. In India, there are currently 5,294 locations for the Pradhan Mantri Bhartiya Jan-Aushadhi Pariyojna (PMBJP) programme, which aims to provide low-cost, high-quality generic medications. When this plan was first introduced in 2008, there were difficulties with supply chain management. The redesigned programme offers store owners financial incentives and boasts a larger product selection with over 1000 pharmaceuticals and 154 surgical supplies.

The JA programme expanded most quickly in urban areas, places with strong literacy rates, and places with a high level of development.

The prospective market size and resulting profitability are taken into account while opening JA outlets. In 2019, the majority of districts had at least one JA store, while few Northeastern and Central districts had none.

0.5% of the Indian pharmaceutical market is made up of online pharmacies. The majority of e-pharmacy sales currently occur in Delhi. Due to expanding internet access and the untapped rural market, the e-pharmacy market segment is poised to explode. Important challenges in this area include the ethical distribution of medications, safe transportation, and prescription verification.

The Jan Aushadhi plan

The Jan Aushadhi (JA) initiative, which was introduced in 2008, aims to distribute high-quality, generic medications at reasonable prices through specialised retailers. The Bureau of Pharma Public Sector Undertakings of India (BPPI) oversees the programme, however these Jan Aushadhi outlets are not directly run by the government. Alternatively, if a person satisfies certain standards, they can register and operate a store.

The state government would grant the space free of charge for the operation of JA stores inside government hospitals or within the grounds of medical colleges by non-governmental organisations (NGOs) or institutions designated by the government. Online applications are also accepted from other NGOs and organisations that have the required expertise, location, and funding to create a store. Individual business owners may also open their own stores as long as they comply with certain regulations.

The pharmaceuticals found at these shops come from producers who adhere to the WHO's Good Manufacturing Practices (WHO-GMP) standards.

Prior to the drugs arriving at store outlets for sale, additional quality checks are performed by drug-testing laboratories authorised by the National Accreditation Board for Testing and Calibration Laboratories (NABL).

Pricing advantages

Each formulation presented in their stores, the prices offered by JA stores, and the prices offered by the top three main brands are listed on the Jan

Aushadhi website. While the average percent savings at Jan Aushadhi outlets can be estimated based on the price savings for each drug, we instead aggregate this information based on the therapeutic classes that have been identified. The product basket provided by the JA scheme16 includes more than 900 medications and 154 surgical products, with significant price benefits for all therapeutic class areas.By therapeutic class, Table 1 displays the typical % decline in medicine pricing (as compared to the top three leading brands). For instance, the average price of the 108 formulations included in the therapeutic class of anti-infective medications decreased by 62.66% when compared to the top three leading brands. Drugs targeting urogenital organs experienced the highest price drops (83.39% for six formulations), whilst treatments addressing water and electrolyte imbalances saw the least price drops (52.35% for two formulations). At the moment, all medications have price reductions of at least 50%, with over 300 medications having price reductions of at least 80%.

Table 5.2 Price listing of various classification of drugs.

Therapeutic class	Percent decrease	Formulations covered
Analgesic and antipyretic /Muscle relaxant	-76.20%	51
Anti allergic drugs	-77.37%	17
Anticancer drugs	-74.69%	16
Anti infective drugs	-62.66%	108
Diuretic drugs	-55.07%	5
Drugs acting on cardio vascular system	-74.47%	82
Drugs acting on central nerve system	-73.12%	54
Drugs acting on endocrine gland including steroids & immune supressant	-59.19%	17
Drugs acting on eye & ENT	-69.98%	14
Drugs acting on female reproductive organs	-78.12%	6
Drugs acting on gastro-intestinal-tract	-68.87%	53
Drugs acting on respiratory tract	-60.33%	16
Drugs acting on skin (Topical/local Application)	-69.66%	29
Drugs acting on urogenital organs	-83.39%	6
Drugs used in diabetes	-68.18%	32
Local/General anaesthetics drugs	-61.34%	4

Table 5.2 ***contd…***

Therapeutic class	Percent decrease	Formulations covered
Miscelleneous	-79.64%	1
Solutions correcting water & electrolite disturbances	-52.35%	2
Vaccine	-52.38%	1
Vitamins, minerals & food supplement	-75.03%	18

Indian Consumerism: Businessmen originally used the term "consumerism" in the middle of the 1960s because they saw the consumer movement as a rival "ism" to socialism and communism that threatened capitalism.

Consumerism is described as social force aimed to protect consumer interests in the marketplace by mobilising consumer demands on business. Consumerism is a form of consumer protest against unethical company practises and other forms of economic injustice.

The unfair marketing practises that include misbranding, fake products, unsafe products, planned obsolescence, adulteration, fictitious pricing, collusion over prices, deceptive packaging, false and misleading advertisements, void warranties, hoarding, profiteering, black marketing, and short weights and measures are all intended to be eliminated.

Consumer advocacy groups may lead coordinated campaigns to combat deceptive marketing tactics and provide consumer protection. In the marketplace, the seller typically has the majority of the power. In order to correct this imbalance in the exchange transactions between suppliers and purchasers, society has turned to consumerism.

The basic foundation of the marketing notion is under attack by consumerism. Can a competitive free market economy meet the legitimate public demands? Is the market process flawed in some way? Should that flaw be fixed through political methods, i.e., through government rules and consumer legislation?

According to P. Drucker, consumerism challenges four important premises of the marketing concept:

(1) It is assumed that consumers know their needs.

(2) It is assumed that business really cares about those needs and knows exactly how to find about them.

(3) It is assumed that business does provide useful information that precisely matches product to needs.

(4) It is presumed that products and services really fulfill customer expectations as well as business promises.

Consumerism in India - In Marketing

Sectors of Consumers' Fundamental Rights:

All marketers need to understand that consumers have "rights." The UK government recently promoted the creation of a citizen's charter that includes a "Patient's Charter" for the National Health Service, a "Passenger's Charter" for rail travellers, as well as numerous other customer-focused initiatives.

The USA was where consumerism really began to take off. Prior to Nader's book, President Kennedy emphasised in his "Consumer Bill of Rights" the responsibility an organisation owes to its customers.

This covered four key areas that ought to be fundamental rights for all customers:

(1) The need for security

(2) The privilege of information

(3) The freedom to decide

(4) A right to an audience.

The concept of rights Thomas Jefferson's inclusion of "inalienable rights" un the US Declaration of Independence is where the concept of rights first emerged. Today's marketing professionals must be aware of these rights and incorporate them into their strategy for promoting goods and services whenever possible. They provide a solid framework for thought.

1. **the right to safety:** Consumers have the right to anticipate that products they buy will be safe to use. The product shouldn't make any false or deceptive pledges and should be able to deliver on its promises. In reality, this "right" is a minefield for the marketing industry. Items that were once thought to be safe for use or ingestion have since been discovered by modern study to not be so.

   When sugar in meals was not advertised on television as being terrible for teeth, cigarettes were not thought to be hazardous to health, and people were told to "go to work on an egg" was this advice still safe in hindsight? There are further instances in medicine, such as the drug Thalidomide, which resulted in deformities in the offspring of mothers who took the drug as prescribed.

   In a number of nations, legislation emphasising "Products Liability" has been introduced. Suppliers now have to think about their accountability as a result. Should businesses, however, continue in a positive direction rather than a negative one? One could argue that this right will be directly impacted by law, which is apparent.

One may argue that this right will be tightly related to legislation and that it is evident that marketers who fail to protect customers do so at their peril. This right will be closely tied to legislation and obvious.

2. **The right to information:** The right to information has broad implications; it covers deceptive pricing and credit conditions, inaccurate information about product ingredients, incomplete information about how to use and operate a product, and false or misleading advertising. But this takes a disapproving stance. Avoiding conflict alone won't enough.

   Any chance to interact with customers and educate them on the advantages and qualities of the merchandise being sold should be seized by any market.

   It shouldn't be a defence to say that customers don't read directions. Marketers are responsible for ensuring complete and efficient customer and supplier communications.

   Yet, this "right" establishes that customers must be provided with sufficient information in order to exercise the following right—the right to choose.

3. **The Freedom of Choice:** The consumer has the freedom to make their own decisions, but marketing undoubtedly tries to sway them. Nonetheless, in the majority of western marketplaces, competition is encouraged and consumers should not be misled by items.

   It has been argued, for instance, that in order to make this right simpler to get, packaging should be modified such that identical goods from various companies are packaged in exactly the same quantities, or at the at least, utilise both metric and imperial weights/measures. It shouldn't be a defence to say that customers don't read directions. Marketers are responsible for ensuring complete and efficient customer and supplier communications.

   Yet, this "right" establishes that customers must be provided with sufficient information in order to exercise the following right—the right to choose and so make it simpler for the client to compare values.

   In actuality, Sainsbury but not Tesco provide this comparative information on shelf tickets. The unsolved question is whether or not customers utilise this information when making decisions.

4. **The Freedom to Speak:** Free expression is guaranteed in all western nations. Do businesses, though, pay attention to their customers? Such

feedback ought to be welcomed in a marketing organisation with a clear purpose, and it ought to be considered a crucial component for the future. Customers have the freedom to voice their opinions following a purchase, particularly if they are unsatisfied. The buyer should anticipate that any issues with their purchase will be fairly and promptly resolved.

Indian Consumerism: Marketing and Consumerism

Every consumer segment has an impact on the marketing landscape in which businesses operate. It should be noted that each pressure organisation is'marketing' its ideas, but this is not taken into account here. One method of getting consumer feedback is through pressure groups. Working with these organisations allows marketers to enhance their influence, which can result in more visibility because the pressure organisations can produce good. PR for supportive vendors. Where consumer preference is involved, such as with beer, the Campaign for Genuine Ale was successful in pressuring producers to fulfil demand.

So, in order to represent customer opinions and shape demand, marketers must collaborate with organised consumer groups and recognize their influence. Today's consumers have a voice in what they buy. The awareness that this is happening is spreading. Businesses who are aware of this and meet these expectations have a significant marketing advantage over their uninformed rivals. The Times stated in 1991 that

This week, the General Synod of the Church of England urged us to stop drinking Nescafe for the benefit of Brazilian infants. But, as far as the Church of England's legislators are concerned, we are still allowed to eat Rowntrees' candies, Eindus fish fingers, and Cross & Blackwell soup, and our kids are still allowed to drink formula.

Yet, these are also Nestle Group products, which activists allege encourages bottle feeding in developing nations, tempts mothers to stop breastfeeding, and raises disease risks. Nestle claims that company is following a 1981 World Health Organization code, but the activists counter that it is in violation of restrictions amended to the code in 1986.

The issue is that, despite the fact that the behavior being criticized is occurring with a different product (dry infant milk) in a different nation, Nestle is being singled out for consumer action directed at their top-selling product (Brazil).

The Management's Reaction to Consumerism in India

The ideal scenario is that consumerism gives a fantastic chance for the forward-thinking, competitive firm management. Marketers are required by consumerism to be more responsible, effective, truthful, and informed. It gives the marketer's challenge and the benchmark by which he assesses his own performance a new social dimension.

The ultimate goal for every marketer is to have a perfect match between the marketing opportunity and effort, as this would ensure consumer happiness and, in turn, profitability, which is the outcome of meeting demand. Bending or adjusting the supply to the demand is the cornerstone of marketing theory.

In the near future, the Indian marketing environment will show extremely fierce competition among sellers and high consumerism.

All marketers will be required to use the societal marketing concept in such a developed market. The Consumer Protection Act is now in effect.

Through better services (better trained travelling salesmen, regional customer-service centres), better products (safer, more nutritious, less polluting, more durable, more reliable, easier to repair and maintain, etc.), direct channels of communication between the company and its disgruntled customers (consumer representation or voice in decision-making), and better customer information, consumerism suggests the prospects of new ways to compete for consumers' preferences. (consumer representation or voice in decision-making), better customer information (informative labelling, trustworthy advertising, personal selling, consumer guidance and education, truthful packaging), and the need to develop many completely new products in order to conserve natural resources, reduce pollution, and allow recycling, where possible.

Indian scenario on consumer protection and consumerism

Because the typical consumer is less knowledgeable and less powerful than the seller, consumer protection is important. Laws and voluntary actions can both be utilised to safeguard consumers. A consumer is anybody who purchases things and uses services for their own purpose. Each person who uses these products and services with the buyer's consent is considered a consumer. More than thirty laws have been passed by the Indian government to help consumers.

The Contract Act of 1882, the Sale of Goods Act of 1930, the Laws of Torts, the Essential Commodities Act of 1955, the Tine Prevention of Food Adulteration Act of 1954, the Standards and Weights of Measures Act of 1976, The Agricultural Product (Grading and Marketing) Act of 1937, the Monopolies and Restrictive Trade Practices (MRTP) Act of 1969, and the Consumer Protection Act of 1986.

Despite the abundance of laws and regulations, India's consumer situation is still appalling. Many laws contain numerous flaws. There have been several laws that have been poorly and slowly implemented. The enforcement apparatus is ineffective and dishonest.

The rights and remedies that consumers have under various laws are unknown to them. Even if a consumer is aware of these rules, the lengthy, expensive, and convoluted legal processes discourage him from going to court. Legislation hasn't helped consumers' lot because there isn't a robust consumer movement. Furthermore, because the focus is on punishing those who break the law, the numerous rules don't directly help the customer.

To better safeguard the interests of consumers, the Consumer Protection Act of 1986 was passed. It offers customers strong protections against subpar products, subpar services, unfair business practises, and other types of abuse.

5.4 INDUSTRIAL MARKETING

The fundamentals of consumer marketing and industrial marketing are interconnected. The industrial market's function is completely different. All of the market's influencing factors have an impact on industrial demand. Industrial market managers must react to changing markets in a variety of ways in order to develop products that address these changes and advertise them in wholly unique ways to target and sophisticated customers while upholding corporate policies. As a result, industrial marketers deal with a variety of unique marketing circumstances that are uncommon in the consumer market. The purchase, which is the outcome of several decision-making processes, is one of many shared elements between the marketing of corporate goods and consumer items. The backdrop of industrial marketing is a complicated, multifaceted field. In organisational markets, the business that purchases goods and services for various purposes such as incorporation, consumption, use, or resale. Global industrial marketing has undergone significant paradigm adjustments, moving from the promotion of goods to the promotion of services. This is due to the fact that customers purchase offerings that provide services and hence create value rather than products or services. The demanding field of industrial marketing offers opportunity for the use of marketing ideas.

Industrial marketing concept

Due to the distinctions in the structure of the markets, the marketing concept is relevant and significant for both the industrial and consumer markets. The marketing model for industrial business organizations. In accordance with the marketing theory, a target market's demands should be identified and defined, and the organization's product or service should be modified to meet those needs. Consumer marketers have adopted the marketing concept more comprehensively than their industrial counterparts, which are supported by the fact that industrial customers, such as organizations, corporations, institutions, and governmental agencies, have specific requirements. More than just facilitating communication with these consumers is part of the industrial marketing strategy. This is due to the fact that it is based on the relationship between the customer and seller. A successful transaction requires an excellent buyer-seller relationship.

For both buyers and sellers to succeed in their corporate objectives, a good connection is essential. Instead of focussing on the additional value for their clients, many technically focused businesses emphasise the technical aspect of their products. Industrial marketers may bring value by efficiently and effectively delivering technical knowledge training. Effective marketing does more than just boost revenue; it also helps businesses build recognisable brands that they may wish to sell in the future. Industrial marketing typically entails huge orders and long-term partnerships between the producer and supplier; the transaction procedure is too challenging or more complex than the transaction between a firm and a single consumer. The interactions between two parties are the main emphasis of B2C sales. Business-to-business (B2B) refers to a scenario where one firm transacts with another business, whereas business-to-consumer (B2C) sales may concentrate on one-on-one interactions between two parties.

When a company is acquiring materials for their manufacturing process, for example: (e.g. a car manufacturer purchasing tyre).

A company requires the assistance of another to function (e.g. a car manufacturer employing an accountancy firm to audit their finances).

A company resells products and services made by others (e.g. a dealer buying the end product from the car manufacturer).

Industrial marketing definition

Business-to-business marketing, business marketing, and organizational marketing are frequently referred to as industrial marketing. Marketing to business entities is known as industrial marketing or business marketing. Manufacturers, governmental agencies, businesses in the private sector, hospitals, schools, and distributors are just a few examples of their clients. Businesses purchase goods and services to achieve objectives including maximizing revenues, lowering expenses, utilizing cutting-edge technology, and so on. Contrarily, consumer marketing entails promoting goods and services to single people, families, and homes. Consumers purchase goods and services for personal use.

The entire process of marketing goods and services to businesses that use them in their manufacturing is known as industrial marketing.

The entire process of marketing goods and services to businesses that use them in the creation of consumer or business goods and services is referred to as industrial marketing. organisations that sell purchasing organizations products and services like steel, computers, machine tools, and courier services. Additionally, they must identify and describe the needs, purchasing power, trade policies, and purchasing procedures of the buyer. The selling companies should concentrate on providing products and services with value additions.

Product of Industry

Products utilized for processing or operating a firm are referred to as industrial products. So, the distinction between a consumer good and an industrial good depends on the use for which the good is purchased. A mixer, juicer, or grinder purchased by a client for household use is an example of a consumer product. Nevertheless, the same mixer, juicer, or grinder sold to a fruit juice vendor is an example of an industrial product. Business Services additionally allows for the implementation of industrial marketing. TCS, an Indian company, offers commercial services to a variety of companies. Several governmental and non-governmental groups might use their services. Three major categories can be used to classify industrial products:

1. Materials and Components

2. Investment items,

3. Goods and services

1. **Materials and Components:** They include raw materials, finished materials, and components. Farm items like cotton, wheat, and vegetables are typically considered raw materials. Finished materials and parts include things like iron rods, linen yarns, wires and cables, etc. Some naturally occurring products include meat, petroleum products, iron, and so forth. Component and parts include things like household appliance motors, PC component parts, and motor vehicle component parts, among others.

2. **Investments:** Capital items are industrial goods that help the buyer's operations and manufacturing. They include ancillary devices, structures, possibly even buildings, and sophisticated computer systems. The accessory equipment that can help the production process, such as forklifts for material handling, equipments & furnishings, etc., are some additional items that can be included. Certain products, such as material handling

forklifts, equipment, and furnishings, among others, last less time than buildings and sophisticated structures.

Some things, like material handling forklifts, furnishings, and equipment, last less time than complex computer systems and structures, as was described earlier.

3. **Services & Supplies:** This is yet another category of commercial goods and services in the context of industrial marketing. These comprises things that are constantly used in the office or at the plant. Cleaning supplies, watercolours, pencils, printer ink, photocopy paper, and other convenience items are easily accessible for purchase. Items like window and furniture cleaning supplies, computer repair materials, etc. are included in maintenance and repair services. Also, there are business counselling services including legal, management, and advertising. In industrial marketing, there are four basic sorts of exchanges that might occur.

Different Exchange Methods

Each company organisation or industrial buyer's nature is to pinpoint and specify the goals of a target market. It is significant because industrial customers, such as organisations, corporations, institutions, and governmental bodies, have particular needs, as opposed to consumers. As a result, multiple exchange processes with these consumers are included in the industrial marketing idea. The following trade mechanisms satisfy the goals and needs of industrial buyers.

1. **Method of Product Exchange:** Each product or service included in the process of product exchange will have a big impact on the industrial exchange process. The ease of trade depends on the seller's capacity to recognize the needs of the buyer and the product's potential to satisfy those demands. Only when the exchange is favorable in terms of price, quality, quantity, and after-sale services will it undoubtedly produce a positive image for the customer's loyalty. Provision of raw materials to the company for processing into finished products for the consumer or end user. Consider the distribution of soap or detergent powder to soap or detergent makers. Suppliers of soap and detergent raw materials provide HUL with the finished goods as Rin Detergent Bar or Surf Excel.

2. **Method of Information Exchange:** Information exchange occurs when one organization provides another organization with technical expertise, economic consulting, or answers to organizational concerns. It consists of pre- and post-sale maintenance and service information that must be shared with the members of business organizations, as well as technical, economic, and organizational questions. Goods and services must be created with the goal of effectively serving customers. In order to

accomplish this, buyers and sellers frequently collaborate and long-distance exchange product-specific information. As an illustration, the installation of sophisticated Information exchange can refer to software in an organization and the operating system of that programme.

3. **The process of financial exchange:** Foreign exchange is the yielding of credit or the requirement to exchange money from one currency to another when dealing with foreign purchasers. Financial exchange occurs when credit facilities are granted to an entity. Financial exchange occurs when two organizations in two different countries exchange money. As an illustration, consider how the Industrial Development Bank of India (IDBI), which provides loans to businesses, operates.
4. **The process of societal exchange:** Social interaction is important for removing uncertainty between the buyer and vendor. preventing immediate problems and, as a result, maintaining a healthier relationship over time. An agreement between buyers and sellers in the industrial market depends on a number of variables. They are neither entirely formal nor predicated on legal standards, but rather on mutual trust and arbitration.

Industrial Customer Types

Commercial Enterprises, Government Agencies, Institutions, and Cooperative Societies are the four categories into which industrial customers are typically divided.

They are as follows, as illustrated:

Business Organizations

Commercial businesses are profit-driven, private sector companies like IBM, General Motors, Computer Land, and Raven Corporation that acquire industrial products and/or services for uses other than their own. rather than making direct sales to final consumers. Since individuals buy items for various purposes, it is more effective from a marketing perspective to describe them in order to comprehend their needs when looking at the varied things they buy and how marketing strategies may be created to satisfy those demands.

The following commercial enterprises should be given more consideration: I industrial distributors or dealers; (ii) original equipment manufacturers (OEMs); and (iii) users. These categories, which frequently overlap, are helpful to industrial marketers because they highlight the various ways that goods and services are used by purchasing organisations.

Industrial Dealers and Distributors

Industrial dealers and distributors take title to the goods; as a result, they serve as the industrial marketer's middlemen, operating similarly to wholesalers or even retailers. In addition to serving the consumer market, intermediaries also work with other businesses, governments, and both public and private institutions. They buy industrial products and resale them to other industrial clients in the same shape.

Original Equipment Manufacturers (OEMs)

These industrial clients buy industrial products so they can use OEMs in the goods they make. For instance, a tyre manufacturer (like MRF) who sells tyres to a company that makes trucks (like TELCO) would classify the truck maker as an OEM in this scenario. As a result, the industrial marketer's (MRF) product merges with the client's (TELCO) offering.

Users

A user is an industrial customer who buys goods or services from an industrial supplier to assist its production process or to streamline business operations. Drilling, pressing, winding, and other manufacturing-related products are an example, whereas computers, fax machines, telephones, and other business-related devices make it easier to conduct business.

In addition to the aforementioned, there may occasionally be overlap across categories, which implies a manufacturer may also be an OEM. For instance, a car manufacturer is considered to as a user when they purchase a drilling machine to help their manufacturing process. The same automaker can also be referred to as an OEM because it purchases batteries that are built into cars.

Public Sector Clients

The Central and State Government departments, undertakings, and agencies, including the Railways, the Department of Telecommunication, the Defense, Director General of Supplies and Disposal (DGS&D), state transport undertakings, state electricity boards, and others, are India's largest buyers of industrial goods. These government entities form a sizable market and buy practically all types of commercial goods and services.

Organizations

Institutional consumers include both public and private institutions like hospitals, schools, colleges, and universities. While some of these institutions have strict limits for purchases, others have more lax guidelines.

To effectively advertise the goods or services, an industrial marketer must be familiar with each institution's purchasing procedures.

Cooperative organizations

A group of people come together to form a cooperative society. Organizations that don't produce anything like cooperative sugar mills, can be involved (e.g. Cooperative Banks, Cooperative Housing Societies). These are also the business clients.

Overview In general, the term "industrial marketing" refers to the practise of selling goods and services to businesses, manufacturing firms, service providers and institutions, businesses in the public and private sectors, and government activities.